THE
BEST
SHORT
PLAYS 1986

edited and introduced by
RAMON DELGADO

Best Short Plays Series

APPLAUSE
THEATRE BOOK PUBLISHERS
211 West 71 St • New York, NY 10023

for Gene McKinney

Copyright © 1986 by Ramon Delgado
All Rights Reserved
Published in New York, New York by Applause Theatre Books
Library of Congress Catalog Card No. 38–8006
ISBN 0-936839-13-9 (paper) 0-936839-14-7 (cloth)
ISSN 0067-6284
Manufactured in the United States of America

1 2 3 4 5 6 7 8 9 0 4 3 2 1 0 9 8 7 6 5

0008-86-086-1M

Contents

Introduction vii

BRUCE BONAFEDE
Advice to the Players 1

P. J. BARRY
Reasonable Circulation 31

MILCHA SANCHEZ-SCOTT
Dog Lady 55

DOUGLAS SODERBERG
The Root of Chaos 77

JANE NIXON WILLIS
Slam! 107

ROMULUS LINNEY
The Love Suicide at Schofield Barracks 123

DAVID KRANES
Going In 157

KATHERINE LONG
Ariel Bright 177

GINA BARNETT
Blood Bond 199

JANET NEIPRIS
The Agreement 215

Cited twice by *Outstanding Educators of America*, Dr. Delgado has taught acting, directing, playwriting, and dramatic literature at Kentucky Wesleyan College; Hardin-Simmons University in Abilene, Texas; St. Cloud State University, Minnesota; and Montclair State College, New Jersey, where he is presently Associate Professor of Theatre.

In 1983 an acting edition of his Cuban-American romantic comedy *A Little Holy Water* was published, and his latest full-length play *Stones*, produced at Montclair State College in December of 1983, stimulated discussion on the toxic waste problems of the environment. Dr. Delgado's acting textbook, *Acting with Both Sides of Your Brain*, was published this year, and he is working now on an acting styles book, an introductory text for theatre appreciation, and is compiling the 1987 edition of *The Best Short Plays*.

BOOKS AND PLAYS BY RAMON DELGADO

The Best Short Plays 1981 (with Stanley Richards)
The Best Short Plays 1982
The Best Short Plays 1983
The Best Short Plays 1984
The Best Short Plays 1985
Acting With Both Sides of Your Brain

The Youngest Child of Pablo Peco
Waiting for the Bus
The Little Toy Dog
Once Below A Lighthouse
Sparrows of the Field
The Knight-Mare's Nest
Omega's Ninth
Listen, My Children
A Little Holy Water
The Fabulous Jeromes
The Jerusalem Thorn
Stones

INTRODUCTION

With this 1986 edition of *Best Short Plays* we welcome a new publisher to the venture. Glenn Young, publisher of *Applause Theatre Books*, has graciously continued the series that had been so carefully husbanded from 1968 through 1985 by Chilton Books. We hope the addition of the new paperback format will make the collection more accessible for greater numbers of students of theatre and literature and more affordable for other fans of interesting and challenging short plays.

When one of the other champions of the short play—the late Alan Schneider—was directing an evening of one-acts for Joseph Papp's Public Theatre in Manhattan, New York in March of 1984, he was quoted as saying, "I like one-acts. My grandmother told me 'Diamonds don't come as big as bricks.'" Hidden beneath this homily lies a more subtle observation. Through the miracles of laser technology the gemologist can now record the traits of any precious stone, preserving a picture of its unique crystalline structure, its size, and its flaws. This "gemprint" is as individual as a fingerprint. A similar individual stamping—an imprint of viewpoint—can be found in one-act plays, even more readily than in full-length plays. This identifying characteristic might be called the playwright's "viewprint."

As I completed the collection for this year's volume of *Best Short Plays*, I surveyed the contents of the series during my six years as editor, and what a range of viewprints can be found in these sixty plays—range of subject matter, range of style, range of sensibility—but all the plays share in some way in that difficult, troubling, and sometimes inspiring question, posed from the beginning of man's awareness, but still challenging us today: "What does it mean to be a finite creature in an infinite universe?"—or as novelist Thomas Wolfe phrased it, what does it mean "to live beneath the senseless stars—and find man's meaning there?"

As I look among the examples in the recent annual volumes of *Best Short Plays* I find such diverse viewprints as Christopher Durang's fervent, iconoclastic challenge to the rigidity of individuals and institutions in *Sister Mary Ignatius Explains It All For You*; David Henry Hwang's viewprint with his insights into art in *The Dance and The Railroad*; Mary Gallagher's probing of loneliness and sharing in the bitter-sweet confection *Chocolate Cake*; John Guare's exploration of the joy and irony of human celebrations in the lyrical, poignant *In Fireworks Lie Secret Codes* ; Beverley Byers Pevitts' rage against the injustice of aging in *Reflections in a Win-*

dow; and Jane Martin's reverent, indelible viewprint of a wistful baton *Twirler* transcending her own earthbound limitations. Examples in this year's collection you will discover for yourself.

Precious viewprints do come in small packages. And as long as sensitive seekers of meaning question the nature and purpose of our brief existence in infinite time, the tradition of the one-act play will stretch into tomorrow, offering us new viewprints with every sociable stranger in our midst—those playwrights who seek their own answers to the mysteries of life, those who look to the stars and find hard-gleaming diamonds, hotly pressed from the passionate dust of their own mortality.

RAMON DELGADO
Montclair, New Jersey

Bruce Bonafede

ADVICE TO THE PLAYERS

Bruce Bonafede

When *Advice to the Players* premiered in Actors Theatre of Louisville's '84 SHORTS festival of one-act plays, reviewer William Mootz of the *Courier-Journal* exclaimed, ". . . the Victor Jory Theatre exploded with the thrill of discovery . . ." Bonafede's play is "blazing with emotional force and moral complexities. His taut, searing inquiry into the iniquities frequently perpetuated in the name of political justice gave '84 SHORTS a stunning moment of dramatic truth." So successful was the play in the '84 SHORTS festival, that artistic director Jon Jory revived the production for the 1985 Humana Festival of New American Plays in which the raves continued for Mr. Bonafede's work.

The play is based on a true incident during the 1981 Baltimore International Theatre Festival. Before the festival had opened, two black South African actors, John Kani and Winston Ntshona, bowed to a political protest and withdrew their production of Samuel Beckett's *Waiting for Godot* that had been scheduled for presentation. The complex issues of freedom of artistic expression versus the political symbolism of their representing the government of South Africa created a real life drama on which Mr. Bonafede based *Advice to the Players*. This publication is Mr. Bonafede's debut in the *Best Short Play* series as well as his first produced play.

Mr. Bonafede studied briefly at the New Playwrights Theatre of Washington, D.C., and is a charter member of the Washington Playwrights Unit. *Advice to the Players* was developed with the help of those groups.

The playwright, who lives in Laurel, Maryland, has been commissioned by the Actors Theatre of Louisville to write another one-act play, and he is also at work on a new full-length play.

Characters:

JOHN TYLER, *male, white, American, about forty*
TONY, *male, white, American, about twenty-five*
OLIVER MANZI, *male, black, South African, about thirty-five*
ROBERT OBOSA, *male, black, South African, about forty*
RANDALL MOORE, *male, white, American, about forty*
EMILY NGOME, *female, black, South African, about forty*

Scene:

The scene takes place on the stage of a theatre in the United States.

Time:

Afternoon. 1981.

The houselights are up. The stage is seen under a work light, set for a production of WAITING FOR GODOT: *there is a low mound to one side; a tree, virtually dead, stands upstage. Downstage is a folding table covered with scripts, markers, paper cups and other rehearsal debris. Before the audience is prepared John Tyler and Tony enter from opposite sides. Both wear casual clothes. Both carry scripts. They meet centerstage. Tyler explains in low tones, and shows in his script, that they will be rehearsing the final moments of the play. Tony nods, goes off in the direction of the theatre's lightbooth. Oliver Manzi and Robert Obosa enter together. They are in costume. As they prepare, Tyler discusses with them, again in low tones, where they will begin. Tyler steps away. Oliver and Robert position themselves. Oliver unties the cord holding his baggy trousers, which fall down around his ankles. He holds the cord out in front of him.*

TYLER: (*Calls to the booth*) Set, Tony?
(*The houselights go down. The work light changes to performance lighting; an exotic red, perhaps; suggestive of sundown on the veldt*)
TYLER: O.K. Whenever you're ready.

OLIVER: *(A beat, as Estagon)* Didi.

ROBERT: *(As Vladimir)* Yes.

OLIVER: *(As Estagon)* I can't go on like this.

ROBERT: *(As Vladimir)* That's what you think.

OLIVER: *(As Estagon)* If we parted? That might be better for us.

ROBERT: *(As Vladimir)* We'll hang ourselves tomorrow. *(A pause)* Unless Godot comes.

OLIVER: *(As Estagon)* And if he comes?

ROBERT: *(As Vladimir)* We'll be saved. *(He takes off his hat, peers inside it, feels about inside it, shakes it, knocks on the crown, puts it on again)*

OLIVER: *(As Estagon)* Well? Shall we go?

ROBERT: *(As Vladimir)* Pull on your trousers.

OLIVER: *(As Estagon)* What?

ROBERT: *(As Vladimir)* Pull on your trousers.

OLIVER: *(As Estagon)* You want me to pull off my trousers?

ROBERT: *(As Vladimir)* Pull *on* your trousers.

OLIVER: *(As Estagon, realizes his trousers are down)* True. *(He pulls up his trousers)*

ROBERT: *(As Vladimir)* Well? Shall we go?

OLIVER: *(As Estagon)* Yes, let's go. *(They do not move. A beat)*

TYLER: They do not move.

(The stage lights fade quickly)

TYLER: Tony! Slower on the fadeout!

(The stage lights come back up, then fadeout more slowly until black. A beat, then the work light comes up again. The houselights also come on)

TYLER: Fantastic. *(Oliver does not move. Robert relaxes, takes off his hat)*

ROBERT: Thank you . . .

TYLER: Thank *you*. Thank you both. It's going to be great.

ROBERT: You think so?

TYLER: Absolutely. *(He and Robert move to the folding table. Neither notices that Oliver has not moved)* I mean it. I've seen at least a dozen productions of *WAITING FOR GODOT*. I've even directed it a couple of times before. But I've never seen it done quite the way you do it.

ROBERT: Thank you . . .

TYLER: It's almost as though it was written for you.

ROBERT: *(Laughs)* Please, I'm not that old.

TYLER: Well, you've hardly seemed to need me at all.

ROBERT: But we do. Especially with your people in the other roles.

TYLER: Yes, I hope you don't consider that too much of a disadvantage—having to use our people.

ROBERT: No, no. They're very good.

TYLER: It's too bad yours couldn't be here.

ROBERT: We knew in London they wouldn't be able to come. Our government's refused to extend the travel permits of the rest of our company before.

TYLER: They do that just to make things difficult for you?

ROBERT: *(Nods)* Oliver and I are accustomed to such . . . small punishments. We've learned to live with them. We couldn't let that stop us from coming to America again. Isn't that right, Oliver? *(He looks around, sees Oliver, who still has not moved)* What are you doing?

OLIVER: *(A beat)* You mean that's it?

ROBERT: What?

OLIVER: That's the end of the play?

ROBERT: Yes, that's the end. Come now. Time to return to reality.

OLIVER: *(A beat)* Well, shit. *(He ties up his trousers with his cord)*

ROBERT: Please excuse my friend. He's very childish. He loves to play these little games. *(Tyler smiles)*

OLIVER: And you love it when I do.

ROBERT: I?

OLIVER: Yes.

ROBERT: So?

OLIVER: So . . . who is more childish?

ROBERT: *(Shrugs)* You are.

OLIVER: I?

ROBERT: Yes.

OLIVER: Not you?

ROBERT: No.

OLIVER: Are you certain?

ROBERT: Ah . . . nothing is certain.

OLIVER: Nothing is certain?

ROBERT: No.

OLIVER: That's terrible. *(A pause)* Are you certain?

ROBERT: Yes.

OLIVER: *(Relieved)* Ah . . . that's reassuring. *(He picks up a cup of coffee from the table)*

TYLER: Are you two ever offstage?

OLIVER: Only when absolutely necessary. (*He tastes the coffee, makes a face*) This coffee is colder than those whores we had in Berlin.

ROBERT: We were never in Berlin.

OLIVER: That's what I mean.

TYLER: (*Laughs*) There should be some hot in my office.

OLIVER: I hope so. I cannot continue to rehearse if my tongue is frozen.

ROBERT: (*Smiles*) Oh, I don't know . . . (*To his surprise, Oliver says the rest of the line an instant before him*)

OLIVER: It might help.

ROBERT: . . . It might help. (*He tries to slap Oliver, who evades him*) How did you know I was going to say that?

OLIVER: (*Laughing to Tyler*) You must excuse my friend. He is very predictable.

ROBERT: Well, anyone would be after nine years.

OLIVER: Especially yourself.

ROBERT: (*Pretends to be insulted*) So, what's the plan for today, Mr. Tyler?

TYLER: Please, I told you—it's John.

OLIVER: (*Brightly*) The plan for today is John.

ROBERT: Be quiet. (*To Tyler*) John.

TYLER: Well, I've scheduled the dress rehearsal for two o'clock.

OLIVER: (*Eager*) And we go on at eight?

TYLER: Yes.

OLIVER: And you think we'll have a good crowd?

TYLER: We're sold out for every performance. I told you that yesterday.

OLIVER: I know. I just like hearing it again. (*Sighs happily*) Such an intelligent people, these Americans.

(*Tony enters from the back of the auditorium. He stops before reaching the stage*)

TONY: John?

TYLER: Yes?

TONY: Sorry to interrupt.

TYLER: That's O.K.

TONY: There's a man here to see you.

TYLER: Now? Who is it?

TONY: I don't know.

TYLER: Did he say what he wants?

TONY: No. (Shrugs) He's wearing a suit.

OLIVER: (*He jumps*) Don't let him in!

TYLER: (*Laughing*) I probably shouldn't. You don't mind, do you?

ROBERT: No, no . . .

TYLER: I'll get rid of him. O.K., Tony. (*Tony exits as he came in*)

ROBERT: When will your people begin to arrive?

TYLER: (*Looks at his watch*) Oh, in about an hour.

ROBERT: We have some time, then?

TYLER: Sure . . .

OLIVER: Enough for a round of golf at the country club?

TYLER: (*Playing along*) I think so.

OLIVER: (*Getting excited*) Followed by cocktails on the verandah . . .(*Slyly*) And maybe a quick one with the governor's wife?

TYLER: (*Laughing*) Well, it would have to be quick.

OLIVER: (*Ruefully*) It would be.

ROBERT: I was thinking more of a few minutes rest.

OLIVER: Rest?

ROBERT: Something we both need. May we use your office, John?

TYLER: Of course.

ROBERT: Thank you. (*He takes Oliver's arm*) Come along, Oliver.

OLIVER: (*He resists*) But, Robert . . .

ROBERT: (*He pulls*) We'll get you some hot coffee.

OLIVER: (*He struggles*) Who wants coffee? We're having cocktails on the verandah!

ROBERT: No, we're not. You're fantasizing again.

OLIVER: (*Knowing full well he is*) I am?

ROBERT: Yes.

OLIVER: But what about the governor's wife?

ROBERT: What about her?

OLIVER: We don't want to disappoint her.

ROBERT: Oliver. She doesn't exist either.

OLIVER: She doesn't?

ROBERT: No.

OLIVER: (*Convinced*) Well, then I think we should call to tell her we're not coming. (*He reverses himself, leads Robert off toward one of the wings. They exit. Tyler watches after them, smiling*)

(*Randall Moore enters from the back of the auditorium. He is dressed in a three-piece suit and carries a briefcase. He mounts the stage*)

MOORE: Mr. Tyler?

TYLER: (*Turns to him. Pleasantly*) Yes?

MOORE: My name is Randall Moore.

TYLER: (*Puts out his hand*) How do you do. Can I help you with something?

MOORE: (*Surprised, he shakes hands cautiously*) Well, yes.

TYLER: What?

MOORE: (*A beat*) I should've realized. I didn't expect to be welcomed. (*A pause*) You don't know who I am, do you?

TYLER: Should I?

MOORE: I've been trying to reach you for several days. (*A pause*) I'm from the Coalition. (*A pause*) The Coalition for the Liberation of the South African People.

TYLER: Oh, I see.

MOORE: Yes. I wish you'd returned my calls.

TYLER: (*A beat, then he moves to the table, tries to appear busy*) Well, we've been extremely busy getting ready for our festival. We're producing a different play each week for six weeks.

MOORE: We're aware of your agenda . . .

TYLER: And the first one opens tonight . . .

MOORE: And are you still planning to have Oliver Manzi and Robert Obosa perform?

TYLER: (*He stops*) They're our guest artists, yes.

MOORE: You intend to ignore the Coalition's request?

TYLER: Well, I wouldn't say ignore . . .

MOORE: Simply not agree to it, then.

TYLER: (*A beat*) I thought I'd made our position clear. I recall speaking to someone—someone else, not yourself. I explained there was nothing we could do.

MOORE: Which is why I was asked to step in.

TYLER: In what capacity?

MOORE: As their attorney.

TYLER: You work for them?

MOORE: I do some work for them. When I'm needed. As a volunteer, of course.

TYLER: Of course.

MOORE: I support the goal of a free South Africa.

TYLER: Well, so do I.

MOORE: (*Smiles*) There, you see? We've already found an area of common agreement. (*He puts his briefcase down on the table*) I'm sure we'll be able to count on your cooperation.

TYLER: (*Very uncomfortable*) Well, actually . . . no. I simply can't do what your Coalition asks.

MOORE: (*A beat*) Let me clarify the lines of authority here. You are the director of this festival?

TYLER: Yes, over-all. I'm also directing the play these two actors are appearing in.

MOORE: I see. But it was your decision which artists to invite?

TYLER: Yes.

MOORE: Then you have the authority to cancel, to, say— disinvite anyone on the program?

TYLER: I suppose so.

MOORE: So you *can* do as we ask. It's only a question of whether you *will* or *not*.

TYLER: (*A beat*) You realize this isn't my theatre. I don't run it. I'm an independent, hired by the Board of Trustees to organize the festival.

MOORE: Should I meet with the Board?

TYLER: Well, you can't . . .

MOORE: No?

TYLER: The members aren't all in one place.

MOORE: Can you call them together?

TYLER: Not on such short notice . . .

MOORE: Why not?

TYLER: It's just not possible . . .

MOORE: And not *really* necessary. The choice *is* yours, isn't it?

TYLER: But I'm answerable to the Board . . .

MOORE: We're all answerable to someone, Mr. Tyler. Can you or can't you make the decision on your own?

TYLER: (*Angry*) I can, yes.

MOORE: (*A beat, smiles*) Good. (*He opens his briefcase, takes out a printed brochure, reads*) "The International Theatre Festival was conceived as a celebration of theatre, and as a means of bringing artists of diverse national origin to the attention of our city for the betterment of our cultural life." (*He puts down the brochure*) Very admirable.

TYLER: (*Sarcastic*) Thanks.

MOORE: The Coalition would like very much to support your festival. We can help you. But we cannot agree with the political statement you are making by including a production by members of the Cape Town Theatre Company.

TYLER: We're not making any political statement.

MOORE: Maybe not deliberately, but the implications . . .

TYLER: What implications?

MOORE: This production will be seen as a sign of approval of the South African government.

TYLER: I don't see why. We're talking about two celebrated actors who've performed practically all over the world.

MOORE: We're aware of their reputations.

TYLER: I've never heard it suggested that their work showed approval of their government. Quite the opposite.

MOORE: They are still South African.

TYLER: But they're *black*. Do you know that?

MOORE: Yes. Even so, to allow them to perform here would show that we're willing to have cultural exchange with South Africa . . .

TYLER: Not with South Africa. With two actors who happen to be South African.

MOORE: . . . And that would be a violation of the boycott. We must maintain the boycott, Mr. Tyler. It's the only way for the civilized world to deal with South Africa.

TYLER: We're not trying to *deal* with anything. We're doing a play.

MOORE: But you could be doing much more. You have a chance here to make a real contribution. (*A pause*) In return, we'll . . .

TYLER: You mean if I cancel the production.

MOORE: . . . Yes . . .

TYLER: I can't . . . I *won't* do that. I won't have these two men become pawns in some political game.

MOORE: This is hardly a *game*, Mr. Tyler. (*A pause*) Let me explain what I'm asking you to do . . .

TYLER: Please don't.

MOORE: But we can help you . . . help the festival . . .

TYLER: I don't need your help, and I don't *want* it. (*A pause*) Look I'm sorry. I'm sure you think you're doing the right thing. But I don't believe you can help the cause of freedom in South Africa by stifling freedom of expression here in America. You'll end up victimizing two of the men you profess to be trying to help.

MOORE: (*Insulted*) We're not stifling anyone's freedom. We're trying to help millions *gain* their freedom, and giving up a single production in a theatre festival seems a very small price to pay.

TYLER: I'm sure it does, to you. And you might be right, if it would somehow lead to what you want, but it won't.

MOORE: We disagree . . .

TYLER: Yes, that's obvious.

MOORE: What happens here will have a major effect on the international situation.

TYLER: You can't really believe that.

MOORE: Yes, we can. And we do. (*He glances at his watch*) I have to advise you that if you're unwilling to agree to our request, we're prepared to take whatever steps are necessary to stop the production.

TYLER: What steps?

MOORE: We'll exercise our right to protest.

TYLER: Well, I can't stop you from doing that.

MOORE: You stop us? It's quite the other way around. If we have to stop this production, we intend to stop the entire festival.

TYLER: Oh? How?

MOORE: By eliminating your audience.

TYLER: (*Sarcastic*) Are you going to shoot them?

MOORE: We have a demonstration ready right now to move in. (*He closes his briefcase*) We are not the ones playing games here, Mr. Tyler.

(*The sound of laughter comes from offstage. Oliver and Robert enter from the wing they had exited to. Oliver is in the lead, trying not to spill the cup of coffee he is carrying. Robert is trying to restrain him*)

OLIVER: John!

ROBERT: Oliver, stop this . . .

OLIVER: (*Turns back to him*) Shh! (*Robert shrugs, lets go of him. He turns to Tyler*) I have to tell you. We were just talking about your lovely theatre. We wish we had a place like this at home. (*He looks about the theatre appreciatingly*) Ah, yes. Ours is nothing like this. You've heard of Shakespeare in the park? We have Beckett in the basement. (*Laughs*) Of course, that's kind of appropriate.

ROBERT: (*A loud whisper*) Oliver, you see? I told you. We're interrupting. (*Oliver notices Moore, shrugs apologetically, begins to follow Robert off*)

TYLER: No, wait. I'm glad you're here. (*Robert and Oliver stop*) I think you should meet . . .

MOORE: Mr. Tyler, I'm not authorized to discuss this with anyone but yourself.

TYLER: Not even the men involved?

MOORE: I'm to speak only to you. Alone.

TYLER: (*A beat, then he continues*) Robert Obosa, Oliver Manzi—this is Mr. Moore.

OLIVER: (*Makes a grand bow*) An honor, sir . . . (*He spills his coffee*) Oh, shit.

ROBERT: How do you do. Are you involved with the festival? (*Moore remains silent*).

TYLER: In a way. You see, there's a bit of a problem.

OLIVER: (*Concerned*) With the festival?

TYLER: Yes. Well, actually, with your part in it.

OLIVER: Oh, no! We're closing before we've even opened!

ROBERT: I told you theatre in America was strange. (*They smile at Tyler*)

TYLER: No. No one's closing.

ROBERT: Then what's the problem?

TYLER: We're involved in a protest. There's a protest against your production.

ROBERT: A protest? By who?

TYLER: By Mr. Moore.

MOORE: By the organization I represent.

OLIVER: (*A beat. Secretively*) Robert, do you think he's a Nazi?

ROBERT: I don't think so.

OLIVER: How can you tell?

ROBERT: No uniform. No swastika.

OLIVER: Ah . . . then he must be from the Ku Klux Klan.

ROBERT: Not necessarily.

OLIVER: No?

ROBERT: He's not wearing a sheet. I've heard they always wear sheets.

OLIVER: Always?

ROBERT: Except in bed. (*He and Oliver break up laughing*)

MOORE: (*To Tyler*) I really don't see the point . . .

TYLER: Yes, please, gentlemen. He's threatening to try to close down the festival if I don't cancel your production.

ROBERT: (*Soberly*) Why are you protesting our production?

MOORE: Because you're South African.

ROBERT: But we're black.

MOORE: That doesn't matter.

OLIVER: It matters to us.

MOORE: The group I represent is opposed to any contact with South Africa.

OLIVER: Well, so am I. (*Shrugs*) I get out whenever I can.

ROBERT: You mean if we were from, say—Zimbabwe—you would not be protesting us?

MOORE: There's no boycott of Zimbabwe. It's been liberated.

OLIVER: Ah. So in South Africa we have race-prejudice, and in America we have nation-prejudice. What is this group you represent?

MOORE: The Coalition for the Liberation of the South African People. (*Oliver laughs*)

ROBERT: (*Smiles*) But you're an American.

MOORE: We're an American organization.

OLIVER: Well, we're South African people. Please liberate us by going away.

MOORE: Not until I have Mr. Tyler's promise to do what we ask.

ROBERT: What has he to do with it?

MOORE: He's in authority here.

OLIVER: Oh, I'm not sure I like that. I always have trouble with the authorities.

ROBERT: You support the cause of democracy in South Africa?

MOORE: Yes, of course.

ROBERT: So do we. Why are you protesting *us*?

MOORE: We're not protesting you personally. But to allow you to perform here would be a violation of the boycott. It would look as though we approve of South Africa.

TYLER: Don't bother trying to convince him that he can't help you by hurting you. He doesn't agree.

ROBERT: Our government has nothing to do with our being here. They didn't sponsor us. They don't even want us here. When our London production was over they cancelled the travel permits of the rest of our company in an attempt to scare us into coming home. But they didn't cancel ours because, thank God, we're well known enough that the publicity might've embarrassed them.

MOORE: That isn't why.

ROBERT: It isn't?

MOORE: Hasn't it ever occurred to you that you're being used as propaganda? If your government allows you to travel and perform as though you're free, the world will see that and then not care so much what's done to your people at home.

ROBERT: (*A beat. Angry*) No. That has never occurred to me. Only a rich, white American who knows nothing at all about our lives could think such a thing.

OLIVER: Robert, I think you're making him angry.

ROBERT: I hope so.

MOORE: (*Goes to Tyler, faces him*) Are you going to cooperate or not?

ROBERT: You're asking the wrong person. You won't stop us by intimidating Mr. Tyler. If we're thrown out of his theatre, we'll perform on the bloody street if we have to.

MOORE: (*To Tyler*) Do you or don't you want to save your festival?

ROBERT: How do you propose to close it down?

TYLER: He claims he's got a demonstration outside waiting to move in.

ROBERT: A demonstration? How large?

MOORE: (*Still facing Tyler*) Large enough. (*He takes his briefcase from the table*)

TYLER: Of course, if they do, I'll be forced to call in the police.

OLIVER: (*He jumps*) The police?

TYLER: Yes.

OLIVER: They're on *our* side?

TYLER: Of course.

OLIVER: Imagine that.

MOORE: That will do you no good.

TYLER: You won't set foot in this theatre.

MOORE: We don't need to. We'll set up a line of demonstrators out front with signs accusing the festival of promoting exchange with South Africa. You can call the police. I've dealt with them before. They'll do nothing. They won't take a chance on the demonstration escalating into a riot. (*A pause*) Meanwhile, your audience will see the whole thing on the news, after we call every station in the city to make sure it's covered. How many of them do you think will face *that*, just to see a play? Think of how it will look as the festival goes on, and your theatre stays empty. Think of what the Board, who hired you, will say. Think of . . .

TYLER: Yes, well, I appreciate your concern. Is that all?

OLIVER: (*Laughs*) I don't think you've convinced him. What do you think?

MOORE: I think you're all . . . incredibly irresponsible. You can't live in your own little world.

OLIVER: We can try.

MOORE: Well, it won't work.

ROBERT: Why, because of a few misguided American whites, who obviously know nothing about us or our country?

MOORE: (*A flash of anger*) That's the second time you've brought up the fact that I'm white.

ROBERT: Yes, for some reason I couldn't help noticing.

MOORE: As a matter of fact, the woman who asked me to come here happens to be South African and *black*.

OLIVER: (*Excited*) Listen, if she's good-looking, by all means send her over.

MOORE: (*Furious*) You wouldn't dare make fun of this person if she were here.

ROBERT: And why's that?

MOORE: Because she happens to be from the South African National Council.

ROBERT: (*A beat*) You really have a talent for saying the most outrageous things.

MOORE: You don't believe me?

ROBERT: The Council would never be involved in a protest against *us*.

MOORE: Maybe that's why she asked me to keep her involvement secret. (*He takes his briefcase, leaves the stage, exits through the auditorium*)

OLIVER: (*A beat*) What do you think, Robert?

ROBERT: (*Looks after Moore, shakes his head, unsure whether to laugh or not*) He's a liar. He's trying to impress us.

TYLER: He said he was here to represent his Coalition. What's this National Council?

ROBERT: The leading anti-government group in our country. They've led the struggle for our people's rights for over thirty years.

TYLER: They've never given you trouble before?

ROBERT: Trouble? We wouldn't've come this far without their help. When we first started, the Council promoted our work in the townships. They got the people out to see us. And they've been with us all along.

TYLER: Why would they turn against you now?

ROBERT: (*Looks after Moore again, then to Tyler. Decides*) They haven't. (*A pause*) When I was young I was sent to prison for anti-governmental activities. My crime was being a member of a banned organization. That organization was this Council.

TYLER: You're a member?

ROBERT: Not now. Not for . . . nine years. Since I left prison.

OLIVER: (*Laughs*) Once Robert met me he didn't need the Council. (*Robert laughs*) We met in prison, you know.

TYLER: Really?

ROBERT: Well, Oliver was only there at the end. Short time.

OLIVER: My crime may not've been as glamorous as yours, but it was a legitimate offense, and I will not allow you to belittle it.

ROBERT: Why don't you tell him what you were in for?

OLIVER: (*Proudly*) I was considered a threat to the national security . . .

ROBERT: Oliver . . .

OLIVER: (*Defensively*) Well, of a sort . . .

ROBERT: He was arrested for indecent exposure.

OLIVER: A clear case of fascist oppression.

ROBERT: He got drunk and took his trousers off in the street.

OLIVER: (*Explaining*) It was summer . . .

ROBERT: And he was seen by two white girls driving by. (*By now all three are laughing*)

OLIVER: Those girls shouldn't've been in that neighborhood anyway. But of course they had to go and tell the police all about the crazy Kaffir they'd seen.

ROBERT: The "crazy Kaffir"—yes. That's what Oliver was called in prison, even by the other blacks.

OLIVER: I used to recite Shakespeare in my cell at night. (*Recites*) O, that this too, too solid flesh would melt, *and slide out between the bars!*

ROBERT: (*Composed*) It was Oliver who introduced me to the theatre. After my release, I found him and convinced him—hey, we start our own acting group.

OLIVER: Well, we all make mistakes.

ROBERT: Oh, has it been so bad? We just finished doing this play in London. Next we go to New York for the Fugard play. (*A pause*) We've come a long way.

OLIVER: (*Sincerely*) That's true.

ROBERT: (*Moved*) Farther than I ever thought we could.

OLIVER: (*Leans close*) Well, you never had much of an imagination. (*Robert tries to slap Oliver, who evades him. They are laughing*)

(*Tony enters hurriedly through the auditorium*)

TONY: (*Calling*) John! We've got a problem!

TYLER: What is it?

TONY: There're people outside.

OLIVER: (*Still cheerful*) Customers?

TONY: Demonstrators. With signs and everything.

TYLER: How many?

TONY: I don't know. I didn't count them. About a dozen, I guess.

TYLER: (*To Robert*) That's not a lot.

TONY: Yes, but they're *blocking the doors!*

TYLER: They are?

TONY: And the alley too.

(*At this point, if possible in the theatre of presentation, Tyler or Robert, or both, should move rapidly offstage and through the auditorium to witness this for themselves. Oliver sits dejectedly on the mound. The following may be delivered from anywhere in the house*)

TYLER: That man from before, Mr. . . .

TONY: Moore?

TYLER: Yes. Did you see him out there?

TONY: No. What do you want me to do?

TYLER: (*Thinking*) Stay by the doors. Keep them locked. Let me know if they try to get in, or if Moore shows up.

TONY: Right. (*He starts off*)

TYLER: (*Calling*) And be careful! (*Tony exits through the auditorium. Tyler, if he left it, returns to the stage*) Well, he's made good on his threat. (*Distracted*) I can't believe this is happening here.

OLIVER: Why should it be different here from anyplace else?

TYLER: What?

ROBERT: (*If he left it, returns to the stage*) How much trouble can they give us?

TYLER: Well, he's right about the publicity. That can't help us. It might very well scare some of our audience away.

ROBERT: But not all of them.

TYLER: Who knows? If things get out of hand, and there's trouble . . .

ROBERT: We don't want anyone hurt.

TYLER: . . . Plus, if they're blocking the doors, we've got a more immediate problem. The rest of our cast and crew will be here very soon. What if these people won't let them in? Are you ready to go on tonight without a final run-through?

ROBERT: We can, if we have to. But if they won't let the crew in. they won't let the audience in anyway.

TYLER: (*A beat, then he starts off*) I'd better call the police.

ROBERT: (*Stops him*) No, don't. Not yet.

TYLER: I don't want to either, but what else *can* we do?

OLIVER: I think we should ignore them.

ROBERT: This is no time for jokes, Oliver.

OLIVER: I'm not joking. If we refuse to deal with them, they will grow discouraged and go away.

TYLER: Don't you believe it. They wouldn't've gone to the trouble of coming here if they were going to leave after a little while.

OLIVER: All right. Then we should call the police at once.

ROBERT: We can't do that.

OLIVER: Yes, we can. We can have them beaten and jailed and be done with them. (*Robert dismisses him with a shrug*) I mean it.

TYLER: The police won't do that.

OLIVER: Well, they should.

ROBERT: I don't believe I'm hearing this. *You* want to call the police on demonstrators?

OLIVER: As long as we have the power on our side, for once, let's use it.

ROBERT: (*Horrified*) *No*, Oliver . . .

OLIVER: *Yes* . . .

ROBERT: You don't really want . . .

OLIVER: Well, what do *you* want, Robert? What do you expect of me? (*To Tyler*) We're on temporary papers. After next month we must go back to South Africa. (*To Robert*) Until when? When will they let us out again?

ROBERT: We'll get out again. What's that got to do with this?

OLIVER: All that time in London—free of having to carry the passbook, free of curfew and being watched by the security police. And all next month ahead of us in New York. That wonderful play. I want to do that play. I just want to be free long enough for that. Is that so much to ask?

ROBERT: No, Oliver.

OLIVER: If it is, then we may as well go back now.

TYLER: Don't talk like that. You're still in America. You're still free.

OLIVER: Am I free *now*?

TYLER: Well, these people outside aren't exactly security police.

OLIVER: Demonstrators, police . . . whatever. They're all the same. They're all . . . politicians. They've all got excuses for what they do. They all pretend they want what's right, but what they really want is power.

ROBERT: Oliver . . .

OLIVER: These people will stop us.

ROBERT: No, they won't. I meant what I said. We'll perform on the street if we have to.

OLIVER: And I know we're in trouble when you begin to believe your own rhetoric.

TYLER: Don't worry. If we keep our heads, we'll work this out.

OLIVER: All our lives we've had to beg the politicians to be allowed to do what we were put here to do.

ROBERT: We've never begged . . .

OLIVER: The power is all they care about. Who has it? Who can hold it? Who can take it away? It's a game to them. They play games with our lives, and we let them.

(*Tony enters through the auditorium*)

ROBERT: It's not that we let them, Oliver. What can we do to stop them?

TONY: (*A beat. Standing in the auditorium uncertain whether to interrupt*) John?

TYLER: Yes?

TONY: Sorry, but there's someone else now who wants to talk to you.

TYLER: Someone else . . . not Moore?

TONY: No. A woman.

ROBERT: (*Struck*) A *black* woman?

TONY: Yes.

OLIVER: You see? It's true.

ROBERT: It can't *be*.

OLIVER: What do we do now?

ROBERT: (*A beat*) Let her in, please.

OLIVER: No! (*Tony hesitates, looks to Tyler*)

ROBERT: (*To Oliver*) Yes. (*To Tyler*) Please.

TYLER: Go ahead, Tony. (*Tony exits through the auditorium*)

OLIVER: We're making a terrible mistake. We shouldn't even talk to her.

ROBERT: We've got to let her explain. I want her to explain *this*. I want to hear it from her mouth.

TYLER: Would you rather speak to her alone?

ROBERT: No, please stay. There's no reason you shouldn't be here. Let her say it out loud to all of us.

(*Emily Ngome enters through the auditorium, with Tony behind her. She is dressed in African clothes, and wears a scarf around her hair. She mounts the stage. Tony hangs back*)

EMILY: Gentlemen. Good afternoon.

ROBERT: Mrs. Ngome.

EMILY: Robert. Oliver. It is good to see you both again.

TYLER: (*A beat*) You know each other?

ROBERT: This is Mr. Tyler, the festival director.

EMILY: (*Goes to Tyler, shakes hands with him*) How do you do. I am Emily Ngome.

TYLER: (*Confused*) Hello.

ROBERT: Emily is . . . much respected in our country. Her husband was Peter Ngome, who was Chairman of the Council when it was banned by the government.

OLIVER: (*Bitterly*) And who later died in police custody.

TYLER: Oh . . . I'm sorry.

EMILY: Thank you, but please do not be embarrassed to speak of it. We must speak of it. (*Tyler embarrassed, does not know what to say*)

TONY: John?

TYLER: Yes?

TONY: Can I talk to you for a minute?

TYLER: (*Grateful*) Sure. (*To the others*) Excuse me. (*He moves to Tony. They speak in low tones*)

EMILY: (*Goes to shake hands with Robert*) Molo. [Hello.]

ROBERT: (*Respectful*) Molo.

EMILY: Unjani. [How are you?]

ROBERT: Ndiyaphila. [I am fine.]

EMILY: (*Turns to Oliver*) Molo. Unjani. (*Oliver shrugs, does not respond*)

ROBERT: How did you get here?

EMILY: Through Lusaka. Our underground got me out of the country.

ROBERT: What about the security police?

EMILY: They think I am very ill, and receiving no visitors. They are watching my empty house. (*Tony exits through the auditorium*)

TYLER: (*Returns*) Our people've started to arrive. They're waiting across the street, away from the demonstrators.

ROBERT: Yes, Emily—what's going on? Why're you protesting our production?

EMILY: We are not.

OLIVER: Your lacky, Mr. Moore, claims you are.

EMILY: Mr. Moore is not our lacky. He is our ally.

ROBERT: We thought we were your allies.

EMILY: We hope you are.

ROBERT: After all this time there should be no question of that.

EMILY: Then help us face this crisis.

ROBERT: We don't know anything about a crisis.

OLIVER: Except the one we're in the middle of.

EMILY: (*A beat*) Two weeks ago, one of our people was murdered in Paris. He was there to meet with an important financial supporter of the Council. (*A pause*) The evidence indicates he may have been killed by agents of the Bureau of State Security.

ROBERT: The government has begun killing Council members in other countries?

EMILY: We believe so.

ROBERT: That could be disastrous.

EMILY: Precisely. (*To Tyler*) We have offices all over the world, with hundreds of members who have operated in the open for years. If the government moves against us now, it could mean a bloodbath. (*To Robert and Oliver*) We must call attention to the incident, create as much public outcry as possible, to demonstrate to the government that they cannot do such things without consequences.

OLIVER: And what has that to do with us?

EMILY: It was decided to ask you to cancel your production here as an act of protest over the murder.

OLIVER: (*Laughs derisively*) You know we can't do that. You know what would happen.

ROBERT: I don't understand. It was decided to ask us? Then why weren't we asked? Why didn't you come to us yourself?

EMILY: I only just arrived from our office in Washington.

ROBERT: So instead you sent a white lawyer to talk to us?

EMILY: No, I sent him to speak to Mr. Tyler. He was supposed to convince Mr. Tyler to cancel your production, without involving the two of you. (*To Oliver*) I thought if the incident was kept strictly between the Americans, our government might not hold you responsible. (*To Robert*) Mr. Moore would announce to the media that he convinced Mr. Tyler to cancel to protest the murder. We would get our publicity, but you would be blameless. (*A pause*) I have sent word to the Council of my plan. Mr. Moore is now waiting for their confirmation.

ROBERT: But the Council didn't think of such a plan. Their first thought was to throw us to the lions.

EMILY: Do not judge them too harshly. They fear they may be fighting for their lives, and the life of our movement. (*Robert and Oliver are both turned from her. She turns to Tyler*) You see how important it is you cooperate.

TYLER: (*A beat*) Well, I still don't like it. (*A pause*) I'm not even sure I understand it. (*A pause*) But I'll do whatever Robert and Oliver want.

ROBERT: What about the festival?

TYLER: Well . . . I want to do what's best for you.

ROBERT: There's no guarantee it'll do any good.

EMILY: But if it does any good at all . . .

ROBERT: I don't know. Oliver?

OLIVER: No.

ROBERT: No?

OLIVER: They're playing games with our lives. I've had enough of it.

ROBERT: But, Oliver . . . It's the Council . . .

OLIVER: I don't care who it is, and neither will the government. They won't care who cancels what. They've been waiting for us to get directly involved for years, and the minute we do, they'll move against us.

EMILY: You've always been involved. Your plays have always made political statements.

OLIVER: On *stage*, in the *theatre*. If we make the same statements ourselves . . . publicly . . . if we cancel this production, or let it be cancelled, they'll use it as an excuse to charge us with supporting a revolutionary organization. And you know the punishment for that. At the very least we'll be banned.

TYLER: Banned?

ROBERT: (*To Tyler*) It's a legal action they use. You're made to stay in one place of the government's choosing, sometimes hundreds of miles from your home. You can't work, or write anything, or be quoted by anyone, and you're forbidden from speaking to more than one person at a time except for members of your family. You cease to exist as a public person.

OLIVER: A fine fate for an actor.

TYLER: But at the trial you could claim *I* cancelled, not you.

ROBERT: There is no trial.

TYLER: (*Horrified*) My god, how long does it last?

ROBERT: A ban? A ban is perpetual.

TYLER: It lasts the rest of your life?

EMILY: No. It lasts until the government falls.

OLIVER: (*To Emily*) For the rest of your life.

TYLER: How're you supposed to live?

OLIVER: Ah . . . that's a good question. Let's ask Mrs. Ngome. (*To Emily*) How did Peter live?

EMILY: My husband . . . refused to obey. He would not be silenced. He continued to speak out . . .

OLIVER: Until they killed him.

EMILY: He did what his loyalty demanded. And we could all learn something from his example.

OLIVER: I agree. I too refuse to be silenced.

EMILY: It is hardly the same thing.

(*Moore enters quickly through the auditorium. He carries a sealed envelope*)

MOORE: (*Calls*) Mrs. Ngome! (*He mounts the stage*) A courier just brought this from the Council office in Washington. (*Emily takes the envelope from Moore, opens it, removes a paper, reads silently*)

TYLER: (*To Robert and Oliver*) I didn't realize something like this was at stake. I won't be a part of putting you in this kind of danger.

EMILY: (*A beat. She finishes reading*) That does not matter, Mr. Tyler. You are no longer involved.

ROBERT: Why? What does it say?

EMILY: I am ordered . . . to proceed as originally instructed.

ROBERT: They still want us to cancel on our own?

EMILY: Yes.

ROBERT: They don't agree with your plan?

EMILY: No.

ROBERT: Why not?

EMILY: They feel . . . if you cancel the production yourselves . . . it will have more of an impact.

OLIVER: (*To Robert*) You see?

ROBERT: I don't believe this.

EMILY: I also . . . have to inform you . . . that if you go ahead with your production here . . . the Council will order a boycott of your future productions at home.

ROBERT: (*Moves toward Emily, furious*) Let me see that!

EMILY: Robert—*no*! (*She holds the paper to herself*) You must do as they ask.

ROBERT: *Ask?*

EMILY: This is one battle they are not willing to lose.

ROBERT: You can tell them that they've lost it already. The whites've never been able to intimidate us. Does the Council think *they* can?

EMILY: Our movement is at stake. You must help. You know what the Council means to us.

ROBERT: I know what it *meant*.

EMILY: Don't speak like that. You cannot abandon them.

ROBERT: They've abandoned *us*.

EMILY: What of your loyalty?

ROBERT: Loyalty? Loyalty works both ways. Anything else is . . . obedience.

EMILY: You can not abandon your people.

ROBERT: Who are my people?

EMILY: You know the answer to that. You know who you are.

ROBERT: Do I? No. No, I don't. Not really. Not anymore. (*A pause*) Yes. Yes, I do. I'm an actor. An actor—that's all.

EMILY: But still South African. Still black. Still Xhosa. What of your country? What of your brothers?

ROBERT: (*Gestures toward the stage*) This is my country. *This*. (*He gestures toward Oliver and Tyler*) And these are my brothers. I'm a part of nothing else.

EMILY: You are still involved, whether you like it or not.

OLIVER: (*A beat. Calmly*) If we perform here, the Council will ruin us as actors at home. If we don't perform, the government will ban us, and we'll be ruined as well. (*A pause*) Either way—we're fucked.

TYLER: (*A beat*) What if you emigrated? Just left it all behind? You've got a career outside. You could work here in America, in Europe, anywhere. I'll help you.

ROBERT: That's very kind, but it's impossible. That's called an exit permit, where they'll let you out, but you can never go back.

TYLER: Well . . .?

ROBERT: We've always had the option to take that, if we were willing to leave our families behind.

OLIVER: Besides, if we emigrated, do you think the Council would let us defy them and go unpunished? They have friends all over the world to help them make our lives miserable. (*To Moore*) Isn't that right, Mr. Moore? (*Moore remains silent*)

ROBERT: Then that's it, isn't it? Either way, we're finished as actors.

EMILY: (*A beat*) Then you will do what they want?

ROBERT: How can we? If we do what the Council wants, and the government bans us, how will we work? And at what? What about our families? How will Oliver support his Lisa and their little ones? You've met my father. Can he work? How will I care for him and my mother? It isn't just us.

EMILY: (*Softly*) I know.

ROBERT: If we perform, and the Council punishes us, ruins us as actors at home, at least we will not be banned. At least we can work. At *something*. We can care for our families.

EMILY: (*A beat*) My final orders . . . are to advise you . . . that the Council disavows any responsibility for the consequences of your decision.

ROBERT: Meaning?

EMILY: They may not be able to control the people.

ROBERT: The Council has always controlled the people.

EMILY: They may not be able to now. (*A pause*) There may be . . . reprisals.

ROBERT: (*Realizing*) Are you threatening us?

EMILY: You are placing yourselves . . . in danger . . .

ROBERT: (*Disbelief*) Emily . . .

EMILY: . . . And your families . . .

OLIVER: Are you threatening our families?

EMILY: (*Torn*) I am saying we will not accept responsibility!

ROBERT: We'd be in no danger unless the Council ordered it.

TYLER: (*He starts off*) This is extortion. We don't have to listen to this.

ROBERT: (*Stops him*) Wait.

TYLER: I'm calling the police.

ROBERT: No. They can do nothing. (*A beat. Tyler relents, stays*) You can't be a part of this.

EMILY: I have no choice.

ROBERT: Of course you do. You always have a choice.

EMILY: No . . .

ROBERT: *Yes!*

EMILY: (*A beat*) Too many years, Robert. Too many dead. Too many who still lead meaningless lives. (*A pause*) Our only hope is the Council. I can't abandon them when they need me most.

ROBERT: You tried to help us.

EMILY: I thought the Council would agree.

ROBERT: Make them agree.

EMILY: It's too late for that.

ROBERT: You could convince them. Emily, if *anyone* could ... (*A pause*) Think of what you're doing.

EMILY: Things must be done, Robert. Things we do not want to do, but we must do.

ROBERT: What about Peter? Would he have done this? If Peter were alive, would he have allowed *this*?

EMILY: He would have made whatever sacrifice was necessary.

ROBERT: Yes, *he* would have, but he would never've asked it of someone else. (*A pause*) You've become inhuman. All of you.

EMILY: Then we will ... be inhuman. Let that be *our* sacrifice. But for it we will win our freedom, and our children's freedom.

OLIVER: Don't believe it.

EMILY: (*A beat*) I must have your answer.

OLIVER: Can you possibly not know what it will be? Do you think we might still perform, knowing what you will do to the people we love?

ROBERT: No, Oliver. She's right. It's still up to us, no matter what she does. (*He moves close to Oliver*) You know, in my last year in prison I was most of the time alone. But once, for awhile, I had a man with me. I never knew who he was. He couldn't tell me his name because when they first threw him into my cell his jaw was already so badly broken he couldn't speak. And it never healed. They made sure they beat him often enough so it wouldn't. (*A pause*) One night they brought him back, and I listened to him die. It took hours. (*A pause*) In the morning, when they brought that shit they fed us, I ate his too. When they came for him again, I dared them to take me instead. They were happy to oblige. Anyway, I kept them from finding out for a few days. I even dragged his body around the cell so when they looked in they'd think he was moving. (*A pause*) But then he started to smell, and ... (*He shrugs*) They thought I'd gone crazy when I refused to give him up. They stood in the door with their guns on me, cursing and shouting their lungs out ... faces all red. I pulled him with me back against the wall, and I waited for them to shoot. (*A pause*) And nothing happened. (*Laughs*) I started to laugh at them standing there, watching me holding this dead man in my arms. The thing was ... they were waiting, waiting for *me*, waiting to see what *I* would do. I still had choices, Oliver. (*A pause*) I could come to my senses, be a good Kaffir, and say "Ja, baas," and give him up. Or I could hold onto him until they came in and beat me. Or ... I could walk straight into their guns. *I* could make them be the monsters they were threatening to be. (*A pause*) Whatever happened would be because of the choice *I* made. Whatever they did would be in reaction to me. They were as bound by me as I by them because we were men in confrontation. (*A pause*) I was still a human being, and that was something all their laws and prisons and guns and power could not take away. Could never take away. (*A pause*) And I knew this was something our people needed to see. Something that would help them live, whether they got this . . . *freedom* they wanted or not.

EMILY: (*A beat*) You cannot still perform. Robert, you cannot.

ROBERT: No . . . we *will* not.

EMILY: (*A beat. To Moore*) Come. (*She starts to leave the stage. Moore does not move. She stops*)

ROBERT: (*Notices Moore*) Did you want something else?

MOORE: (*Barely audible*) I didn't want . . . (*A pause*) No. (*Emily leaves the stage without looking back. Moore goes out behind her through the auditorium. Robert and Tyler watch them go. Oliver drifts to the mound, sits on it*)

ROBERT: John, thank you for all your help. (*He puts out his hand*)

TYLER: (*Takes his hand*) Do you have to leave now?

ROBERT: There's no reason to stay.

TYLER: (*Embraces him, pulls back*) I wish there was more I could do.

ROBERT: You did as much as anyone could ask.

(*Tony enters through the auditorium*)

TONY: John? The protesters are leaving.

TYLER: Yes, it's over.

TONY: Should I tell our people to come in? (*Tyler looks at Robert*)

ROBERT: We'd rather not see anyone, if you don't mind.

TYLER: I understand. I'll send them home.

ROBERT: No need for them now anyway.

TYLER: No. (*A pause*) Come on, Tony. (*He leaves the stage, goes out through the auditorium. Tony follows him*)

ROBERT: (*A beat*) Oliver, are you all right? (*He goes to the mound, sits beside Oliver*)

OLIVER: (*Dreamy*) Have you ever wondered, my friend, in all these years, how different things would've been if they couldn't touch us?

ROBERT: What do you mean?

OLIVER: If we'd given ourselves over wholly to our art. If we were without wives, or children . . .

ROBERT: (*Slight laugh*) Without parents?

OLIVER: Yes.

ROBERT: (*Puzzled*) Without homes?

OLIVER: Then they could not get at us.

ROBERT: They would get at us . . . through our friends.

OLIVER: If we were without connection to this world at all, if we lived only on stage . . . then we would be free.

ROBERT: Then they would round up our audiences, and who would we act for?

OLIVER: We would act for each other . . . as we did in prison.

ROBERT: Then they would kill one of us. (*A pause*) It's a beautiful thought, but it's got nothing to do with this real world.

OLIVER: That's why it's a beautiful thought.

ROBERT: (*A beat*) Let's go. (*Oliver nods. They stand. Robert goes to the folding table*)

OLIVER: (*Stands looking at the tree*) We should've taken the final exit permit a long time ago. (*A beat. Then Robert gets an idea, moves toward the tree, untying the cord holding up his baggy trousers, which fall down around his ankles as he moves. He gestures to Oliver to help him tie the cord to a branch of the tree*) Don't try to make me laugh.

ROBERT: Would *I* do that?

OLIVER: (*A beat*) Well, if we're going, we'd better change our clothes.

ROBERT: Why?

OLIVER: *Why?*

ROBERT: This is the way I'm going home. (*He gestures at his costume*)

OLIVER: You are?

ROBERT: Yes.

OLIVER: Well, you don't want to be arrested for indecent exposure, do you? Pull on your trousers.

ROBERT: (*Smiles*) What?

OLIVER: Pull . . . (*Realizes what Robert is doing*) . . . on your trousers.

ROBERT: (*Slowly*) You want me to pull . . . *off* my trousers?

OLIVER: (*Loud*) Pull on your trousers!

ROBERT: True . . . true. (*He quickly pulls up his trousers, stands belting them with the cord*)

OLIVER: You're very childish, you know that?

ROBERT: I?

OLIVER: Yes.

ROBERT: More than you?

OLIVER: Much more than me.

ROBERT: Ah . . . are you certain?

OLIVER: (*Stares at him*) Nothing is certain.

ROBERT: Nothing is certain?

OLIVER: (*Daring him to go on*) No.

ROBERT: That's terrible. (*A pause*) Are you certain?

OLIVER: (*Ready to strike*) Yes.

ROBERT: (*Relieved*) Ah ... (*Very deliberately*) ... that's ... reassuring. (*Oliver lashes out, trying to slap Robert, who evades him. They break up laughing. Then, as they compose themselves, they collect their things from the table. Finished, they stand looking around the theatre*)

OLIVER: (*A last joke*) Well? Shall we go?

ROBERT: (*A long beat*) Yes, let's go.

(*They do not move. Then they put an arm around each other as they exit together to one of the wings. When the stage is empty, all the lights fade out*)

The End

P. J. Barry

REASONABLE CIRCULATION

P. J. Barry

P. J. Barry makes his debut in this series with *Reasonable Circulation*, a delightful satire on the private behavior of people in the corporate publishing world. The play appears for the first time in print in this anthology.

Mr. Barry's full-length play *The Octette Bridge Club* was such a hit in the 1984 Humana Festival of New Plays, presented by the Actors Theatre of Louisville, that it was subsequently produced on Broadway in the spring of 1985 with an all-star cast consisting of Peggy Cass, Nancy Marchand, Anne Pitoniak, Bette Henritze, Gisela Caldwell, Elizabeth Huddle, Lois de Banzie and Elizabeth Franz. Though the New York run was not a lengthy one, *The Octette Bridge Club* promises to have an extensive life in regional and community theatres.

Born in Rhode Island, P. J. Barry graduated from La Salle Academy in Providence. He then moved to New York City, where he enrolled in the American Academy of Dramatic Arts, receiving his graduation certificate at the end of their three-year program.

During the Korean War, Mr. Barry served as an entertainer and director in the 10th Special Services Company, for which he received the Commendation Ribbon with Medal Pendant. After release from the service under the G.I. Bill, he attended the University of California at Berkeley, where for two years he majored in English. At that time he began writing, first producing three novels, which he considered his apprenticeship in the writing craft.

Upon returning to New York Mr. Barry became artistic director of the Hudson Guild Theatre, a position he held for seven years. During the same time he also turned his hand to playwriting. Within his tenure at the Hudson Guild, six of his own plays were produced by that organization: *The Brownsville Raid, 1916, Actortines and Actorettes, The Kiss of Life, Light Me a Candle,* and *She Played Good Piano.* Other groups were producing his plays during this period as well: *The Love Man's Gone Away* , produced by the Maine Theatre Arts Festival in 1971; *Heritage,* produced at the Theatre de Lys in Manhattan in 1971; *Toast and Jelly* , produced by the George Street Playhouse in New Brunswick, New Jersey in 1979; and *Good Bargains,* produced at the American Theatre of Actors in Manhattan in 1981.

Mr. Barry's family has been influenced by his life in theatre. His son Matthew co-starred with Jill Clayburgh in Bertolucci's *Luna* and has appeared on the television series *Cagney and Lacy* and *Family Ties.* His son Neill appears in the feature films *Joey* and *O.*

C. and Stiggs. His daughter Nina, fifteen, is not yet in show business, but with the other members of the family so active in the profession, it may be only a matter of time before she joins them.

Since leaving the Hudson Guild Theatre, Mr. Barry has directed at regional theatres and resumed his career in acting for the theatre and television. And, of course, he continues to write new plays.

Characters:

SANDRA HOROWITZ, *twenty-four, attractive, a glorified clerk*
COLLEEN DUGAN, *nineteen, pretty, buxom, a glorified clerk*
MARTA PEREZ, *twenty-two, petite, a secretary, but actually functioning as the department manager's assistant*
JOHN TRAINOR, *thirty-five, handsome, a temporary typist*
NORMAN KENT, *well-dressed department manager*

The Setting:

The action of the play takes place in the regional circulation department of Ketchum Publishing Directory, New York City.

A clean, shining office. A tight little island of desks. Each desk has a telephone. Downstage right and downstage left are two desks with typewriter attachments. John sits at right, Marta sits at left. Center stage, slightly upstage are two desks, each with an adjoining table. Through the play Colleen and Sandra work at their desks, covered with 5-by-5 cards, which they sort, and work at their tables with large galley sheets and ledgers. They then rotate a lot in their chairs from desk to table.

Time:

The time is the present. Late morning, spring.

All lights rise:

John is busy typing, Colleen and Sandra are working diligently, and Marta is checking her makeup.

COLLEEN: What did your mother say?

SANDRA: That I shouldn've got engaged to a Vietnam veteran because they're all unstable.

COLLEEN: What did your grandmother say?

SANDRA: She said that my mother was wrong. She said that Lenny isn't unstable, it's just that he wasn't in a war like World War II which was patriotic, so that's what makes Lenny automatically neurotic.

COLLEEN: What did your father say?

SANDRA: He says that I should never have got engaged to anybody so much older in the first place, ten years, he says, is too much difference in years, same old thing . . . and he said that the reason that Lenny sometimes has those moody spells is because he had to fight a war that wasn't a war, just a meaningless . . . conflict, that's it, conflict. My father was in the Korean War, and he says that was a war and Lenny told me it wasn't a war but a police action whatever that is . . . like all that P.L.O. and Israel and Argentina and the Falklands and all that back and forth stuff like that, I think.

MARTA: What did your Aunt Shirley say?

SANDRA: Oh, her. "Engaged to be engaged is not engaged, Sandra. Show me that ring, sweetie, then I believe." She's so vicious.

(*Telephone rings*)

COLLEEN: My father was in the Korean War, too.

MARTA: (*Answering the phone*) Regional Circulation.

SANDRA: Yeah?

COLLEEN: Yeah.

MARTA: (*On phone*) He's at a meeting right now. Can I help you?

COLLEEN: He loves "M.A.S.H." I mean he loves it. He watches it religiously. He wouldn't miss an episode. Even the reruns.

MARTA: (*On phone*) No, I'm not his secretary. I'm his assistant.

SANDRA: My father hates "M.A.S.H."

COLLEEN: How come?

SANDRA: He says it makes him sick to his stomach.

MARTA: (*On phone*) Fine.

COLLEEN: How come?

SANDRA: My Uncle Sam—my father's younger brother, his only brother—he was killed in Korea.

COLLEEN: Oh, that's sad.

SANDRA: I know.

MARTA: Bye, bye. (*She hangs up*)

COLLEEN: Do you remember your Uncle Sam?

SANDRA: How could I? I wasn't even born before he was dead.

(*Telephone rings*)

COLLEEN: Oh, that's right.

MARTA: (*On phone*) Regional Circulation.

SANDRA: But we have pictures of him. He was handsome
. . . even though he did have a harelip.

MARTA: (*On phone*) No, he's at a meeting now.

COLLEEN: Oh, that's so sad.

MARTA: (*On phone*) Fine.

SANDRA: But you wouldn't know he had it because he wore a moustache from the time he was fifteen, and so you hardly noticed unless someone told you. My father said it never bothered my Uncle Sam.

MARTA: (*On phone*) Bye, bye.

COLLEEN: My father still has shrapnel in his leg . . . from being hit by a bomb. (*Telephone rings*) His leg recovered . . . but there's still a little piece they never got out so that's what makes him limp when it's foggy.

MARTA: (*On phone*) Regional Circulation.

SANDRA: Hey.

COLLEEN: What?

SANDRA: How could your father go to Korea? I thought he was born in Ireland. I thought he grew up there.

COLLEEN: He did. But when he got over here at seventeen he had to join the army so he could become a citizen.

MARTA: (*On phone*) Norman is at a meeting right now.

SANDRA: Oh. Oh, now I see.

MARTA: (*On phone*) Can I have him call you back?

SANDRA: Did you see that old movie on Channel 9 last night? With John Wayne about Ireland. *The Quiet Man*?

MARTA: (*On phone*) Uh huh.

COLLEEN: Oh, yeah. My father always watches it.

SANDRA: Oh, it's good. My father likes it, too.

MARTA: (*On phone*) Bye, bye.

COLLEEN: My mother likes it, too.

SANDRA: My Aunt Shirley hates it. She says John Wayne was an old right-wing fart. But she has a bad attitude about most everything.

(*Telephone rings*)

COLLEEN: A lot of those old movies on TV are better than most of the new ones, you know that?

SANDRA: I know.

MARTA: (*On phone*) Regional Circulation.

SANDRA: They had stories.

MARTA: (*On phone*) Oh, hello, Mrs. Kent.

SANDRA: I love those old war movies . . . with a romance back home . . .

MARTA: (*On phone*) No, Norman's at a meeting right now.

SANDRA: . . . someone waiting, someone caring . . . and like that . . .

COLLEEN: Yeah, me, too. They're corny, but they're good.

MARTA: (*On phone*) How's the baby?

SANDRA: There's one—I don't remember the name—about a blind war veteran and he doesn't want this girl to love him because he's got blind and he drinks with his old buddies in a bar and he's drunk and falls and then she comes to rescue him and then he sleeps it off and in the morning he knows he can love her even if he is blind.

COLLEEN: I didn't see that. What's the name of it?

MARTA: (*On phone*) Oh, how cute.

SANDRA: Something, something, I can't remember. Oh, and the one about the nurses on some island, I think it's called *Bataán* . . . and this one nurse has a hand grenade and she puts it in her shirt right under her left boob right against her heart and she walks right toward the Japs so the other nurses can get away and she gets blown up and saves their lives. I loved that.

COLLEEN: I saw that. That was good. What was the name of it?

SANDRA: Something like *Stars and Stripes Forever* . . . something like that.

JOHN: (*Drawn in for the first time*) *So Proudly We Hail*.

MARTA: (*On phone*) Oh, how cute.

SANDRA: Was that it? Was that the title? I think so, I think you're right, John.

COLLEEN: The one I like is the one with Marlon Brando and he's a paraplegic and his girl still loves him anyway . . . and he wants to stay in the hospital and keep suffering with all the other paraplegic guys from the war and he feels real sorry for himself and she says they'll be all right and she cries, then he cries, then they both hug and cry.

MARTA: (*On phone*) Of course.

COLLEEN: It was terrific.

SANDRA: That Marlon Brando was in that one about Vietnam.

COLLEEN: Yeah, *Apocalypse Now*.

SANDRA: That sucked. Did you see that, John?

JOHN: Yes.

SANDRA: Did you like it? I hated it. Have you ever been in a war movie?

JOHN: No. Not yet.

COLLEEN: But that commercial you said you did was for the Army . . . so that's sorta like being in a war movie.

MARTA: (*On phone*) I'll tell him. Bye, bye. (*She hangs up*)

SANDRA: It's two hours, Colleen. Don't forget to take your medicine.

COLLEEN: Oh, yeah. Thanks for reminding me, Sandra.

MARTA: How many bridesmaids are you going to have, Sandra?

SANDRA: Four.

MARTA: Will you be wearing white?

SANDRA: Of course.

MARTA: What colors will your bridesmaids wear?

SANDRA: Powder blue. I'd like them all in powder blue. The maid of honor can wear either gold or lemon.

MARTA: Gold or lemon? Won't that clash with powder blue?

SANDRA: No. My mother and I are going to start working on the guest list this weekend.

COLLEEN: Aren't you getting ahead of yourself?

SANDRA: Colleen, we're getting married in a year. What's wrong with pre-planning?

COLLEEN: You're just engaged to be engaged. No ring yet.

SANDRA: You sound like my Aunt Shirley.

COLLEEN: Well . . .

SANDRA: Colleen, yesterday you told me that when you and Marco get married, you want two of your bridesmaids in pink and two of your bridesmaids in peach.

COLLEEN: I said if and when I get married to Marco.

MARTA: Where will you get an apartment? Queens?

SANDRA: No, I think it would be good for both of us to be away from our parents. Maybe Brooklyn.

COLLEEN: We live in a section that's still decent.

SANDRA: We're not going to live in Lenny's apartment, I'll tell you that. It's as big as a peanut.

MARTA: You'd love Long Island. It's the only place to live.

SANDRA: Lenny wants to live right here in Manhattan. (*She gets moans*) I know, I know. He says he hates traveling an hour to work every day.

COLLEEN: I wouldn't want to live here.

MARTA: Me either. It's a jungle.

COLLEEN: You can say that again.

SANDRA: He says he'd like to live in Greenwich Village.

COLLEEN: Oh, no.

MARTA: Would you?

SANDRA: I don't know. You see he goes there twice a week. That's where his therapist lives.

COLLEEN: Lenny goes to a therapist?

SANDRA: Yeah.

MARTA: Why?

SANDRA: He says it helps keep him balanced.

COLLEEN: He has to keep balanced if he's going to marry you. (*Telephone rings*)

SANDRA: Oh, shut up, you.

MARTA: (*On phone*) Regional Circulation . . . oh, hi, Lenny . . . Yes, she is . . . Hold on. (*She switches call to Sandra . . . a buzzer sounds*)

SANDRA: (*On phone*) Hi, honey.

NORMAN: (*Entering*) Marta, did those brochures get here from Printing?

MARTA: Yes, they did, Norman. How was the meeting?

NORMAN: The computers will not be here on Monday. It will take another month. I should have known.

MARTA: Your wife called. She said your son took his first steps.

NORMAN: About time. He's almost two. (*Examining the brochures*) What is this? I ordered beige, lavender, olive and cerise.

MARTA: Yes.

SANDRA: (*On phone*) Lenny, you didn't say I couldn't tell Mom and Dad.

NORMAN: Well?

MARTA: Well, what?

NORMAN: This is brown not beige, this is purple not lavender, this is green not olive, and this is . . .

MARTA: . . . Red not cerise.

NORMAN: Exactly. I'll show you the color wheel in my office. Those dunderheads in Printing. (*Confidentially*) That dumb midget and that dumb Chink. They mangle everything. But we have to have our Senior Citizen representation, don't we. (*Starts off, stops*) Oh. These labels. (*Removes them from a large interoffice envelope he is carrying*) They must be retyped today.

MARTA: What's wrong with them?

NORMAN: (*Drawing her aside*) That temp we had before John. She typed them on large labels instead of small labels.

MARTA: Oh, these. I thought you wanted them on the large labels.

NORMAN: No, I wanted them on the small labels, not the large labels, and I wanted them addressed to the Purchase Manager, not to the Personnel Manager. Shall I give them to you to give to John or shall I give them to him directly myself?

MARTA: You can give them to him if you like, Norman, or I can give them to him if you prefer.

NORMAN: I'll give them to him, Marta.

MARTA: All right, Norman.

SANDRA: (*On phone*) Lenny, you didn't say I couldn't tell my brother or my Aunt Shirley.

NORMAN: You're sure? Your official title is now Regional Circulation Assistant, not secretary, and I don't want you to feel that I'm infringing on your new responsibilities.

MARTA: Oh, not at all, Norman.

NORMAN: I'm glad to hear that, Marta.

SANDRA: (*On phone*) I didn't think you meant my family or my closest friends.

MARTA: (*Handing Norman the envelope*) Then you'll give these to John?

NORMAN: This is correct. I'll give them to him right now.

SANDRA: (*On phone*) That's not true. I can be trusted.

NORMAN: John, how are you doing?

JOHN: Fine, thank you.

NORMAN: I wanted you to know how much we've appreciated your work in the last four weeks.

JOHN: Thank you.

NORMAN: You're a whiz. The best temporary typist we've had in six months.

JOHN: Thank you.

NORMAN: I know you need extra time some days to go on your little acting auditions . . . rough racket, show business. I know you have taken your lunch hour at odd times . . . so if you do need extra time for your little acting auditions please just let us know and take that time, buddy.

JOHN: Thank you.

NORMAN: Of course you get paid by the hour, no change on that. But in your need for an extra hour or two we can make adjustments for you if the need arises.

JOHN: Thank you.

NORMAN: You're welcome, buddy. Now would you put that work aside and complete these labels. Retype them all on small labels, not big labels . . .

SANDRA: (*On phone*) I am, Lenny.

NORMAN: . . . Addressed to Purchase Manager, not Personnel Manager. I'd like them completed by five.

JOHN: There are a lot of labels here.

NORMAN: Give it your best shot. If we bend a little for you, bend a little for us. I'm sure you'll manage, buddy.

SANDRA: (*On phone*) I am an honorable person.

NORMAN: (*Returning to Marta*) Marta, I *want all of us* to start cutting down on excessive telephone calls.

JOHN: The telephone tempers the tension of the tedium.

NORMAN: What?

JOHN: The telephone . . .

NORMAN: I heard you. Type the labels, John.

JOHN: That's why I'm here, buddy. (*He begins to type*)

NORMAN: (*After a brief pause*) Marta, come into my office . . . and bring those ugly brochures. (*He starts off*)

MARTA: In a second, Norman.

NORMAN: *Now* . . . Marta. (*He exits*)

(*John begins to dial*)

MARTA: I'll be right there, Norman.

(*Norman exits. Marta is about to follow as the telephone rings*)

COLLEEN: I'll get it, Marta. Go ahead.

(*Marta nods her thanks and goes*)

SANDRA: (*On phone*) Lenny, you're unreasonable.

COLLEEN: (*On phone*) Regional Circulation.

JOHN: (*On phone*) Any messages for John Trainor?

COLLEEN: (*On phone*) Oh, hi, Marco.

SANDRA: (*On phone*) I'm upset.

COLLEEN: (*On phone*) I'm better.

SANDRA: (*On phone*) You're going to make me cry.

COLLEEN: (*On phone*) Yes, I'm taking my medicine . . . like a good little girl.

JOHN: (*On phone*) John Trainor.

COLLEEN: (*On phone*) Marco, I'm nineteen.

SANDRA: (*On phone*) I did not break a promise.

COLLEEN: (*On phone*) I'm too young to get an ulcer. Aren't I?

SANDRA: (*On phone*) I simply took people into my confidence.

COLLEEN: (*On phone*) Any arrests today?

SANDRA: (*On phone*) This is not breaking a promise.

COLLEEN: (*On phone*) I know you are. Thanks for calling, Marco. You're nice.

SANDRA: (*On phone*) Lenny?

JOHN: (*On phone*) No messages?

COLLEEN: (*On phone with a subdued kiss*) Me, too.

SANDRA: (*On phone*) *Lenny?*

JOHN: (*On phone*) Thank you. Bye.

COLLEEN: (*On phone*) Bye.

(*The three hang up at the same time, Sandra slamming down her receiver. John resumes typing*)

SANDRA: Lenny hung up on me.

COLLEEN: Is anything wrong?

SANDRA: He hung up on me.

COLLEEN: Something's wrong.

SANDRA: He never did that before. I think I'm gonna cry.

COLLEEN: Don't. Norman will see you.

SANDRA: He's talking to Marta, he won't see me.

COLLEEN: If you have to cry, Sandra, go to the ladies room and cry. I did it last Thursday after I was mugged. It helped.

SANDRA: Oh, it's so awful!

COLLEEN: What's so awful?

SANDRA: I can't talk about it now.

COLLEEN: Go on, talk about it.

SANDRA: I can't, Colleen, I can't.

COLLEEN: Let it out, Sandra, let it out.

SANDRA: I can't, I can't, I just can't.

COLLEEN: Let it out or you'll get gastritis . . . like me.

SANDRA: Lenny broke our engagement to be engaged.

COLLEEN: Oh, no. Is that why he hung up on you?

SANDRA: I've got to call my mother.

COLLEEN: Sandra, don't. Norman is in a piss-ant mood today. Look at him, look at him with Marta, look at that face. Don't get on the phone again right away.

SANDRA: Lenny was so awful, Colleen. (*She picks up phone, puts it down*) I said I wouldn't tell anyone except my mother and my father and my grandmother and my brother and my Aunt Shirley . . . she can't keep her mouth shut about anything, but I had to tell her even though she responded negatively which isn't unusual for her . . .

COLLEEN: Want a Kleenex?

SANDRA: No, I refuse to cry over him. And Rachel, I had to tell Rachel, she's my maid of honor . . . and Leah called, and if she found out I'd told Rachel and not her, she'd be on my case for weeks . . . Leah's one of my bridesmaids. Well, I blame Leah. She was my mistake. Because on the subway this morning Lenny said three people congratulated him from the neighborhood on his engagement . . . and at the office he got four phone calls. He said he knew he couldn't trust me. I tried to reason with him, and he said I was unreasonable, that I was not a reasonable person. What a thing to say! Maybe I should've kept going with his brother, Moses.

COLLEEN: Maybe.

SANDRA: No, no, Colleen. Moses is immature. He's only twenty-four, my age. A man is very immature at twenty-four, you know that, we all know that, not like a woman. Lenny's mature. He's neurotic, but mature. You see he didn't want to announce our engagement to be engaged until after he got the results of his exam at the veteran's hospital yesterday. He's worried, you see, about

Agent Orange because his hair is beginning to fall out. He's losing his hair, I never told you.

COLLEEN: A lot of men lose their hair young. My father was all the way bald when he was thirty-five.

SANDRA: Lenny's only thirty-four. Should I call his mother? Why call her? She's such a pain in the ass. She is ... but she might know something that I don't know, right?

COLLEEN: What's Agent Orange?

SANDRA: Maybe I should call my father?

MARTA: (*Returning, smoking a cigarette*) Easy on the phones today. Norman's ready for war ... let's not aggravate him any more than necessary.

COLLEEN: They must be hiring a new black girl to replace Felena. He hates blacks.

MARTA: He does not, Colleen. He just doesn't tolerate them very well.

COLLEEN: He hated Puerto Ricans, too ... until you came.

MARTA: I'm not Puerto Rican, I'm Spanish.

COLLEEN: Okay, okay.

MARTA: There's a big difference.

COLLEEN: Okay, don't get touchy.

SANDRA: I won't cry over that bastard.

MARTA: Lenny?

SANDRA: Son-of-a-bitch.

MARTA: (*To Colleen*) Lenny?

(*Colleen nods*)

SANDRA: Prick.

MARTA: What happened?

SANDRA: I don't want to talk about it.

MARTA: What happened with Lenny?

SANDRA: I refuse to cry.

COLLEEN: After they got engaged to be engaged last night Sandra promised that she wouldn't tell anyone except her mother, her father, her grandmother and her brother.

SANDRA: And my Aunt Shirley.

COLLEEN: And her Aunt Shirley. And her best friend Rachel who ...

SANDRA: ... is going to be my maid of honor and also Leah who is going to be one of my bridesmaids.

COLLEEN: Leah was the mistake. On the subway five people congratulated Lenny, and at his office *ten* people called.

SANDRA: And he hung up on me.

COLLEEN: He didn't want to announce they're engaged to be engaged until after the results of his examination at the vet's hospital yesterday. He's worried about Agent Orange because his hair is falling out. Sure you don't want a Kleenex, Sandra?

MARTA: What's Agent Orange? Like herpes?

SANDRA: No. Agent Orange is something our government used in Vietnam, some kind of spray that's bad.

MARTA: Spray? You mean like a chemical?

SANDRA: Something like that.

JOHN: Agent Orange is a herbicide they used in Vietnam to defoliate the jungle.

COLLEEN: What does defoliate mean?

JOHN: It would strip the trees of leaves so you could see your way, see the enemy. Since then, veterans have died of cancer . . . some have loss of hair . . . some have become impotent . . .

SANDRA: Lenny's not that.

COLLEEN: I know what that means.

JOHN: All of it comes under the heading of war-related defects. And in some cases, because of exposure to it, children are born deformed.

COLLEEN AND MARTA: Deformed?

SANDRA: Ich. He didn't tell me about that.

JOHN: He probably didn't want to scare you.

SANDRA: I'm calling him back.

COLLEEN: Go to the ladies room first, Sandra.

SANDRA: Why?

COLLEEN: Just to sit and think and pee a little, so you don't regret what you have to say if you did call him back without taking the time to put yourself together.

SANDRA: I guess. Come with me.

COLLEEN: No. Norman will have a heart attack if we're both
. . .

SANDRA: Oh, fuck him. Come on.

MARTA: No . . . Colleen's right. Look at him looking at us through his window.

COLLEEN: Look at him stare.

MARTA: Smile.

(*The three smile*)

SANDRA: Oh, that face. Like a rat.

COLLEEN: (*Tilts her head*) Sort of.

SANDRA: Colleen, I'm not going into the bathroom and cry. I know, I'll have some water. And I don't care what Norman rat face thinks about that. Colleen, come with me to the water fountain. Don't stand there. Come with me to the water fountain, please.

(*Colleen goes with Sandra. John is busy typing again. Marta is busy typing*)

MARTA: John, how did you know all that about Agent Orange?

JOHN: I was in the army.

MARTA: Vietnam?

JOHN: Yes.

MARTA: Was it terrible?

JOHN: Yes.

MARTA: Did you have to kill anybody?

JOHN: Yes.

MARTA: How many?

JOHN: Too many.

MARTA: Do you think we'll have a nuclear war next?

JOHN: If there is, we'll all get dead.

MARTA: Oh, there'll be some safe places. There'll be places on Long Island.

JOHN: What makes you say that?

(*Phone rings*)

MARTA: Because Long Island is like that. (*Answering phone*) Regional Circulation ... she's away from her desk right now ... Yes, I will ... Who's calling please? ... Thank you, Mrs. Dugan ... Bye, bye.

NORMAN: (*Returning*) Where did Colleen and Sandra go?

MARTA: To the water fountain.

NORMAN: Really?

MARTA: Yes.

NORMAN: How odd.

MARTA: Is it?

NORMAN: Thirsty at exactly the same time?

MARTA: Sandra said she was thirsty, and because she said it, then Colleen discovered that she was, too.

JOHN: Like yawning.

NORMAN: Oh, you mean the power of suggestion?

JOHN: Yes.

NORMAN: You think that being thirsty is the same kind of thing as yawning? Yawning is much more contagious than being thirsty.

JOHN: Maybe.

NORMAN: It is, John.

JOHN: Maybe.

NORMAN: I said it is, and it is. (*To Marta, confidentially*) Marta, call that dumb midget or that dumb Chink about the brochure colors and get it corrected.

MARTA: I thought you wanted to handle it.

NORMAN: You're the Regional Circulation Assistant, Marta. You need new responsibilities to stretch. (*He picks up the phone, and hands it to her*) Stretch.

(*Marta takes phone from him, Norman exits*)

JOHN: That man is an asshole.

MARTA: (*Nods*) Every day. (*She dials*)

SANDRA: (*Returning with Colleen*) I'm going to call him back right now and confront him face to face.

MARTA: Colleen, your mother called. (*She hands her the message*)

COLLEEN: Thanks, Marta.

MARTA: (*On phone*) Hello, Tiny, this is Marta.

SANDRA: (*On phone*) I'd like to speak to Lenny.

MARTA: (*On phone*) Marta, from Regional Circulation.

SANDRA: (*On phone*) Lenny Silverstein.

MARTA: (*On phone*) I'm Norman Kent's assistant, you know me.

SANDRA: (*On phone*) Sandra Horowitz.

COLLEEN: (*On phone*) Hello, Ma? This is me.

SANDRA: (*On phone*) Miss. (*Her hand over the receiver*) "Miss or Mrs." She always asks that. And she knows who I am, the bitch.

COLLEEN: (*On phone*) Better, Ma. I'm taking the medicine.

SANDRA: She always keeps me waiting.

COLLEEN: (*On phone*) Marco called, too.

SANDRA: I think she has the hots for Lenny.

COLLEEN: (*On phone*) To ask about my gastritis. Wasn't that sweet of him?

SANDRA: He says I'm imagining things.

(*John dials*)

COLLEEN: (*On phone*) Yes, he was on duty.

SANDRA: I know I'm not.

COLLEEN: (*On phone*) He just arrested some guy for beating his wife with a hammer.

JOHN: (*On phone*) Hello, Eve. This is John Trainor. Is Adam there?

COLLEEN: (*On phone*) Cops are entitled to breaks like everybody, Ma, so he got a coupla minutes, so he called me because he's concerned about me.

SANDRA: (*On phone*) Yes, I'll hold on until he's off the other line.

JOHN: (*On phone*) Sure, Eve, I'll hold on.

SANDRA: (*Her hand over receiver*) Bitch.

MARTA: (*On phone*) I am calling for Norman because he wanted me to explain to you what he ordered.

COLLEEN: (*On phone*) Why are you being so nasty about Marco? He does his job, Ma, he's a good cop. He hardly takes any graft.

MARTA: (*On phone*) Tiny, I have a Xerox copy here in front of me of the original order.

SANDRA: She said: "Are you still there?" Is she to be believed? Fat bitch.

COLLEEN: (*On phone*) What are you saying?

SANDRA: Lenny says she's fatter than fat. You know what I said to him? I said some men prefer an overabundance of flesh.

COLLEEN: (*On phone*) I am not pregnant!

JOHN: (*On phone*) I'm holding on, Eve.

COLLEEN: (*On phone*) Dr. O'Keefe said it was gastritis and that's all. What's the matter with you?

MARTA: (*On phone*) He ordered the following shades: beige, lavender, olive, and cerise.

SANDRA: Oh, please god, don't let me start crying when Lenny gets on, please. Let me be adult.

COLLEEN: (*On phone*) Ma . . .

MARTA: (*On phone*) He got brown for beige . . .

JOHN: (*On phone*) Thanks, Eve.

MARTA: (*On phone*) . . . Purple for lavender . . .

JOHN: (*On phone*) Hi, Adam.

MARTA: (*On phone*) . . . Green for olive, and red for Cerise.

JOHN: (*On phone*) This is John.

COLLEEN: (*On phone*) Oh, Ma, you're not making any sense.

JOHN: (*On phone*) John Trainor, Adam.

MARTA: (*On phone*) It doesn't matter what I think, Tiny. It's what Norman ordered and what Norman orders, Norman gets.

JOHN: (*On phone*) I'm fine. Did you hear any more on that movie Universal would be shooting here in July?

MARTA: (*On phone*) He did not order brown, purple, green or red, he ordered *beige, lavender, olive and cerise*.

COLLEEN: (*On phone*) Don't you call me that.

MARTA: (*On phone*) Yes, Tiny, he wants them all redone.

SANDRA: (*On phone*) Hello, Lenny. Remember me?

MARTA: (*On phone*) You won't lose your job.

SANDRA: (*On phone*) Why did you hang up on me and hurt me so?

MARTA: (*On phone*) We all make mistakes.

JOHN: (*On phone*) Adam, they said they liked the screen test.

SANDRA: (*On phone*) Now will you please explain more about this Agent Orange and how it effects you? I know it's a defoldiate, but . . .

MARTA: (*On phone*) Tiny, you'd better let me speak to your boss.

SANDRA: (*On phone*) Defoliate, sorry.

COLLEEN: (*On phone*) Ma, you're talking crazy.

MARTA: (*On phone*) Let me speak to Mr. Wong. I don't want my boss to go on the warpath either.

JOHN: (*On phone*) I definitely don't have the part?

COLLEEN: (*On phone*) If you don't stop talking like that, I'm gonna move out.

SANDRA: (*On phone*) Oh?

COLLEEN: (*On phone*) Marco is a good man and a good cop and good to me.

JOHN: (*On phone*) Adam, why didn't you call me and tell me that I'd lost it?

MARTA: (*On phone*) Hello, Mr. Wong. This is Marta Perez, Regional Circulation.

JOHN: (*On phone*) Don't give me that crap, you knew I'd been waiting to hear.

SANDRA: (*On phone*) I'm listening, Lenny.

MARTA: (*On phone*) About the colors.

JOHN: (*On phone*) You bet your ass I'm overly sensitive. I've been here a month typing name after name . . .

COLLEEN: (*On phone*) Italians are just as good as the Irish.

JOHN: (*On phone*) . . . address after address, and it's goddamned grim.

COLLEEN: (*On phone*) You have a fault, Ma. You watch too many soap operas. You're addicted to them . . . like an alcoholic.

MARTA: (*On phone*) I'm trying to explain it to you now, Mr. Wong, if you'd give me the chance.

JOHN: (*On phone*) My unemployment ran out, my savings are almost gone, it's been the pits.

COLLEEN: (*On phone*) Don't you dare call me that again.

SANDRA: (*On phone*) I said I'm listening.

JOHN: (*On phone*) Instead of doing your best, Adam, do a little better.

COLLEEN: (*On phone*) Then I'm an Irish slut's daughter.

JOHN: (*On phone*) I don't like your attitude either. (*He hangs up*)

MARTA: (*On phone*) He ordered beige, lavender . . . What?

SANDRA: (*On phone*) Oh?

MARTA: (*On phone*) I'm sorry, Mr. Wong, I'll go slower. (*Slowing up*) Beige . . .

COLLEEN: (*On phone*) I will move out.

MARTA: (*On phone*) Lavender . . .

COLLEEN: (*On phone*) I hope God forgives you.

MARTA: (*On phone*) Olive . . .

COLLEEN: (*On phone*) Bye. (*She slams down receiver*)

MARTA: (*On phone*) Cerise.

(*John begins to dial again*)

SANDRA: (*On phone*) Uh huh.

COLLEEN: My mother wants me to move out. She says I only give twenty dollars a week anyway, and my sisters need my room.

MARTA: (*On phone*) The colors he did not want are . . . no, no, I won't go fast, Mr. Wong.

JOHN: (*On phone*) Hello, Eve, John Trainor again. Can I speak to Adam?

SANDRA: (*On phone*) So all you've been telling me comes down to this: that you are no longer engaged to be engaged to me, that you don't want to marry me and that you're moving from your apartment in Queens to something even more expensive in Greenwich Village.

JOHN: (*On phone*) Yes, I'll hold on, Eve. (*He continues to type*)

MARTA: (*On phone*) Brown . . .

SANDRA: (*On phone*) You will not save that much money on transportation, Lenny.

COLLEEN: You don't tell your daughter to move out when she's got gastritis.

SANDRA: (*On phone*) Sell your car? How will we get any place if you sell your car?

MARTA: (*On phone*) Purple . . .

SANDRA: (*On phone*) Do you know what I think? Do you really want to know what I think? You're using this Agent Orange stuff as an excuse to end our relationship.

MARTA: (*On phone*) Green . . .

SANDRA: (*On phone*) Well, if you're worried about it, I can share that worry with you, Lenny.

COLLEEN: Father Fitzpatrick would say: "Mrs. Dugan, you've wronged your daughter."

SANDRA: (*On phone*) Yes, if you feel the need to make changes, Lenny, I can make those changes with you, Lenny.

MARTA: (*On phone*) Red . . .

COLLEEN: But then Father Fitzpatrick would say to me: "Forgive your mother, Colleen Frances."

SANDRA: (*On phone*) If you want me to live with you in Greenwich Village without a wedding ring or an engagement ring, I'll live with you . . . for better or worse.

COLLEEN: The problem is my mother is going through the change.

MARTA: (*On phone*) Yes, Mr. Wong . . . Thank you. Bye, bye. (*She hangs up and moans*) Oh, do I need a cigarette.

SANDRA: (*On phone*) You still love me?

JOHN: (*On phone*) Yes, I'm holding, Eve.

SANDRA: (*On phone*) Yes, I love you, too.

MARTA: Where are my cigarettes?

SANDRA: (*On phone*) I'll see you tonight, honey. Bye, honey. (*She hangs up*)

MARTA: Where the hell are my cigarettes? (*She begins to rummage*)

SANDRA: Lenny is moving to Greenwich Village, and he wants me to move in with him. Don't say it . . . Don't! Don't say I shouldn't, because I'm going to. You know how handsome he is, Colleen. All those faggots in Greenwich Village give good head. I'd better be there, or he'll be eaten alive. Besides, I've lived with my parents long enough. They'll be glad to have the room for my brother. And don't either of you say anything about that Agent Orange stuff and deformed babies because . . . because I never said I wanted a baby.

JOHN: (*On phone*) Yes, I'm still holding, Eve.

SANDRA: Oh, I'm just so glad I called him back. I'd be miserable without him. He still loves me. He wants me to be with him day after day, night after night.

MARTA: I must have left them in his office. Shit. (*She storms off*)

SANDRA: Whatever that Agent Orange does to him . . . (*The telephone rings*) I'll be by his side. (*Answering phone*) Reasonable Circulation.

COLLEEN: (*Having dialed again*) Hello, Ma, it's me . . . Colleen Frances, Ma, you know . . .

SANDRA: (*On phone*) Sorry, you have the wrong number. (*She hangs up, giggles*) Did you hear me? I answered the phone and said *reasonable* circulation. Isn't that a riot? (*She laughs and goes about her work*)

JOHN: (*On phone*) Hello, Adam . . . I'm calling you back to tell you I'm not signing with you, you scumbag, I'm . . .

SANDRA: We should try that for the rest of the day.

JOHN: (*On phone*) What?

SANDRA: Say: "Reasonable Circulation" instead of Regional.

COLLEEN: (*On phone*) Ma, I'm sorry.

SANDRA: See how many people would catch it. Not many I bet.

COLLEEN: (*On phone*) I'm really sorry, Ma.

SANDRA: Know why? Because people don't listen . . .

JOHN: (*On phone*) You're kidding . . . That much?

SANDRA: They just don't really listen to each other.

JOHN: (*On phone*) Wow.

COLLEEN: (*On phone*) Ma, I'm not ready to go live on my own.

JOHN: (*On phone*) Wow.

COLLEEN: (*On phone*) I didn't say you were an alcoholic, Ma. If you need a drink at 11:45 in the morning, am I to say that you shouldn't have it? That's for Doctor O'Keefe to decide, wouldn't you say?

JOHN: (*On phone*) Wow.

(*Marta returns, smoking*)

COLLEEN: (*On phone*) So I can keep my room? I won't have to move out yet?

JOHN: (*On phone*) Wow!

SANDRA: Wouldn't it be a good idea, Marta. Just answer "Reasonable Circulation" for the rest of the day. See what happens?

MARTA: What are you talking about?

COLLEEN: (*On phone*) Thanks, Ma. God bless. Bye.

SANDRA: Why do I feel unhappy?

JOHN: (*On phone*) Bye. (*He hangs up*) Holy Christ! (*He rises*) I read for a series. Months ago. They flew me out to L.A. to read for it, ABC. They thought it had hit the dust. But they just called my agent. It was called the *Boston Dispatch* about a group of soldiers during the revolution who form their own newspaper. But that premise, they figured, was dated. So they rewrote it, updated it to a headquarters unit in Vietnam. It's called the *Saigon Dispatch* now, and it's about a group of G.I.'s who form this newspaper to get to the public the truth about the war. The pilot is sold without being filmed. And thirteen more episodes. Sold! And I'm sold. I start working the first of next month. Holy Christ! (*He kisses Sandra, Colleen, and Marta and jumps up on the desk in his excitement*)

COLLEEN: You've had good news.

JOHN: Yeah.

(*Norman enters*)

NORMAN: What's going on?

SANDRA: John has good news.

MARTA: He's going to be on a TV series.

COLLEEN: ABC.

JOHN: In the fall.

NORMAN: Congratulations, John. Glad to hear it, buddy. (*He shakes his hand*)

JOHN: Thanks, buddy.

NORMAN: But a word of caution, John. Have you signed a contract yet?

JOHN: I just got off the phone.

NORMAN: Wait until you sign that contract before you jump for joy. The fickle finger of fate booms in show business. One day you're on top, the next day the bottom. Time to get down and get back to reality.

JOHN: You mean typing?

NORMAN: You want to get paid on Friday? Finish those labels. Down, buddy, down. (*John gets down*) Very good. Back to work everyone. (*He takes Marta aside, confidentially*) Marta, I've changed my mind. Call the midget or the Chink and tell them I think the solid colors of the brochures might be best after all.

MARTA: But . . .

NORMAN: No "buts." I don't want any "buts" today, Marta. Tomorrow maybe, but not today. Do it. And you'd better cut down on those cigarettes before you wind up a corpse. (*He exits*)

MARTA: (*She dials*) Someday, soon, I will be in a position to fire that man.

COLLEEN: My stomach hurts. Should I take more medicine?

SANDRA: Maybe I shouldn't move in with him.

MARTA: (*On phone*) Hello, Tiny. It's Marta again. Can I speak to Mr. Wong, please?

SANDRA: All that Agent Orange and everything.

MARTA: (*On phone*) Mr. Wong, it's me again, Marta.

SANDRA: Who knows what else can happen inside his body, in his bloodstream?

MARTA: (*On phone*) Regional Circulation . . . Norman Kent's assistant.

COLLEEN: Anybody want an M & M?

SANDRA: Lenny just may be too old for me. My father may be right.

MARTA: (*On phone*) The order can switch to the way you made up the brochures.

JOHN: (*Typing*) Purchase Manager . . . Mentor Electric Sewer . . .

SANDRA: My father always liked Lenny's brother, Moses. And Moses is my age.

JOHN: (*Typing*) 24 Power Horn Terrace . . . Kalamazoo, Michigan, 49224 . . .

MARTA: (*On phone*) Yes, Mr. Wong. The exact opposite of what we discussed a few minutes ago.

JOHN: (*Typing*) P.S. See *dynamic* John Trainor . . .

SANDRA: Even my Aunt Shirley liked Moses . . . and she doesn't like anybody. Moses isn't as sexy as Lenny . . . but

Moses at twenty-four makes almost twice as much as Lenny makes at thirty-four.

JOHN: *(Typing)* . . . in the *Saigon Dispatch* . . . coming this fall on ABC. *(He chuckles to himself)*

SANDRA: Maybe I should back off from Lenny and reconsider Moses? For my own sanity, for my own peace of mind . . . I mean, I do want healthy children someday.

COLLEEN: I feel like I'm getting a cold on top of everything else.

MARTA: *(On phone)* All right, all right, Mr. Wong. Get a pencil.

SANDRA: Lenny would probably be better off with that fat receptionist who has the hots for him anyway.

MARTA: *(On phone)* Good. *Brown* . . .

JOHN: *(Typing)* Purchase Manager . . .

SANDRA: My best friend, Rachel? She really looked forward to being my maid of honor. She wasn't even opposed to my choice for her to wear gold or lemon.

MARTA: *(On phone)* *Purple* . . .

JOHN: *(Typing, more gleefully)* Mohawk Excavating Industries . . .

SANDRA: She may not even want to hang out with me after this.

COLLEEN: I should've called Marco before I called my mother back. Why didn't I think of that?

MARTA: *(On phone)* *Green* . . .

JOHN: *(Typing)* Candlewood Corners. Berlin, Connecticut, 95418.

SANDRA: Actually . . .

JOHN: *(Typing)* P.S. See . . . *electrifying* John Trainor . . .

SANDRA: Actually, I'm confused.

(The telephone rings)

I'll get it, Marta.

JOHN: *(Typing)* . . . In the *Saigon Dispatch* . . .

MARTA: *(On phone)* *Red* . . .

SANDRA: *(Answering the telephone)* Reasonable Circulation.

(Blackout)

The End

Milcha Sanchez-Scott

DOG LADY

Milcha Sanchez-Scott

Milcha Sanchez-Scott makes her debut in this anthology with *Dog Lady*, a charming satire on the achievement of success through athletics, which features an Hispanic marathon runner. Herbert Mitgang of the *New York Times* describes the play from its 1984 production by the Manhattan Hispanic theatre INTAR: "In *Dog Lady*, a runner is given a healing potion to make her go faster; the twist is that the religious mumbo-jumbo in the barrio causes her to run, like an animal, on all fours." The INTAR production was directed by INTAR's artistic director Max Ferra with sets designed by Ming Cho Lee. The production teamed the play with the writer's companion piece, *The Cuban Swimmer*. The two short plays had been developed in 1982 by the author as a special project of the L.A. Theatre Works, and in 1983 the plays won the Vesta award, which is presented each year to a woman artist living on the West Coast.

Ms. Sanchez-Scott's first play, *Latina*, was premiered by the L.A. Theatre Works in 1980 and received seven *Dramalogue* awards. The play also received a grant from the California Arts Council to tour the state.

In 1983-84 Ms. Sanchez-Scott was selected as one of the Playwrights-in-Residence for the workshop sponsored by INTAR and conducted by playwright and director Maria Irene Fornes. During her New York residency Ms. Sanchez-Scott began writing a full-length play, *Roosters*, which she has now completed, and presently she is working on three one-act plays grouped under the collective title *City of Angels*.

Born in Indonesia of Mexican and Asian parents, Ms. Sanchez-Scott lived in Mexico, Colombia, and England before immigrating with her family to the United States when she was thirteen years old. She now lives in Los Angeles where she has worked with the group Artists in Prison and Other Places. Also in Los Angeles she has taught a writing workshop at Nostros Theatre.

Characters:

RAPHAEL
ORLANDO, *mailman*
ROSALINDA LUNA, *the runner*
MARIA PILAR LUNA, *Rosalinda's mother*
JESSE LUNA, *Rosalinda's younger sister*
LUISA RUIZ, *the Dog Lady*
MRS. AMADOR, *a neighbor*

Time:

Summer.

Place:

Los Angeles. A small barrio off the Hollywood freeway.

1st Day:
Early summer morning. The residential section of Castro Street.
There is a large sun, and the sunlight has the particular orange
hue that indicates the Santa Ana weather condition.
  We see two front yards, enclosed by a low stone or cement
fence. One yard is very neat, tidy, almost manicured, with a ro-
tating sprinkler watering the green lawn. The other yard is
jungle-like, with strange plants in odd places, rubber tires, all
other kinds of rubbish, and a sign in front that reads: "CU-
RANDERA—HEALER." Each yard has a mailbox and on the
far side of the neat house, there is a jacaranda tree.
  Leaning against the fence is Raphael, a dark, brutal-looking
young man of eighteen or nineteen. He has smoldering dark
eyes. He is wearing a Cuban T-shirt, khaki pants, a dark felt
hat. He is staring at the neat house.

RAPHAEL: (*Like music*) Rosalinda!
(*Enter Orlando, the mailman, carrying his bag. Raphael runs*
away before Orlando can see him)
  ORLANDO: (*Walking*) Neither rain, nor sleet, nor snow . . .
Says nothing about the heat . . . not one word about the heat.
(*Orlando opens the mailbox of the messy yard and rummages*

through his bags) Nada, ni modo, nothing for you, Doña Luisa. *(Reading sign)* "Curandera . . . healer." *(Shakes his head)* It takes all kinds.

(Rosalinda comes out of her house. She is eighteen years old, wearing a jogging shorts outfit. She is quite pretty and feminine. She does some warm-up stretches)

Hola Rosalinda, ay qué hot! . . . It's a scorcher . . . it's a sauna . . . you could fry eggs on the sidewalk . . . it's so hot that . . . You gonna run? Today?

ROSALINDA: I'm gonna win, Orlando.

ORLANDO: You're gonna die! This heat could affect your brain.

ROSALINDA: *(Getting into starting position)* I'm going to run around the world. Today Africa, tomorrow India and Saturday
. . .

ORLANDO: "The Big One."

ROSALINDA: Rome!

ORLANDO: On your mark. Get set. The whole barrio's behind you . . . Go!

(Rosalinda runs off. Orlando yells to Rosalinda)

May all the Angels come down and blow you over the finish line. *(Walking off)* Wish we had some rain, some sleet, some snow.

(Exit Orlando. The sun moves up a fraction in the sky to indicate passage of time. In front of the neat yard of the Luna family we see Maria Pilar Luna, Rosalinda's mother, wearing a fresh housedress and apron. She is standing on the newly swept cement path that leads to her front porch. She has a very determined look as her eyes scan the street. The Luna's neighbor, Luisa Ruiz, is slowly making her way through the rubble and rubbish in her front yard. She is dressed in a torn, stained, dingy white bathrobe. Although her lips are painted a bright red, her hair has not been combed. The overall effect is that she looks not unlike her front yard)

MARIA PILAR: Rosalinda! Rosalinda!

LUISA RUIZ: Buenos días, María Pilar. It's a beautiful Santa Ana day, que no?

MARIA PILAR: Buenos días, Doña Luisa. Si, si it's a beautiful day. Rosalinda! Ay dónde está, esa muchacha? Rosalinda!

LUISA RUIZ: Are you looking for Rosalinda?

MARIA PILAR: No, I'm doing this for the good of my health.

LUISA RUIZ: Oh. Maybe a tea of wild pepper grass.

MARIA PILAR: I'm only joking, Doña Luisa, I'm already under the doctor's care, thank you.

LUISA RUIZ: Oh. You're welcome.

MARIA PILAR: Rosalinda! Rosalinda!

LUISA RUIZ: Where is she?

MARIA PILAR: Ay, Doña Luisa, believe me, if I knew where Rosalinda was, I wouldn't be calling for her. (*Calling*) Rosalinda!

LUISA RUIZ: Sometimes if you whistle, they come. El Bobo only comes when I whistle.

MARIA PILAR: El Bobo?

LUISA RUIZ: The big one. He's a ... a ... Labrador retriever. He only comes when I whistle. Once the people complained so I got one of them ultrasonic dog whistles, but when I blow it, Mr. Mura says it opens up his garage door.

MARIA PILAR: Doña Luisa, my daughter is not a dog to be whistled for.

LUISA RUIZ: Oh. Now El Pepe, he's the cockapoo, they're not so independent, you know. He comes whenever you just call him.

MARIA PILAR: Rosalinda! (*Holding her stomach*) Ay this screaming is making me acid. (*She yells toward the house*) Jesse! Jesse! Andale, baby, get me the Rolaids. They're on top of la llelera. You hear me, Jesse?

LUISA RUIZ: You just say "Pepe, Pepe" and he just comes running, wagging his tail, happy to see you. Not like Esmerelda, she's the collie that stays in the window all the time.

MARIA PILAR: Jesse! The Rolaids!

JESSE'S VOICE: (*Offstage*) I can't find them, Mom.

MARIA PILAR: On top of la refrigerator, I said.

JESSE'S VOICE: (*Offstage*) There's only bananas on top of the refrigerator.

MARIA PILAR: Ay San Fernando de los Flojos, when will you cure that lazy child? Con permisso, Doña Luisa.

(*Maria starts to leave, but Luisa Ruiz grabs her by the sleeve and points to the window of her house*)

LUISA RUIZ: There she is. There's Esmerelda. You see her? Eh, you see her?

MARIA PILAR: Yes, yes Doña Luisa, I can see her.

LUISA RUIZ: I call her "La Princessa," she's a real snob, that one, just like royalty. Sits there all day.

MARIA PILAR: That's because the dog is blind, Doña Luisa. And you should ...

LUISA RUIZ: (*Interrupting*) They gave her to me that time I was an extra in the movies ... the man said that she was the daughter of Lassie and she had belonged to La Liz Taylor.

MARIA PILAR: You should take that animal to the veterinarian and ...

LUISA RUIZ: (*Interrupting*) It's the cataracts in her eyes. I can cure that. I know there is something I can use to cure that.

MARIA PILAR: (*Walking briskly to house*) Jesse! Jesse! María de Jesus.

(*Jesse comes out the back door. She looks disheveled*)

JESSE: Mom! Don't call me that.

MARIA PILAR: Ay, if your Sainted Father que Dios lo tenga en la Gloria ... (*Crosses herself*) ... could see you now. Jesse, por favor, stand up straight and comb your hair. (*Maria Pilar exits into house*)

JESSE: What for? I'm not going anyplace. I never go anyplace. Nobody even knows that I am alive. (*Jesse slumps her way to Luisa Ruiz, who is busy studying the sky*) I'm just drifting.

LUISA RUIZ: (*Looking at sky*) Like a cloud.

JESSE: (*Looking at sky*) Yeah.

LUISA RUIZ: (*No longer looking up*) It was such a little cloud.

JESSE: (*Still looking at sky*) A baby cloud, all fat and happy . . .

LUISA RUIZ: But it got bigger and bigger . . .

JESSE: (*Looking up*) It didn't know what to do, what to say. It wasn't ready . . .

LUISA RUIZ: And bigger until it blinded her.

JESSE: (*Looking at Luisa Ruiz*) Huh?

LUISA RUIZ: The clouds in Esmerelda's eyes.

JESSE: The cataracts.

LUISA RUIZ: I put the pollen of the yellow passion flower on them, which is very strong, Jesse, they say within the flower are the symbols of the crucified Christ.

JESSE: I knew you were talking about the cataracts.

LUISA RUIZ: But it had no effect. I made a tea of that weed they call Juan Símon . . .

(*Raphael appears, lurking around the edge of the yard*)

It had no effect, but I still have the ginseng root in the shape of a cross . . . (*She starts walking back to her house, mumbling to herself*) The ginseng root with the leaf of the aloe plant . . . (*Exit Luisa Ruiz*)

JESSE: (*Yelling to Raphael*) My sister's not home! She's not interested in you. She's going to see the world. So you can stop hanging around the house.

(*Jesse and Raphael stand, stare at each other for a beat, Jesse picks up a rock. Exit Raphael. Jesse shouts after Raphael*)

And you can stop calling on the phone and hanging up. I know it's you . . . (*Softly*) I recognize your breathing.

(*End 1st Day*)

1st Night:
Lights change to night.
The stage is dark, except for a large three-quarter moon and the small light in the bedroom window of the Luna house. We hear crickets and the howling of a dog.
Enter Rosalinda, in sweatshirt and pants, from house.
ROSALINDA: (*Running in place*) I'm going to run around the world, over oceans and islands and continents. I'm going to jump over the Himalayas, skip the Spanish Steps and dip my toes in the blue Nile. I'm going to see places I've never seen and meet people I've never known, Laplanders, Indonesians, Ethiopians ... (*Pointing and waving to imaginary people*) Ay, mira los Japoneses, y los Chinitos and who are those giants? Ay, Dios, los Samoans! And I will speak many tongues like the Bible ... (*Shaking hands with imaginary people*) Mucho gusto yo soy Rosalinda. Je suis Rosalinda, comment allez vous? Io sono Rosalinda. Jumbo! Me Rosalinda from America.
(*Jesse appears in window. The alarm clock in Jesse's hand goes off*)
Shhhh! Somebody might hear me.
JESSE: Somebody might mug you.
ROSALINDA: I'm too fast. (*Rosalinda gets into starting position*)
JESSE: Jeez, I wish we had a stopwatch. It's hard with this alarm clock ... Which way are you going tonight?
ROSALINDA: The northern route. Over the Pole.
JESSE: Say hello to the Eskimos.
ROSALINDA: Oh, please, Jesse, hurry up.
JESSE: O.K., O.K. When the little hand hits twelve ... on your mark ... get set ... go!
ROSALINDA: (*Running*) There's Fresno ... San Francisco ... Portland ... (*Exit Rosalinda*)
JESSE: Weird.
(*Enter Raphael. Seeing him, Jesse hides behind window curtain. Raphael paces up and down front of house, looking at the window. He picks up a small stone and throws it through the window. We hear a loud "Hey!" from Jesse*)
RAPHAEL: Psssst ... Rosalinda ... Rosalinda ...
JESSE: (*In a breathy, sexy voice*) Yeeesss?
RAPHAEL: Rosalinda, I know you got things on your mind with your big race on Saturday, pero a man can only be ignored so much. (*Pause*) Listen, Rosalinda, me voy a declarer. Sí, I'm going to declare myself. (*Pause*)

"Rosalinda: a poem by Raphael Antonio Piña."
"You are once
You are twice
You are three times a lady
And that is why you'll always
Be my one and only baby.
When I see you running
Running through the barrio
With your legs so brown and fine,
Oh Rosalinda, Rosalinda,
Won't you be mine?"

JESSE: (*Throwing a shoe out the window*) Oh, Christ.

RAPHAEL: Ay, Rosy, don't be mean.

JESSE: Her name isn't Rosy. So stop calling her Rosy. She's not gonna answer to Rosy.

RAPHAEL: Oh, you again.

JESSE: Ay Rosalinda! Quick somebody hold me back, I'm about to declare myself.

RAPHAEL: Listen you . . . you . . .

JESSE: My name is Jesse. I live here too ya' know.

RAPHAEL: Where is Rosalinda?

JESSE: She's not home. She's running. She's in training and she doesn't see boys when she's training.

RAPHAEL: I'm not a boy, I'm a man.

JESSE: Oh yeah! . . . Well . . . eh . . . er . . . you're not her type.

(*Raphael starts to exit*)

Hey Raphael!

RAPHAEL: Yeah.

JESSE: You know your poem?

RAPHAEL: Yeah.

JESSE: It wasn't bad.

RAPHAEL: Thanks . . . good night, Jesse. (*Raphael exits*)

JESSE: Goodnight, Raphael Antonio Piña.

ROSALINDA'S VOICE: (*Offstage*) Mexico City, Alcapulco, Puerto Vallarta, La Paz, Santa Rosalia, Encinada . . .

(*Enter Rosalinda*)

Tijuana, San Diego, La Orange County, Los Angeles . . . Castro Street. (*Looking up at Jesse*) How did I do?

JESSE: Huh . . .? I . . . I lost track.

(*Rosalinda sighs and gets into starting position again*)

ROSALINDA: O.K., one more time.

JESSE: Go!

ROSALINDA: (*Running*) Santa Barbara, San Jose, San Francisco . . . (*Exit Rosalinda running*)

ROSALINDA'S VOICE: (*Offstage. Sounding further and further away, as lights slowly change to day*) Seattle, Portland, Vancouver, Alaska, the Bering Strait, Russia . . .

(*End 1st Night*)

2nd Day:

Early morning. Same large sun as 1st day. Maria Pilar Luna, wearing a fresh housedress and apron, is standing in front of her house, scanning the street. Luisa Ruiz, wearing the same outfit as 1st day, is coming out of her house.

MARIA PILAR: Rosalinda! Rosalinda!

LUISA RUIZ: Buenos días, María Pilar.

MARIA PILAR: Buenos días, Doña Luisa.

LUISA RUIZ: It's a beautiful day con mucho viento. Some people call it the Santa Ana wind. Some people call it the Devil Wind. Some people call it El Scirocco. And some people . . .

MARIA PILAR: Sí, sí, it's a very windy day. Rosalinda! Running, running, that's all that girl thinks about. Ay, and my stomach secreting the acid all morning.

LUISA RUIZ: Running, running, that's all El Bobo and Pepe think about too. They wake up, sniff the air and off they go. I think it's something they smell in Mrs. Amador's rose garden. Maybe it's a dead bird. (*She sniffs the air*) No. Maybe Mrs. Amador is making chicharrones . . . (*She sniffs the air*) No . . . (*She sniffs more thoughtfully*) It must be that patch of wild peppermint. They say the scent is very invigorating. Maybe that's where la Rosalinda is.

MARIA PILAR: Doña Luisa, my daughter does not have the custom to go smelling things in other people's garden.

LUISA RUIZ: Oh.

MARIA PILAR: She runs to practice.

LUISA RUIZ: Oh.

MARIA PILAR: She runs because this Saturday she is entered in Our Lady of a Thousand Sorrows Marathon.

LUISA RUIZ: No! . . . Sí?

MARIA PILAR: Sí, Father Estafan himself went from door to door to collect money for her entrance fee.

LUISA RUIZ: Oh, pero he didn't ask me for money. He never came to my door.

MARIA PILAR: Válgame Dios, three hundred young girls from all the Catholic Diocese in California. Ay, I don't know what those priests can be thinking. All that running shakes up a woman's insides.

LUISA RUIZ: He never came to my door ... I didn't give anything ... This Saturday? ... That's tomorrow.

MARIA PILAR: They are making them run from Elysian park to the Mission downtown.

LUISA RUIZ: Oh. That's far ... El Bobo could run that far.

MARIA PILAR: It's not for dogs. It's for Catholic girls.

LUISA RUIZ: Maybe it's not too late for me to give ...

MARIA PILAR: I cannot give to her the things she wants. I am a woman alone. Now if her sainted father, que Dios lo tenga en La Gloria ... (*Crosses herself*) ... were down here with us today ...

LUISA RUIZ: But it is important to give.

MARIA PILAR: To give, ah sí, to give, mira no más, it's easy for you to say give ... and for him, my husband ... (*Raising her hand to heaven*) ... charlando up there, playing the big macho with all the angels and the saints ... does he listen when Rosalinda says she wants to be educated ... she wants to see the world? Does he lift a finger? Does he put in a good word for us? No, se hace sordo, he pretends not to hear me. Gracias a Dios, Rosalinda knows how to work. She gets that from me.

LUISA RUIZ: She looks so pretty working at La Dairy Queen in her white uniform, just like a nurse. She always gives me free cones, soft serve she calls it. She goes up to that big steel machine, she presses the red button, and zas! out comes the ice cream, like a clean white snake it comes round and round and round. Rosalinda twirls the cone. She never spills a drop. When it just gets so high she stops, just like that. She never spills a drop. Then she leans over the counter, with a big smile, and says, "This is for you, Doña Luisa." That girl knows how to give.

MARIA PILAR: I cry, I beg him, "Juanito, mi amor," I say, "help us. It's our duty as parents to provide for our children. Por favor, papacito lindo, I'm already sewing ten hours a day just to put food in our mouths." Did I hear from him? Nothing. Ni una palabra. Condenado viejo ... It took Father Estafan to put her in this race. Just think if she wins el gran premio it is a trip to Rome and all the expenses paid ... but he ... (*Indicating husband in heaven*) ... didn't even help me with the entrance fee or the Nike running shoes. Father Estafan himself had to go door to door.

LUISA RUIZ: (*To Maria Pilar's husband in heaven*) I swear he never came to my door.

MARIA PILAR: She has to run like a dog to get somewhere in life. Ay, this acid is killing me. Jesse!

LUISA RUIZ: Run like a dog . . .?

MARIA PILAR: Jesse, the Rolaids.

(*Jesse coming out the back door, looking more disheveled than usual*)

JESSE: I can't find them, Mom.

MARIA PILAR: María de Jesús! Look at you! Por favor, do something. Comb your hair. Stand up straight. Be a señorita.

(*Exit Maria Pilar into house. Jesse walks to the fence and Luisa Ruiz*)

JESSE: Please stop calling me that! It's weird . . . I was real cute until I was twelve . . . people always pinching my cheeks. (*Pinching her own cheeks*) "Ay qué preciosa!" "Ay qué belleza." But now it's all this pressure.

LUISA RUIZ: Run like a dog . . .

JESSE: Yeah, far away . . . No, wouldn't do any good, I think it's some kinda contagious disease, no matter where you go people expect you to comb your hair and stand up straight. I try but my hair keeps falling into my face and my body just has this . . . terminal slouch . . . it's like I got a hunchback's blood . . . or . . .

MARIA PILAR'S VOICE: (*Offstage*) Jesse! Jesse! What is this porquería under your bed?

JESSE: Maybe I wasn't meant to be a señorita.

MARIA PILAR'S VOICE: (*Offstage*) Dr. Pepper, Twinkies, Cheetos . . .

(*Jesse sighs and slumps her way into the house*)

LUISA RUIZ: She has to run like a dog . . . (*Luisa Ruiz exits slowly toward her house*)

MARIA PILAR'S VOICE: (*Offstage*) Snickers, Ding Dongs, Ho Hos, Susie Qs, a pizza! (*Voice fades. Light changes to night*)

(*End 2nd Day*)

2nd Night:
Moon is fuller than 1st night, but not yet full. There is a soft, low energy sound under this scene, like something vibrating.

Luisa Ruiz, wearing a dark kimono, is standing in front of her doorway. She is holding her hands in front of her body, with a red flannel cloth over her hands. Raphael appears, lurking around the edges of the yard. Seeing Luisa Ruiz, he hides behind jacaranda tree. As Rosalinda comes out of her house in her running outfit, Luisa Ruiz beckons her to come with both hands and the red flannel cloth. This gesture is slow, as though she is hypnotizing Rosalinda.

LUISA RUIZ: Ancho y profundo en pasos, en el corazón, en el Espíritu Santo, Espíritu Bendito.

(Rosalinda slowly waves to Luisa Ruiz and stands before her. Luisa Ruiz makes the sign of the cross on Rosalinda. Rosalinda kneels in front of Luisa Ruiz, who then opens her hands and carefully holds out a special yu-yu amulet—a small red flannel bag, the size of a large book of matches, which is filled with special herbs and potions, with a drawstring which is hung around the neck. Luisa Ruiz holds the yu-yu high above her own head)

Niño Santo Lobo.

(She brings the yu-yu down and hangs it around Rosalinda's neck and starts her chant over and around Rosalinda)

Christo Santo de los Lagos y Las Montanias dice—

(She claps)

Madre Santa de Las Valles dice—

(Claps)

Padre Santo de la Sombra y El Sol dice—

(Clap)

Virgensita de la Niebla dice—

(Clap)

Niño Santo de las Criaturas dice—

(Clap)

Santa Ana de los Vientos Secos dice—

(Clap)

Espíritu Santo de la Chupa Rosa dice—

(Clap)

Espíritu Santo de la Mariposa dice—

(Clap)

San Bernardo de los Perros dice—

(Clap)

Dios te bendiga,

Christo Santo te bendiga.

(A dog howls. Raphael exits. Energy sound fades into sound of TV cartoons as lights change to morning)

(End 2nd Night)

3rd Day:
Early morning. Same large sun as days 1 and 2. Sound of TV cartoons. Maria Pilar comes out from her house.

MARIA PILAR: Rosalinda! (*Yells toward house*) Jesse! Jesse! Turn off those cartoons, you hear me? I want you to go after your sister.

JESSE: (*In the window*) Mom . . . it's seven o'clock. It's Saturday.

MARIA PILAR: Now, Jesse. Do you hear me?

JESSE: Jeez, what's the big deal? (*Jesse disappears from the window. Sound of cartoons goes off*)

MARIA PILAR: Your sister has to come back here and have a good breakfast. Then we have to go to la special mass for the runners where Father Estafan is going to bless her feet before the race. Andale, Jesse. Hurry up.

(*Jesse comes out, looking very sleepy, wearing her pajama top and bottom with a skirt*)

JESSE: I don't believe this.

MARIA PILAR: You don't believe anything y mira no más, how you look. At your age I was up at five. I was already washed, dressed and making tortillas for all the men in the house.

JESSE: (*Rolling up pajama legs*) Take it easy, Mom, I'm going. (*Jesse exits*)

MARIA PILAR: (*Calling after her*) And stop at the market and get some orange juice for your sister. Tell them to charge it to my account . . . and tell them I'll pay them next week. (*To husband in heaven*) Ay, Juanito, you better keep your eye on that child.

(*Enter Orlando*)

ORLANDO: *Reader's Digest* . . . Bill from Dr. Mirabel . . . Buenos días, Maria Pilar. (*Handing her mail*) Well, today's the big day . . . eh. And the whole barrio's gonna be there. How's Rosalinda?

MARIA PILAR: Ay, Orlando, how do I know? I am only her mother, I am the last person to know where she is or how she is. Have you seen Rosalinda?

ORLANDO: Now don't start worrying, she's just warming up for the big race . . . whew! Qué hot . . . looks like it's going to be another scorcher.

MARIA PILAR: Running, running. The whole thing is affecting my nerves.

ORLANDO: It's the Santa Ana winds, they affect people.

MARIA PILAR: Por favor Orlando, if you see her tell her to come home.

ORLANDO: Of course, María Pilar, "Go home at once", that's what I'll tell her. (*Turning to go*) See you at the race. (*Exit Orlando*)

MARIA PILAR: (*Walking to house*) Big race or no big race a person should tell their mother, a person should eat their breakfast.
(*Exit Maria Pilar. The sun moves up a fraction in sky to indicate passage of time. Rosalinda zooms past the house. Enter Jesse, running, carrying a paper bag, one of her pajama legs has fallen down*)
JESSE: Amaa! Amaa!
(*Maria Pilar comes out of the house*)
MARIA PILAR: Ay, por Dios, Jesse, walk como una dama . . . un lady.
JESSE: Ma, wait'll I tell you what Rosalinda did.
MARIA PILAR: And where's your sister? Did you tell her about la special mass?
JESSE: I tried, Mom, but she just barked at me. O.K., I'm walking down Castro Street. I'm right in front of Arganda's Garage. When Manny Arganda slides out from under a '68 Chevy, stands up and says, "*Hey* Essé, what's with jur seester?" I tell him to drop dead. He says, "O.K. Essé, hab a nice dey." He thinks he's so cool.
MARIA PILAR: Jesse.
JESSE: O.K., O.K. That's when I see Rosalinda, with Pepe and Bobo. I yell at her, I say, "Rosalinda, Mom says to come home," that's when she barked at me. Then she turns around and runs up to this car . . . It was a black Impala with a little red racing stripe all along the side and real pretty red letters on the door that said "Danny Little Red Lopez."
MARIA PILAR: Por favor, Jesse.
JESSE: O.K., O.K. So she runs up to the car, and Mom . . . you won't believe this . . . She jumps over the car! . . . The black Impala, she jumps over it! . . . Just like la Wonder Woman . . . and she wasn't even breathing hard.
MARIA PILAR: Jesse, why do you lie?
JESSE: Mom, it's exactly what happened. And when I went to the market, they said Rosalinda charged a pound of chopped meat and bones.
MARIA PILAR: That's ridiculous. Your sister never eats meat. Didn't you tell her to get home and about the mass?
JESSE: I couldn't catch her. She's so fast. The last time I saw her she's standing by the stop light going like this . . . (*Does an imitation of a dog running in place. Paws out, tongue out like a dog panting*)
MARIA PILAR: Ave María Santísima, I told her never to bounce like that. She's gonna break her eggs.
JESSE: Not eggs, chopped beef.

MARIA PILAR: I'm talking about her ovaries.

JESSE: Ovaries?

MARIA PILAR: She's going to ruin her ovaries running like that.

JESSE: Ah, Mom, I'm sure . . .

MARIA PILAR: La verdad! Any doctor will tell you bouncing and riding a motorcycle is going to break your eggs.

JESSE: Uuggh. Disgusting. I'm going in for a soda.

MARIA PILAR: No, señorita, not before your breakfast.

JESSE: Eeewww, Mom, please, I don't want breakfast. I just want a soda.

MARIA PILAR: All right baby, all right. You stay here in case your sister runs by and I'll get you the soda . . . but don't drink it too fast. If you drink ice cold soda too fast, it gives you bad gas.

JESSE: Mom!

MARIA PILAR: Ah sí, you laugh, pero I've known people who have died of these things. (*Maria Pilar exits to house*)

JESSE: Oh, yeah? When I'm eighteen, I'm going to ride a big black Harley Davidson motorcycle that has "La Jesse" painted on the side of the gas tank. I'll be jumping over cars, zooming along dusty, bumpy desert trails, and doing loop-de-loos on the Ventura Freeway. All this, while drinking an ice . . . cold . . . soda real fast before breakfast!

(*There is the sound of a pack of dogs barking, and Rosalinda runs from upstage left to upstage right—a flash of her flying wild, black hair as she runs by*)

Rosalinda! Rosalinda! (*Jesse exits, running after Rosalinda*) Rosalinda, Mom says for you—(*More barking*) Rosalinda wait . . . !

(*Maria Pilar runs out the back door with a bottle of soda and a glass in her hands*)

MARIA PILAR: Jesse . . . ! Rosalinda . . . ! Come back here. This is no time to be playing.

(*Maria Pilar runs to back and around the house and comes out in front. Enter Mrs. Amador. She is out of breath, her hair is askew. She is splattered with mud and rose petals. She carries a broken rose bush. She leans against the fence, trying to catch her breath*)

Señora! Que le pasa?

(*Out of breath, Mrs. Amador struggles to speak*)

Andale, Mrs. Amador, make an effort. Speak to me.

MRS. AMADOR: Rosalinda! . . . The dogs! . . .

MARIA PILAR: Qué? Qué? Qué dices de Rosalinda?

MRS. AMADOR: Rosalinda y los perros destroyed my rose garden.

MARIA PILAR: No . . . no . . .

MRS. AMADOR: Sí, sí, all my roses. La Yellow Rose de Texas
... las tea roses, La Eleanor Roosevelt ... La Jacqueline
Kennedy ... y esta ... (*Holding up broken rose bush*) ... La
Mamie Eisenhower.
(*The sounds of dogs barking is heard*)
Here they come ... here they come ...
(*Rosalinda runs through upstage right to upstage left followed
by a worn-out Jesse*)
JESSE: (*Running to her mother*) Mom, Mom, you should see
Rosalinda! She's chasing cars down Castro Street! She's ...!
MRS. AMADOR: (*Interrupting*) You should see what she did to
my rose garden!!
MARIA PILAR: I'm telling you, it was those dogs next door.
MRS. AMADOR: Pero Rosalinda was with them! She was one
of them. All wild looking she was así, mira ... (*Baring her teeth,
imitating Rosalinda's wild look*) Ay! And blood all around her
mouth. (*Crossing herself*) It makes me tremble to think of it.
MARIA PILAR: Blood around her mouth.
JESSE: Aw, Mom, that was just from the raw meat she was
eating.
(*Enter Orlando, in a state of disarray, strap on mailbag broken,
pants leg torn*)
ORLANDO: La Rosalinda se freakió.
MARIA PILAR: Where is she!? Where did she go?
JESSE: She's O.K., Mom, she's over at the park catching fris-
bees between her teeth. She's really good. You should see her.
MRS. AMADOR: She's on drugs. I've seen it. They go crazy.
JESSE: She's not crazy.
MARIA PILAR: (*Crying*) She can't even take Contac.
MRS. AMADOR: That's how they start. First the Contac and
then the ...
(*Luisa Ruiz enters to her front yard*)
LUISA RUIZ: Pepe! Pepe! Bobo!
(*Enter Raphael running*)
RAPHAEL: Jesse! Jesse! Rosalinda's in ... (*Seeing Luisa
Ruiz and pointing at her*) She's the one! La Dog Lady! She gave
her something. She put a curse on her. She turned her into a dog!
I seen her do it.
MARIA PILAR: (*To Luisa Ruiz*) What have you done to my
daughter?
MRS. AMADOR: Drugs! She gave her drugs. She's a pusher.
RAPHAEL: I seen her. She put something around her neck.
And said spooky words over her.

MARIA PILAR: (*Taking Luisa by the shoulders, shaking her*) What did you do to Rosalinda? What did you give her?

MRS. AMADOR: Speed! I bet that's what she gave her.

ORLANDO: (*Pulling Maria Pilar away from Luisa Ruiz*) Give her a chance to talk. Orale Doña Luisa. Did you give Rosalinda something?

LUISA RUIZ: She had to run like a dog . . . I gave her the Spirit . . . the Dog Spirit. It won't hurt her.

MRS. AMADOR: (*Crossing herself*) Devil's work. Ave, Dios, she's a bruja, a witch. Where's my cross? (*Searching for cross at neck*) Jesse! Don't look at her. (*Pulling Jesse's face away*) Nobody look at her eyes.

(*All shield their eyes, except Orlando*)

ORLANDO: Cálmanse! Y stop talking nonsense.

MRS. AMADOR: Qué nonsense and qué nada! Didn't Father Estafan himself say that she made the dog in the window blind with all those herbs she put in the dog's eyes? Didn't he? Didn't he?

MARIA PILAR: Sí, sí, he said to keep away from her. (*Crying*) She's turned my daughter into a dog.

JESSE: Mom!

(*Raphael, shielding his eyes, pulls a switchblade and points it at Luisa Ruiz's throat*)

RAPHAEL: Turn her back, Dog Lady.

ORLANDO: Raphael . . . put it away. Now everybody calm down. It's just these damn Santa Winds. It drives people crazy.

JESSE: She's not crazy.

MARIA PILAR: Por favor, Doña Luisa, you're a powerful woman . . . I beg you, bring me back my daughter.

(*Luisa Ruiz rummages into her pockets and pulls out an ultrasonic dog whistle. As she pulls it out, everybody stands back. She blows it. Mrs. Amador crosses herself, gasps, and points across the street*)

MRS. AMADOR: Ay! Mira, Mr. Mura's garage door opened all by itself.

(*They all turn around and look in shocked silence. Raphael drops his knife. One by one they cross themselves except for Luisa Ruiz and Jesse. Jesse stands up on fence and looks up and down the street*)

JESSE: Here she comes. Wow! Rosalinda that was great.

(*Rosalinda enters running. She continues running in place. Her hair is messy and wild. She is splattered with mud and rose petals. She has a keenly determined look in her eyes and holds a frisbee between her teeth*)

MARIA PILAR: Rosalinda, where were you? And why didn't you come when I called?
(*Rosalinda drops frisbee at Maria Pilar's feet*)
No Señorita, I'm not playing games with you.
MRS. AMADOR: (*Passing her hands before Rosalinda's face*)
Rosalinda ... how do you feel?
JESSE: Fine! She feels fine!
ORLANDO: You're all right, eh, Rosalinda?
JESSE: Of course, she's all right.
MARIA PILAR: Rosalinda, I want you to go to bed.
JESSE: Not now, she'll be late for the race. Ready? Rome, here comes Rosalinda.
(*Rosalinda exits, running. They look at each other and then run offstage after Rosalinda, except for Luisa Ruiz and Raphael, who lags slowly behind*)
RAPHAEL: (*Exiting slowly*) A man can only take so much. She's never home, she's a lot of trouble, running, jumping, barking. Women!
(*Luisa Ruiz stands onstage alone for a beat. We hear the sounds of dogs barking. She goes to the alleyway*)
LUISA RUIZ: Pepe! Bobo! No, you can't go ... it's only for Catholic girls. We're not invited.
(*She runs offstage after the dogs*)
(*End 3rd Day*)

3rd Night:
There is a full moon. The sound of a mariachi band playing "Guadalajara" and other party sounds. Maria Pilar in a party dress, in front of her house, hanging a banner proclaiming "Rosalinda Number One." Enter Mrs. Amador carrying a big plate.

MRS. AMADOR: Tamales estilo Jalisco.
MARIA PILAR: Just think, she's going to Rome and all the expenses paid.
MRS. AMADOR: What about the woof! woof!
(*Rosalinda comes out of the house. Mrs. Amador jumps back and looks at Rosalinda very cautiously*)
ROSALINDA: She hasn't come yet? She said she would come.
MARIA PILAR: Now don't get excited, if Doña Luisa said she would come, then she will come.
MRS. AMADOR: Sí, don't get excited. Nothing to get excited about.

ROSALINDA: Oh Mom, isn't it wonderful! I'm going to see the world. (*Looking up at the sky*) I'm going to see the universe . . . I am going to dance on Venus, skate on Saturn's rings, dive into the Milky Way and wash my hair with stars.

MRS. AMADOR: Is she getting excited?

(*Rosalinda and Maria Pilar are looking up to the sky. Seeing them, Mrs. Amador very cautiously starts to look up*)

MARIA PILAR: Ay, Juanito . . . I feel your soft brown eyes on me . . . on Rosalinda . . . on Jesse . . . Jesse? Rosalinda, where's Jesse?

ROSALINDA: (*Still gazing at the sky*) I don't know, Mom.

MRS. AMADOR: (*Eyeing the sky with great suspicion*) Is somebody there?

(*Mrs. Amador continues to stare straight up to the sky throughout the rest of this scene. Enter Orlando and Raphael. Both very dressed up. Raphael carries a big bouquet of flowers*)

ORLANDO: Orale, Rafa, give her the flowers.

RAPHAEL: Now?

MARIA PILAR: Ay, look Rosalinda, it's Orlando and Raphael . . . Pasen, pasen . . . ay, where is Jesse?

ROSALINDA: I'll get her.

(*Rosalinda goes toward house as Luisa Ruiz comes out of her house in a faded cocktail dress, a large flower in her hair*)

MARIA PILAR: Ay, qué bonita se ve, me da tanto gusto a ver La Doña Luisa.

LUISA RUIZ: Oh! Thank you, María Pilar. (*She looks up to the sky*) It's a beautiful night.

MARIA PILAR: Sí. God works in mysterious ways, Doña Luisa. (*Enter Jesse. She has been transformed into a beautiful young princess. She stands next to Rosalinda. Raphael stands before them, holding the bouquet of flowers, awestruck at Jesse. All stare at Jesse in silence except for Mrs. Amador, who is still staring at the sky*)

ORLANDO: Look at La Jesse!

MARIA PILAR: Ay, Juanito. (*She crosses herself*) She combed her hair.

LUISA RUIZ: She looks just like a princess.

ORLANDO: (*Nudging Raphael*) Now, Rafa! Now.

(*Raphael, staring at Jesse, tears the bouquet of flowers in half, giving half to Rosalinda and half to Jesse*)

Y la fiesta pues? . . . I am gonna dance with you, Doña Luisa.

(*Orlando takes Luisa Ruiz arm-in-arm and exits into the house as Maria Pilar takes Mrs. Amador, who is still staring into the sky, holding the plate of tamales*)

MARIA PILAR: Andale, Mrs. Amador, it's time for the tamales.

MRS. AMADOR: (*Still looking at the sky*) Is somebody watching us?

(*Maria Pilar takes Mrs. Amador into the house, followed by Raphael*)

ROSALINDA: I'm proud of you, Jesse.

JESSE: (*To Rosalinda*) You're going to see the world . . . all those places . . . all the things that will happen to you . . .

ROSALINDA: I'll be back.

JESSE: You'll be different.

ROSALINDA: We're sisters forever.

JESSE: Rosalinda? . . . Can I see it?

(*Rosalinda brings out the yu-yu from under her blouse*)
Can I touch it? . . . Did . . . did you really turn into a dog?

ROSALINDA: (*Taking the yu-yu off her neck and holding it in her hands*) You have to work very hard.

JESSE: I know.

(*Rosalinda puts the yu-yu around Jesse's neck. She exits into the house. Jesse turns around and stares at the moon. She slowly walks up Castro Street toward the moon. The lights slowly fade, as from offstage . . .*

MARIA PILAR'S VOICE: Jesse! Jesse!

The End

Douglas Soderberg

THE ROOT OF CHAOS

Douglas Soderberg

Douglas Soderberg made his professional debut as a playwright in the Actors Theatre of Louisville's '84 SHORTS festival of one-act plays with *The Root of Chaos* , published here for the first time. Inspired by the uncontrollable underground fire beneath Centralia, Pennsylvania, Mr. Soderberg uses the image as a metaphor for the fears that ruin individual, family, social, and political relationships. Reviewing the play for the Louisville *Courier-Journal*, William Mootz writes, " . . . it is a madcap black farce that mixes horror and laughter in about equal proportions . . . Each of [the family's] four members is trying to escape the ravages of a personal fear, and each, in the end, becomes fear's victim. But Soderberg brings to *The Root of Chaos* a manic sense of humor that constantly contrives jokes as disorienting as bolts of lightning."

Mr. Soderberg received an M.F.A in playwriting from Carnegie-Mellon University in 1981. While a student there, three of his original plays were presented: *The Big Placebo*, *Giantism in America*, and *Mother Tongue*. In 1983 a staged reading of another play, *Liberal Arts*, was presented at the Pennsylvania State University. His most recent production, *Modern Love*, was produced in December, 1984 at the University of Minnesota in Duluth. He has also written a new one-act play about women and pornography, *Making the Beast*, and is now writing a full-length play, *Food from Home*, about Yuppies and cannibalism.

Born in Louisiana, raised in Minneapolis, Minnesota, and Eugene, Oregon, educated in Oregon and Pennsylvania, and now living in St. Louis, Missouri, Mr. Soderberg has had contact with many areas of the country, which gives his work the sensibility of a broad background of American culture.

Characters:

JOE CERNIKOWSKI, *the father, forty*
WILMA CERNIKOWSKI, *the mother, thirty-eight*
DOUBLEMINT CERNIKOWSKI, *the daughter, thirteen*
SKEETER CERNIKOWSKI, *the son, nine*
OFFICER OF SURFACE MINING, *deus ex machina*

[*NOTE: The ages of the children are suggested through costuming and the performances. The actors portraying them should be adults.*]

Scene:

The kitchen and dining area of the Cernikowski house in Centralia, Pennsylvania.

Time:

The present. Dinner time.

Setting:

Three entrances lead to the Cernikowski kitchen. A screen door—the back door of the house—opens out onto a small stoop; characters standing on the stoop are visible through the screen. This entrance also has a heavy, windowless wooden door which opens onto the stage and remains open until indicated. An archway of some sort leads to the rest of the house. And an elaborately locked door, preferably upstage center, is access to the cellar.

There are various, vague-looking boxes mounted on the walls, some with dials and meters, some with metal casings; also a telephone and a countertop radio; a kitchen table, oven, sink, pantry, etc.

At Rise: Darkness. The cellar door opens slowly of its own accord. A dusky orange light glows in the doorway, illuminating dimly the rest of the stage. We hear the voice of the Officer of Surface Mining, at first impersonal and forbidding, but gradually rather chummy.

VOICE OF OFFICER: Centralia, Pennsylvania, located in the southern tip of Columbia County—population one thousand, approximately—has, for the past twenty-two years, been the site of an underground mine fire burning out of control. The fire was discovered in May of 1962 in an abandoned coal stripping pit on the edge of town. The Centralia Borough had been using the area to dump their refuse. The fire quickly spread into a network of mine tunnels throughout the town. Now more than a third of the town's residents are threatened by the unseen blaze. Six point six million dollars have been spent to extinguish the fire. All in vain. Things are looking up, though. Half the town is considered geologically safe from the spreading inferno. Combustion scientists in Pittsburgh some three hundred miles away are experimenting with burnout control, a process by which, instead of dousing the fire, the flames are fanned to accelerate burning and exhaust the fuel supply. While at the same time producing commercial heat and power! Hell of an idea. Of course, plans are continually underway to relocate the whole blasted town. And when it gets to be just too damned much, the residents take Highway 61 into Shamokin for dancing and first-run movies.

WILMA: (*Offstage*) Doublemint!

VOICE OF OFFICER: Yes, sir . . . everything seems to be under control.

WILMA: (*Offstage*) Skeeter!

(*The cellar door slams shut, and the stage is flooded with late afternoon light. Wilma enters through the archway, crosses to the screen door and calls out*)

Children! I've been calling five minutes! Are you deaf and dumb?

SKEETER: (*Offstage*) Mom! Come settle this!

WILMA: No, and don't make me shout.

SKEETER: (*Offstage*) Doublemint's hitting!

WILMA: Skeeter, I want you inside. It'll be dark soon.

SKEETER: (*Entering*) And she's calling names again, too.

WILMA: Bring it up with your father. (*Kissing him*) You haven't seen my thing, have you?

SKEETER: No, ma'am.

DOUBLEMINT: (*Entering; to Skeeter*) Mouthbreather!

SKEETER: There! See?

(*Wilma backhands Doublemint soundly across the side of the head*)

WILMA: I don't want you fighting in front of your father.

DOUBLEMINT: He's bugging me!

WILMA: I don't care. Be friends.

DOUBLEMINT: I was merely waiting for Daddy. Skeeter had to come butt in.

SKEETER: It's a free country.

DOUBLEMINT: Drop dead. Mother, are you looking for your thing?

WILMA: Yes, I am. I've gotten behind.

SKEETER: For the fifty-second time, it isn't a "thing."

DOUBLEMINT: Skeeter was using it to measure his tree fort.

SKEETER: It's called a carpenter's level.

WILMA: Skeeter, honey, I've asked you not to use my good tools outside. I spent a month of your father's salary on that one. Now, I know you like to watch those bubbles . . .

SKEETER: I was checking to see . . .

WILMA: . . . If you need some extra allowance to buy yourself a nice play ruler, bring it up with your father.

SKEETER: All right. I'm sorry, Mom. I'll get it. (*He exits out the back door*)

DOUBLEMINT: I'm gonna start not wearing underwear, okay?

WILMA: Over my dead body. (*She goes to a box mounted on the wall, opens the casing and reads some figures*)

DOUBLEMINT: Marcia Ledbetter says in a true accident, *no* one ends up with clean underwear. I guess I'll bring it up with Daddy.

WILMA: I said "no." Help me remember this: Zero point zero two.

DOUBLEMINT: I could help you read some of those jobbers.

WILMA: Thanks just the same. (*Calling*) Skeeter! I need that, and I need that now!

DOUBLEMINT: It's true, by the way. What I said. Practically the entire school calls him "Mouthbreather" Cernikowski. Gives the family a reputation. I don't need that. I want to start light petting.

SKEETER: (*Entering with the level*) Here, Mom!

WILMA: Thank you, dear. (*She proceeds to lay the tool along baseboards, countertops, etc.*)

DOUBLEMINT: Incidentally, Mother, I forgot to tell you what happened today. During Skeeter's Local History class. Apparently, he tried to stop it, tried to actually breathe through his nose, and it made this terrible sucking sound. No one could concentrate. Mr. Tedd was up writing on the board, but there was this sucking sound, so he had one of his epileptic conniptions and they had to bring in a substitute.

SKEETER: I can't help my deviated septum.

WILMA: Doublemint, stop ridiculing your brother.

DOUBLEMINT: These happen to be facts.

SKEETER: Well, you know what they say about you.

DOUBLEMINT: That's just a rumor.

SKEETER: The school nurse announced it over the P.A.

DOUBLEMINT: Where'd she hear it from?

SKEETER: Beats me.

DOUBLEMINT: Mother, Skeeter has been telling everyone that I'm a . . .

WILMA: Now, look, I don't have time for it. Your father'll be home any minute, so cut it out.

DOUBLEMINT: Aren't you gonna do something? You never punish him. (*To Skeeter*) You don't even know what words mean.

SKEETER: That's what you think.

WILMA: Skeeter, honey, go fetch my pad.

SKEETER: Yes, Mom. (*He exits, runs, through the archway*)

DOUBLEMINT: You never do anything anymore. 'Cept measure stuff. Zero point zero two. E equals MC squared. The angle of the dangle is proportionate to the heat of the meat . . .

WILMA: Young lady, I'm trying to concentrate.

DOUBLEMINT: Tell me. Am I really a bastard?

WILMA: (*Measuring*) Yes, Doublemint. That's why your father married me. Look at this. Six millimeters. He's not going to like this.

SKEETER: (*Entering, with a yellow legal pad*) Here it is!

WILMA: Thank you, dear. (*Writing*) He's not going to like this at all.

SKEETER: What is it?

WILMA: In the first place, I haven't written anything down today. I barely got dinner in the oven. And now this.

DOUBLEMINT: What's for dinner?

WILMA: Tuna and macaroni.

DOUBLEMINT: Daddy's favorite!

SKEETER: Mine, too!

DOUBLEMINT: Yes, only you like the potato chips crispy on top. Daddy prefers them soft and wet. That's how he prefers them.

SKEETER: Mom, how do you prefer your chips?

DOUBLEMINT: Daddy *loves* them soft.

WILMA: Christ on a crumb heap! I knew I'd forgotten something! I haven't gotten to the fissure yet.

DOUBLEMINT: You left out the tuna?

SKEETER: She means the fissure in the basement wall.

WILMA: Your father will blow his stack.

DOUBLEMINT: Oh . . . that stupid crack.

WILMA: He'll think I've been dawdling. There's still time. Skeeter! I've left the set of keys upstairs. Hurry, run and get them!

SKEETER: (*Exiting*) I'm going!

DOUBLEMINT: I'll help! (*Running after Skeeter*) They're in Daddy's dresser drawer! With his briefs!

SKEETER: (*Offstage*) I know where they are!

WILMA: Joe . . . Joe, my darling provider. Don't be angry. I've tried to do everything. Tried to measure and record everything. But it isn't helping. It's not stopping the . . .

DOUBLEMINT: (*Offstage*) Mother!

WILMA: . . . the progress.

SKEETER: (*Offstage*) Ouch! Mom! She's hitting again!

(*Wilma slaps the legal pad on a countertop in disgust and exits through the archway. After a moment, Joe appears in the screen door entrance. He carries with him a surveyor's level mounted on a tripod*)

JOE: I'm . . . home! (*Silence*) Daddy's here! (*Pause. He enters the kitchen, leaving the tripod out on the stoop*) Kids? Wilma? (*A beat*) This has never . . . Where is everyone?

(*Doublemint and Skeeter race in, holding hands and pouncing on Joe together*)

DOUBLEMINT: Daddy!

SKEETER: Hello, Dad!

JOE: (*Kissing them both*) Doublemint. Skeets.

DOUBLEMINT: We were just searching in your drawers, and Skeeter said you have skid marks, so I hit him. Then Mother came and cuffed me. Now we're the best of friends. See? (*She pats Skeeter's head*)

JOE: That's wonderful. Where is your mother?

WILMA: (*Entering*) Here I am.

JOE: Boy, was it quiet. (*He kisses his wife*) How is everyone?

(*The following three lines are delivered simultaneously. All three end on the same beat*)

WILMA: Well, dear, I was driving home from the store, and I got to that sink hole on Walnut Street. You know the one. There was a dog in the other lane, and I had a choice between hitting the dog or driving into the sink hole. Anyway . . . the station wagon's demolished.

DOUBLEMINT: Well, Daddy, I got sent to the principal's office today because I'd written on the board "MR. OSTERMAN IS A CRIPPLE." When I got to his office—I really don't know what made me, but it seemed natural—I took off my clothes. Anyway . . . I got expelled from school.

SKEETER: Well, Dad, I was coming home for lunch because someone stole my lunch money again. The MacGregor boys were behind the Tasty Freeze, and they stripped me. They had boners

and everything, and they said, "We're bigger than you, kid."
Anyway ... it looks like I was raped.
JOE: Terrific! And to think I was worried just now.
SKEETER: 'Bout what, Dad?
JOE: Nothing special. So? Everything's okay?
WILMA: Yes, fine.
DOUBLEMINT: No problems.
SKEETER: Everything's great.
JOE: Good.
WILMA: The house has sunk another six millimeters.
JOE: (*A beat*) The house?
WILMA: The southwest corner.
JOE: Six?
WILMA: Five point nine.
(*There is a tense pause*)
SKEETER: Dad? Dad, are we ... gonna move?
JOE: Hey, Skeets! I brought home a surprise for you!
SKEETER: What is it?
JOE: It's on the back stoop.
(*Skeeter goes out through the screen door*)
WILMA: Joe, I'd really like to discuss ...
JOE: Don't worry about it.
SKEETER: (*On the stoop*) Oh! This is neat!
JOE: The house is your affair, Wilma. I'm sure you can handle
it.
WILMA: That's what I want to discuss. I can't. For all I've
done, nothing is ...
JOE: Honey, everything's going to be all right.
SKEETER: (*On the stoop*) Thanks, Dad!
DOUBLEMINT: What did you bring me, Daddy?
JOE: (*To Doublemint*) Well, honey, there's not much of
anything at work you'd like.
DOUBLEMINT: But ... ?
JOE: But I did bring you this. (*He picks her up in a massive
hug*)
WILMA: Skeeter, you bring your toy inside now. Come to the
table. Dinner's ready.
DOUBLEMINT: Thank you, Daddy. It's the best present in the
world.
JOE: That it is.
(*Skeeter brings the surveyor's level into the kitchen*)
SKEETER: Do I get to keep it?
JOE: I brought it home for you, didn't I?
WILMA: What on earth ...?

JOE: Now I know what you're going to say. You're going to say I'll spoil the boy.

WILMA: I'm going to say we don't have room for this thing.

SKEETER: These legs can break off, I think.

WILMA: What am I going to do with this thing?

(*The four of them are gathered equidistantly around the tripod*)

SKEETER: Please, Mom, can I keep it? I'm gonna be a surveyor like Dad when I grow up.

WILMA: I don't know what to do with this thing.

JOE: Dear, it's not yours to do anything with.

WILMA: If it's going to be in my house . . .

SKEETER: Mom! Dad!

JOE: You can put the goddamned thing in the cellar, for all it's worth!

DOUBLEMINT: Excuse me. I happen to know that this "thing" is called a sextant.

JOE: Uh, no, Doublemint. A sextant is hand-held. We don't use those anymore.

WILMA: Well, what's this one called? Not that I care.

SKEETER: A theodolite, isn't it?

JOE: I . . . I don't remember.

(*Pause. They all stare at the level for a moment, as if expecting it to do something*)

WILMA: Dinner!

JOE: I'm starved!

DOUBLEMINT: I'm ravenous!

JOE: (*Sitting at the table's head*) Then help your mother by setting the table.

DOUBLEMINT: Yes, sir.

JOE: Skeets, come sit down.

SKEETER: (*Looking at them, in turn, through the viewer*) I see Mom in the kitchen. She's real tiny, though. And, Sis, I see two of you. Maybe if you move back there with Mom, you'll come into focus.

DOUBLEMINT: Drop dead twice.

SKEETER: And, Dad, you're a blurry mess.

WILMA: Your father said now, son, and he means now. You can play with it later.

SKEETER: (*Sitting*) Yes, ma'am.

(*A low rumbling noise is heard*)

WILMA: That'll be that fissure acting up again. It's been talking to us all afternoon.

JOE: It hasn't grown, has it?

WILMA: I don't know. That's one thing I was wanting to tell you. I forgot to check it today.

JOE: Well, you can do it later.

WILMA: I forgot, Joe. Honestly. I just forgot.

JOE: I believe you, Wilma. Now get on with dinner. (*The noise grows rapidly in volume*) So tell me. One at a time. What did you all do today?

(*The rumbling has grown deafening. The following is done in pantomime; the characters speak to and hear each other, though their attempts to do so shouldn't seem inordinately animated. Wilma goes to the oven. Skeeter performs a forward roll and then a backward roll. Joe and Doublemint applaud. Doublemint lifts her sweatshirt and shows off her bra. She indicates with her thumb and index finger some measurement in inches. Joe and Skeeter applaud. Wilma brings a Dutch oven to the table. The others applaud, and the children sit. Joe leads them in grace. Quite abruptly, the rumbling stops*)

JOE: (*Shouting*) . . . For what we are about to receive from the booty through Christ our Lord, for thine is the Kingdom and the Power. Amen.

EVERYONE: (*Shouting*) Amen!

WILMA: (*Shouting*) How was *your* day, dear?

JOE: (*Still shouting*) Fine! We went door to door to take up a collection for Ivan Flugar's widow. First time I've been out of the office in three months. I still can't get over them giving me that desk in the old fire hall! (*Screaming*) Doublemint, pass me your plate!!

DOUBLEMINT: (*Shouting*) Off the top, please!

JOE: (*Shouting*) No one's building, of course. And what fool would ever try to put a road across this land? Yep! All in all, a pretty fair day! Let's eat!!

(*Joe, Wilma and Doublemint take a bite of food. At this point, they no longer shout*)

JOE: Mmmmmm!

WILMA: You like it?

JOE: Did it look like a giant woman?

(*All four throw back their heads and laugh fondly. There is another moment; they eat in silence*)

SKEETER: Say, Dad?

JOE: Yes, son?

SKEETER: Why do we always say that?

DOUBLEMINT: Yeah, and then laugh?

JOE: It's a family catch phrase. That's what they call it. Goes back to your mother's and my courtship. On our first date, I took her to see this movie called *The Attack of the Fifty-Foot Woman* . It was our first date, see, and we were both a little nervous to begin with. We weren't terribly involved in the movie. We weren't scared by it, that is. Well, there came this one part where the mutant title character was, you know, sort of marauding over the country-side. Looking for some mate her own size, I think. You can just imagine why. Anyway, hot on her tail was this sheriff and his goofy deputy sidekick. The infamous tall gal had just terrorized some people parked in a lover's lane, and the sheriff and his deputy come up and ask this teenaged boy and his chippie in a white con-vertible, "What happened?" Well, the girl is no help at all. She's crying and carrying on and saying, "Oh, it was awful, it was awful!" And the sheriff's asking, "What? What was?" But the girl won't answer. So then the goofy deputy sidekick pipes in with this line: (*Goofy voice*) "Did it look like a giant woman?" (*Skeeter and Doublemint howl*) Your mom and I just about died. Doublemint, you were conceived later that night. And now, whenever something is really obvious, we say that. A family has got to have catch phrases.

SKEETER: Gee, Dad, you know so much.
DOUBLEMINT: Say, Daddy?
JOE: Yes, dear?
DOUBLEMINT: Do all men masturbate?
JOE: Yes, Doublemint.
DOUBLEMINT: Do you masturbate?
WILMA: Doublemint!
DOUBLEMINT: What? I was just asking.
WILMA: What did your father just say?
DOUBLEMINT: That all men masturbate.
WILMA: And is your father a man?
DOUBLEMINT: Yes.
JOE: Yes, what, young lady?
DOUBLEMINT: Yes, *ma'am*.
WILMA: And what does that mean?
DOUBLEMINT: (*Hanging her head, contrite*) Daddy masturbates.
WILMA: You should learn to think before you speak.
DOUBLEMINT: Yes, ma'am.
JOE: That's what they mean by "look before you leap."
SKEETER: What's masturbate? Who are "they"? My ears hurt. Why do we have funny names? When are we gonna move?
JOE: Ah, now there's another family tradition. Doublemint was my grandmother's name. When my great grandmother, who was pregnant, got off the boat, she didn't know any English, and . . .
SKEETER: Where's mine come from?

JOE: Your mother named you. Pass the popcorn, Doublemint.

SKEETER: Mom?

DOUBLEMINT: I do, too, think before I speak.

WILMA: I once had a dog named Skeeter.

DOUBLEMINT: (*Indicating the food*) Didn't we have this last night?

(*Everyone stops moving. Pause*)

WILMA: What was that remark?

DOUBLEMINT: This casserole. We had it last night. Also, last Friday and Wednesday.

WILMA: Joe, would you please slap your daughter for me? I can't get her good from this side.

(*Joe slaps Doublemint across the face*)

JOE: You are getting a bit sassy.

DOUBLEMINT: Daddy . . .?

WILMA: Who wants more?

JOE: Wait a minute. You know, Wilma . . . I think the girl's right.

(*The telephone rings. Automatically, the four of them reach under their chairs and pull out gas masks. They strap the masks on as the phone continues to ring*)

DOUBLEMINT: Not again.

JOE: Wilma, turn off the alarm.

(*Wilma goes to a small metallic box and opens the casing. She reads a gauge*)

WILMA: I don't understand. There's no carbon monoxide reading. We're at a safe level.

JOE: Are you sure?

SKEETER: I think it's the telephone.

WILMA, JOE, *and* DOUBLEMINT: What?

SKEETER: The phone!

WILMA: So it is.

(*Wilma removes her mask. She answers the telephone. Joe and Doublemint remove their masks and eat*)

WILMA: Hello? Cernikowski residence . . . Yes . . . Oh, hi! Uh-huh . . . When? . . . No! . . .

DOUBLEMINT: (*To Skeeter*) You can take off your mask now.

WILMA: (*Into the phone*) But why?

SKEETER: I like it in here.

WILMA: (*Into the phone*) Is that a fact?

DOUBLEMINT: Daddy, make him. It's creepy.

JOE: Son, do as your sister asks.

SKEETER: Not until we move.

JOE: (*To Wilma*) Who's on the phone?

WILMA: One of the neighbors.

SKEETER: I thought you told us you were gonna move the town.

JOE: Buster Brown, I am getting damned tired of that question. I can't very well move a whole town single-handedly, now can I? But I'm working on it. We're all thinking about it. We're thinking about it a lot. We're thinking about it all the time. And if we do leave, what of it? Centralia's a fine town, but we'll still be a family. Simply someplace else. We'll still have each other. That's the only important thing. How many times do I have to say it?

WILMA: (*Into the phone*) Thanks for calling. Good-bye. (*She hangs up and returns to the table*)

JOE: What's cooking?

WILMA: Strange. The widow down the block, Mrs. Eggenweiller, was arrested this afternoon and taken off to jail.

DOUBLEMINT: How come?

WILMA: No one knows.

DOUBLEMINT: Did she do anything wrong?

WILMA: I don't possibly see how. She always seemed so dull.

JOE: Nice breasts, though. I've seen them. Uncovered.

SKEETER: When, Dad?

JOE: About eight years ago. Her husband had just been killed, and you were a tiny baby in your mother's arms. So I had an affair with her.

SKEETER: (*Removing his mask*) Neat!

DOUBLEMINT: Really? What was she like?

JOE: Her hair was brunette. It's blond now, isn't it, Wilma? Anyway, she was . . .

DOUBLEMINT: No, I mean . . . what was she *like*?

WILMA: Hold it a second. I didn't know anything about this.

JOE: Yes, you did.

WILMA: No, I didn't.

JOE: I told you about it.

WILMA: You did not.

JOE: I did. I remember you were nursing late one afternoon. I came home and said, "How are you?" And you said, "Fine. How was work?" And I said I hadn't been, but was down the block putting it to Sally Eggenweiller.

WILMA: In a pig's valise!

JOE: No, I remember it clearly.

WILMA: I don't remember the conversation at all.

SKEETER: Mom! Dad!

WILMA: Okay. What did I say?

JOE: Huh?

WILMA: What was my response? What did I say to you?

JOE: Oh, something about getting Skeeter on the formula as soon as possible.

WILMA: Are you sure you're not making this entire exchange up?

JOE: Yes.

WILMA: I suppose you're right, then.

(*A mild rumbling from the cellar is heard*)

I'd better measure that crack now.

JOE *and* SKEETER: Right in the middle of dinner?

WILMA: You can all finish without me. (*She goes to the counter and rummages through a drawer*) I meant to get it done earlier. I don't know. I just don't know . . .

JOE: Wilma. Come sit down.

SKEETER: Aw, Mom, please?

WILMA: I whip myself into a minor frenzy, everyday it seems, worried to death you'll be angry I haven't gotten something done. Despite the fact that I've darn well memorized every baseboard and mantle and ledge and . . . and vortex of this house. But still I'm convinced it'll be something. And then you come home, and the kids suddenly behave, and it's the same old thing. I could have merely vacuumed the place, for all it matters. Well, this is for me. I'm going to go measure that fissure now because the truth—the truth, actually—is that what I've been doing today is putting it off. (*She turns to Joe, a large soup ladle in her hands*) Sally *Eggenweiller?*

JOE: Don't be hard on yourself.

WILMA: Yes, putting it off! Joe, I'd been measuring the fissure with that old coffeespoon. You wouldn't buy me a decent pair of whatever they are . . .

SKEETER: Calipers.

WILMA: Calipers. I'd been sticking the handle of that old spoon in to see how much space was left. How much the crack had grown. And yesterday . . . well, I didn't tell you this, it worried me a little . . . yesterday the whole wall kind of shuddered. The bowl of the spoon got extremely hot, actually started to glow, and I let go. It got sucked right up into the hole. It disappeared! My guess is that the fire is . . .

DOUBLEMINT: Mother!

WILMA: You be quiet. The fire is . . .

JOE: Wilma!

WILMA: *It's ten feet from our house!*

JOE: Not in front of the boy.

DOUBLEMINT: You're not supposed to call it by name.

WILMA: I'm going down. Skeeter . . . my Coleman.

SKEETER: Yes, Mom. (*He gets a gas lantern from a cupboard*)

WILMA: Children, mind your father. I'll be back in a minute. (*She goes to Joe, who is seated, and gives him a small kiss*) I'm sorry to interrupt your dinner.

JOE: Now that you bring it up, honey, I've been meaning to talk to you. About the vacuuming.

WILMA: I'll clean house tomorrow.

JOE: You're a grand wife.

(*Wilma kisses Joe again. This time it's a long, passionate, rather involved kiss*)

SKEETER: (*After a moment*) Doublemint?

DOUBLEMINT: Shhh! I'm busy.

SKEETER: See how far I can stick my tongue out? (*He demonstrates*)

DOUBLEMINT: Shut up.

(*Wilma and Joe stop kissing*)

Skeeter, get me a cigarette.

SKEETER: All right.

(*Skeeter goes to a drawer for cigarettes. Wilma proceeds to unlock the cellar door. She speaks with her back to the others and to the audience; she may be crying*)

WILMA: I'm just so afraid, Joe.

JOE: What of? Don't say that.

WILMA: I'm afraid of someday losing you. (*She has the door open*) I'll be right back. (*She exits down the cellar stairs*)

SKEETER: (*Handing cigarette pack to Doublemint*) Hurry back, Mom!

DOUBLEMINT: Daddy?

JOE: Yes, dear?

DOUBLEMINT: . . . Light my cigarette?

JOE: Sure.

(*Joe draws a book of matches from his pocket and lights her cigarette. A loud "Boom!" is heard, and a fierce flash of orange light goes off in the cellar doorway. Skeeter is thrown from his chair*)

DOUBLEMINT: (*Exhaling smoke*) Wow!

SKEETER: What was that?

JOE: (*Calling down the stairway*) Wilma?

SKEETER: (*Joining him*) Mom, what happened?

DOUBLEMINT: Daddy, did you feel that?

JOE: It felt like an explosion.

DOUBLEMINT: I know, I felt it, too.

SKEETER: Mama! Answer!

JOE: Wilma? (*A beat*) I think your mother might need some help.

DOUBLEMINT: I'm not going down there.

SKEETER: Neither am I. It smells like B.M.

JOE: I don't know my way down there. Somebody's got to go. (*He and Doublemint slowly turn to Skeeter*)

SKEETER: Oh, all right. I will.

JOE: That's a good boy.

SKEETER: Maybe she's hurt.

JOE: I'm sure she's fine.

DOUBLEMINT: Look, this is what you do: just go down and find out what happened. And then yell up the stairs and tell us.

JOE: And then bring your mother back up.

SKEETER: Okay.

DOUBLEMINT: Let us know how you're doing.

SKEETER: I will, Sis.

JOE: And be careful.

SKEETER: Can I take my mask?

DOUBLEMINT: Daddy, he's dawdling.

JOE: Run along, Skeets.

SKEETER: Yes, sir. (*He exits down the cellar steps*)

DOUBLEMINT: And tell us everything you see.

SKEETER: (*Offstage*) I heard you! I'm not a baby!

JOE: Be careful!

DOUBLEMINT: (*Moving to the table*) Would you care for seconds?

JOE: Seconds?

DOUBLEMINT: More tuna.

JOE: Oh. No, dear, let's wait till your mother joins us. (*Calling*) Skeeter! Are you there yet? What's going on?

SKEETER: (*Offstage*) I don't see the lantern. It's hard to see down here. And to breathe.

JOE: How's your mother? (*Pause*) Can you see her?

SKEETER: (*Offstage*) Now I see her!

JOE: Is she all right? (*Pause*) Son?

SKEETER: (*Offstage*) Dad?

JOE: Yes, son?

SKEETER: (*A beat; offstage*) She looks like a giant woman.

DOUBLEMINT: Very funny.

JOE: What do you mean, son?

SKEETER: (*Offstage*) Well, she's kind of puffy looking. And I've seen pictures . . .

JOE: What kind of pictures?

SKEETER: (*Offstage*) Negro ladies south of the equator.

JOE: Is she unconscious?

SKEETER: (*Offstage*) She's not moving.

JOE: Can you bring her upstairs? Try.

SKEETER: (*Offstage*) She's stuck.

DOUBLEMINT: Stuck?

SKEETER: (*Offstage*) I can't move her. She's half in and half out.

JOE: What are you talking about?

DOUBLEMINT: Daddy, we shouldn't have sent him down. He's not helping at all. He's not talking sense.

JOE: . . . Unless he means that fissure.

DOUBLEMINT: Ooo! That thing in the wall has got a hold of mother? This I gotta see. (*She heads for the doorway*)

JOE: (*Stopping her*) No. Whatever you do, stay here with me.

SKEETER: (*Offstage*) Hey! I got her glove!

DOUBLEMINT: (*To Joe*) Glove?

JOE: (*To Doublemint*) Mommy wasn't wearing gloves. (*Calling down the stairs*) Skeeter, come upstairs.

SKEETER: (*Offstage*) But Mama's . . .

JOE: Come upstairs now! There's nothing you can do. I'll take over from here. I'm going to have to deal with this. Doublemint, sweetheart . . .what should I do?

DOUBLEMINT: Call the sheriff, Daddy.

JOE: An ambulance. We need an ambulance. I'll have him send one over. Hell, Centralia has more of them per capita than any other American city. I'll have Pete send an ambulance over right away.

DOUBLEMINT: We just need a sheriff.

JOE: Why don't you just dish up some food?

(*Joe goes to the phone and dials. Skeeter enters from the cellar; he is hiding something behind his back*)

DOUBLEMINT: There you are. Sit down, Mouthbreather.

JOE: (*Into the phone*) Sheriff, please.

SKEETER: Dad?

DOUBLEMINT: I know what. Maybe you could learn to breathe through your ears.

SKEETER: Leave me alone.

DOUBLEMINT: What have you got there? (*Skeeter holds out what resembles a black, misshapened glove*) Yuck! Throw that thing back downstairs!

SKEETER: Dad?

JOE: Not now, son. (*Into the phone*) Yes, Pete? Joe Cernikowski.

SKEETER: Is Mama going to heaven?

JOE: I think so, Skeeter. (*Into the phone*) You'd better get over here, Pete, right away. There's been an incident. It's Wilma . . . Well, I don't know if I ever mentioned it, but we've had this small problem in our basement. Apparently not as small as I thought. A rather heated situation, you might say, and it's just blown up on us. Do you read me? (*Pause; to the children*) How are you two feeling?

DOUBLEMINT: We're fine.

JOE: (*Into the phone*) No, no one else is hurt. Can you come over right away? . . . Well, sure, after your dinner would be fine, too. And could you call an ambulance for me? I don't have the number. You'd better bring along Terry and Mike with you. Tell 'em to bring those pneumatic pliers they got . . . You know, that think they've got to pry folks out of car wrecks . . . Okay . . .See you in an hour. Enjoy your meal.

(*Joe hangs up the telephone. Skeeter is sobbing softly at the kitchen table*)

DOUBLEMINT: Daddy, Skeeter's crying.

JOE: It's all right.

DOUBLEMINT: It's not manly.

JOE: No, now they've changed their mind about that. Let him cry.

SKEETER: What about you, Dad? Don't you feel like crying?

JOE: I look at it this way, son. You've known your mother all your life. I only knew her thirteen years of mine. And besides, don't you see? We've still got each other. That'll get us through. We'll survive. I'll see to that. Don't you worry. Come give your Dad a big hug and a kiss. You'll see . . . everything's going to be all right. (*Skeeter kisses him*) I've still got you both.

SKEETER: I'll miss Mama, though.

JOE: We all will. Won't we?

DOUBLEMINT: I guess so.

SKEETER: I had a feeling this was going to happen.

JOE: No one could have forseen it. Doublemint? (*Offering his arms*) Give your Daddy a gigantic hug.

(*Doublemint kisses him, but it is the same kiss her mother gave Joe moments ago. Skeeter sees this and cries anew, even louder than before*)

DOUBLEMINT: It's okay, Skeeter. Our father's right. Everything's going to be fine. (*She goes to Skeeter and puts her arms around him, rocking and cradling him, and speaking low*) Shhh . . . hush. It's all right. It's all right.

(*She sings; a Stephen Foster ballad*)

Let us pause in Life's pleasures

And count its many tears

While we all share sorrow with the poor.
There's a song that will linger
Forever in our ears:
O, Hard Times,
Come again no more!
(*Joe and Skeeter join her in three-part harmony*)
'Tis the song,
The sigh of the weary:
Hard Times, Hard Times,
Come again no more!
Many days you have lingered
Around my cabin door.
O, Hard Times,
Come again no more . . .!
JOE: Not bad.
DOUBLEMINT: But he's still crying. What is it, Skeeter? What do you want?
SKEETER: (*Crying*) I want . . . I want . . .
DOUBLEMINT: You want your mommy.
SKEETER: . . . I want to change my name!
JOE: Why?
SKEETER: Just want to.
JOE: That sounds fair. What do you want to change it to?
SKEETER: Well . . .
DOUBLEMINT: Let me think. We'll call you . . . I've got it! We'll call you "Popocatepetl." How's that?
SKEETER: (*Sniffling to a halt*) Okay, I s'pose.
(*Laughing warmly, Joe wraps his arms around the two children*)
JOE: There, now. See? It's like a brand-new start. Can't you just sense from the feelings in this room that things are going to look brighter?
SKEETER: No. Anyway, it's gotten dark in here.
DOUBLEMINT: So it has.
JOE: I can see fine.
DOUBLEMINT: Daddy, I think it's probably a good idea to keep this room lit up. Well-illuminated. (*She moves about the room, switching on a few lights*) We want people passing by to know there's someone at home. 'Specially here in the kitchen. Forget the living room. Here's where all the instruments are. Am I right, Daddy? I know what this one is. It's a carbon monoxide monitoring device. It always seemed to be Mother's favorite. And this one over here . . . this one reads debacles.
SKEETER: Decibels.
DOUBLEMINT: What?

SKEETER: Decibels!

DOUBLEMINT: Whatever. I used to watch Mother, you know. This here is a temperature doodad.

SKEETER *and* JOE: Thermometer.

DOUBLEMINT: Thermometer, yes. There's even an extra feeler out on the back stoop, so this thing measures both interior and exterior temperatures. Of the house, that is. (*She is at the cellar door*) Don't you think we should keep this door closed?

JOE: Go ahead and shut it.

DOUBLEMINT: (*Doing so*) I'll lock it later. (*Picking up the legal pad from the counter*) Here's most of what's left of her. Hey, listen to what she's got written down. Something about the pull of the moon. "Tide: Definition two. Stress exerted on a body or part of a body by the gravitational attraction of another, specifically that of the sun and moon, the lunar effect being the more powerful." (*Standing at the screen door, she reaches over and snaps on a clock/radio—a slow waltz is heard*) The sun's down, of course. But, boy, is the moon bright! It looks like it's throbbing up there in the sky, the whole circle of it. Makes the horizon look like a big, fat orange line. It's fiercely pretty.

SKEETER: Are you gonna sing again?

JOE: Doublemint? Honey, are you all right?

(*Doublemint moves the theodolite to the porch door, aiming the viewer outside. She peers through it during her speech, her back to the others and to the audience*)

DOUBLEMINT: Last week in school—in home room—we had geography, introduction to physical sciences, how to garnish a meal, and feminist poetry. And then for the health portion, Miss Hedgepeth began talking about premenstrual syndrome. It's something brand-new. A lot of the girls in the class have already started their periods, so they were shaking their heads up and down and shouting stuff like, "Tell me about it!" and "Ain't it the truth!" But you know I haven't started mine yet. So I was quiet. 'Cause I was thinking to myself, "*That's* what it is! *That's* what's been wrong with me for the past couple of years!" Daddy, you must have wondered why I was so mean and irritable and . . . restless, I guess. Didn't you?

JOE: Not really. I hadn't noticed.

SKEETER: I have.

JOE: Did you tell Miss Hedgepeth what you were feeling?

(*Doublemint turns to face them, seeming no longer a child, but a woman of twenty-five. Unaffected, self-confident, handsome. Her walk is different, and her speech pattern is calm*)

DOUBLEMINT: No. I didn't have time. Two days later some men came into the classroom and took her away to an asylum. (*A beat*) This fire's starting to worry me a little.

JOE: Come to the table, honey.

DOUBLEMINT: Outside it smells like ... like what? Is it nitrogen? Funny how things have smells and names and meanings. (*Going to Joe, kissing him on the forehead*) No, Father, I'm going outside to watch the sky and the ground for a bit. (*Kissing Skeeter*) Be good for your father.

SKEETER: Yes, Sis.

DOUBLEMINT: What's this? (*Picking up the piece of charred skin from the table where Skeeter has left it*) I THOUGHT I TOLD YOU TO PUT THIS DOWNSTAIRS!! (*She slaps him viciously with it*)

SKEETER: Dad!!

JOE: No fighting, kids. Your mother wouldn't like it.

SKEETER: (*To Doublemint*) Bastard! You're just the same!

DOUBLEMINT: (*Stunned, dropping the "glove"*) What?

SKEETER: A moment ago, you sang that song and held me. It was so nice. I thought you were gonna be different. But you're not! You'll never change! You're just the same as always!

DOUBLEMINT: I thought you meant something else. (*Slowly backing toward the porch door*) Oh, my God. Oh, God ... I'm scared. I'm afraid.

JOE: Honey, you heard what your mother said. The fire may be ten whole feet from the house. And if it's moving as slow as they say it is ... well, we've got plenty of ...

DOUBLEMINT: Not the fire, for Pete's sake! We've *lived* with it!

JOE: Then what?

DOUBLEMINT: I'm afraid of growing up to be just like her. Exactly like her! And I don't want to! I don't! (*She dashes out onto the stoop where, in the moonlight, her silhouette can be seen*)

SKEETER: I don't like this.

JOE: She'll be fine in a minute.

SKEETER: I feel sick.

JOE: How 'bout playing some catch in the moonlight?

SKEETER: I can't, Dad.

JOE: We can look through your theodolite. C'mon.

SKEETER: My head aches.

JOE: Your head?

SKEETER: So do my arms.

JOE: Well, take a goddamn aspirin.

(*The waltz music from the radio has crescendoed. A brilliant flash of light is seen through the screen door, a loud CRACK! of thunder, and Doublemint is struck dead by a bolt of lightning*)
SKEETER: What was that?
JOE: Sounds like it's going to storm. Doublemint! Come inside now. (*Pause*) Doublemint? (*Pause*) Skeeter, go ask your sister to come inside.
SKEETER: (*Going*) She sure is acting all grown up.
JOE: She's a woman now.
SKEETER: (*At the door*) She's smoking.
JOE: She can smoke inside.
SKEETER: She's smoldering, Dad.
JOE: She's angry?
SKEETER: I think she's dead.
JOE: Huh?
SKEETER: I think she's dead.
JOE: (*Not looking*) I'll bet you think that's mighty smart. (*Black smoke billows in through the screen*) If your mother was here, she'd tie you up till you had something to complain about. Nobody likes a whiny, vindictive little crybaby.
SKEETER: Why don't you come look for yourself?
(*A cacophonous buzzer goes off. Joe runs to the door, looks out, and slams the heavy inner door closed. He leans, wide-eyed, against it*)
JOE: (*Shouting over the buzzer*) Move away from the door! Stay away from the windows!
SKEETER: Told ya!
JOE: What's that noise?
SKEETER: Just like I told you about Mama!
JOE: Never mind! That's not important! What's that buzzer?
SKEETER: Smoke alarm!
JOE: We've got to turn it off! Do you know how?
SKEETER: Wait for the smoke to clear out!
JOE: No! Do something now!
SKEETER: I can unplug the battery!
JOE: Well, do it!!
(*Skeeter crosses to a round plastic screen mounted on the wall. He removes the cover and yanks out a battery. Small sparks shoot from the device. The buzzer, the radio, and the lights go out*)
SKEETER: (*After a beat*) Oops.
JOE: Brilliant.
SKEETER: It wasn't my fault, Dad.
JOE: Things aren't bad enough?

SKEETER: How would this little nine-volt battery make the electricity go?

JOE: Don't ask me. Where does your mother keep the plumber's candles?

SKEETER: Under the sink.

JOE: Get one and light it on the table. I'll call Pete.

SKEETER: Yes, sir.

JOE: (*Picking up the phone receiver*) Damn! Phone's out, too.

SKEETER: That doesn't make sense.

JOE: I suppose it's for the best. What would I have said? "Say, uh, as long as you're loading up the truck with tools and all, you wanna include a scoop shovel to scrape my daughter off the back porch?"

SKEETER: (*Lighting the candle*) Dad, is Doublemint going to heaven?

JOE: I don't know, son.

SKEETER: Is she going to hell?

JOE: Probably. I think so. (*Holding onto Skeeter tightly*) It's going to be tough, son. I've got to tell you that right now. This is the tough part coming up. You know what they say, don't you? You can't live with 'em, and you can't live without 'em.

SKEETER: Who are "they," Dad?

JOE: Women.

SKEETER: No, the other "they" you always talk about.

JOE: Never mind. We're going to have to live without the women. There's no other choice. It's as simple as that.

SKEETER: Are we going to move now?

JOE: Be quiet. Our only option seems clear. There's you, and there's me, and . . .

SKEETER: Are we going to *move*?

JOE: No. But I see what you're getting at. There are precautions we can take. Precautions to stay safe. I'll stay home with you every day. Look at it this way: I'm practically drawing unemployment as it is. Only I go someplace else to do it. Yeah, I'll stay home. And you'll stay home, too. I'll take you out of school. And as for sports . . . well, forget it. Absolutely not. We can play catch, maybe. The two of us, in the living room, with that sponge football. We can . . .

SKEETER: Mama's got that room cordoned off.

JOE: Huh? What? She's got it what?

SKEETER: Cordoned. Off.

JOE: Can you cook?

SKEETER: I don't know.

JOE: You don't have any friends, do you?

SKEETER: Two. Three, counting Doublemint.

JOE: Lose 'em. We've got to keep our priorities straight. (*Hugging him once again*) I'm not taking any chances. This family is still fifty percent here.

SKEETER: It won't be if you don't stop holding me so tight. You're hurting.

JOE: (*Releasing him*) Why did this have to happen to me?

SKEETER: It's all of us, Dad. Everybody. It's the fire.

JOE: Skeeter, don't.

SKEETER: Face it, Dad. I . . .

JOE: No!

SKEETER: . . . I *know* about the fire. And I don't mean just knowing of its existence. I know more about it than you do. Or than Mama and Sis did. You all tried to hide it from me. The realities.

JOE: Big words.

SKEETER: I didn't have to read anything in the papers, or see anything on the news. I knew—I absolutely knew—something from the beginning. Clear back in kindergarten. I used to take myself on little field trips. I went to that stripping pit outside of town and watched the fire. The orange glow. The progress. And smelled the fumes. And felt the heat underneath my shoes. And what I knew at that point was this: it would get to us. Eventually.

JOE: Son . . .?

SKEETER: And knowing made me not afraid.

JOE: Why didn't you tell me any of this before?

SKEETER: Well, for one thing, I'm only nine years old. No one would have listened. And secondly . . .

JOE: Yes?

SKEETER: Secondly . . .

JOE: Tell me. Secondly what?

SKEETER: I would have gotten a spanking.

JOE: (*Going to the table*) I'll tell you, Buster Brown, I could give you one right now the way you're talking.

SKEETER: Something just occurred to me.

JOE: (*Eating*) All this talk of doom.

SKEETER: The fire didn't kill Doublemint.

JOE: Exactly. So you can just forget about theories and reasons.

SKEETER: And have you noticed? People around town? Somebody's always dropping in the middle of the day. Not waking up in the morning. Getting taken away. Why do you suppose there are so many widows and orphans?

JOE: I don't.

SKEETER: Dad! Sis was killed by *lightning*!

JOE: So?

SKEETER: Not the fire!

JOE: Maybe it was some geo ... thermal ... attraction, or something.

SKEETER: No ... no. It wasn't. What if it was something else? Something else entirely. What if it was ...

JOE: (*Offering a bowl*) Popcorn?

SKEETER: What if it was just plain old fear?

JOE: Huh?

SKEETER: (*Grabbing Joe by the shoulders*) Dad, tell me! Please! I know you're really smart. You must be! But tell me something!

JOE: What do you want to know?

SKEETER: What if ... what if there really *isn't* life after death?

JOE: Uh ... I don't know.

SKEETER: Mmmmmmmmrphh!

(*His eyes roll back in his head. He has a small fit, then a massive—quick-cerebral stroke and dies in his father's lap*)

JOE: I suppose you think that's funny, too. What's that supposed to be, anyway? A stroke, or something? (*Pause*) Skeeter? Skeets? Son? (*Pause*) Boy, that's rich. That's a hot one. You're just a baby. A *stroke*?! What a corker! Perfect! Hysterical! While I'm on the subject of really great laughs I've had in the past hour, what about your mother getting fried in the basement? And your sister getting struck down by lightning like that. Now that was really funny. Of course, I shouldn't have been too surprised. And ... and my own mom and dad—I haven't thought about this in six years—my own mom and dad in that supermarket explosion. That was truly a riot. When that happened, I wanted to lay down and laugh so hard. Till I had tears in my eyes. You know what I mean? And I only had one brother, but he was born dead. That made me an only child. (*Pause*) Son? Are you really gone? (*He moves away*) Go ahead, then! Take off! Leave! See if I care! You stupid, stupid, stupid! All of you!! (*Stopping*) This means I ... this means I'm alone. (*A beat*) Except for in-laws.

(*Singing:*)
While we seek mirth and beauty
And music light and gay,
There are frail forms fainting at the door.
Though their voices are silent
Their pleading looks will say,
"O, Hard Times,
Come again no more!"

(*Propping Skeeter's body on a chair at the table*)
They say we're individually always alone. Always, no matter what. But now . . . now I'm afraid.
(*A series of three soft knocks is heard on the wooden porch door*)
Who's there? (*No answer*) Pete? (*The three knocks are repeated*) Pete, is that you? (*No answer*) Oh . . . shit, God. Skeeter! Skeeter, what did you mean about "plain old fear"? (*Knocks*) Your sister said she was afraid to grow up like Mommy. That was just before . . . (*Knocks*) And your Mom. She was afraid I'd leave her. (*Louder knocks*) What about you? What was it you . . . (*Yet louder knocks*) That's right. You were afraid there might not be a heaven or a . . . (*Three very loud knocks; he whispers*) That's for me. (*The knocking becomes a relentless tattoo*) No! I didn't mean it!! A family!! One lousy little family! Big deal! They were all scared of their own shadows, anyway! Alone? So what! Go away! (*He takes the theodolite and props it under the door handle. The knocking is now augmented —magnified and echoed*) Leave me alone! Never mind what I said! I'm not really!! I'M NOT!! *I'M NOT AFRAID*!!
(*Suddenly, the room lights flash back on. The knocking on the door ceases, and a lilting polka is playing on the radio*)
OFFICER: (*Offstage*) Joe?
JOE: You have a voice?
OFFICER: (*Offstage*) What in hell is goin' on in there? Joe?
JOE: Who is it?
OFFICER: (*Offstage*) Jackson. From the Office of Surface Mining.
JOE: Sam?
OFFICER: (*Offstage*) Yeah.
(*Holding the theodolite as a weapon in one hand, Joe throws open the door with the other. The Officer is a handsome, all-American, twenty-five years old*)
JOE: (*After a moment, pumping the man's hand*) Sam! What a relief! Boy, am I glad to see you!
OFFICER: What the fuck's goin' on?
JOE: I can't begin to tell you who I thought it was.
OFFICER: I tried the front doorbell. Must not be workin'. So I come the fuck 'round to the back and hear you screamin' and yellin'. Know you must be pretty fuckin' upset about the wife. Yeah, Pete called me. Fuck, that's why I come over. Figgered you might, you know . . . need someone to be the fuck here.
JOE: I'm fine. Really. I'm fine now.
OFFICER: (*Indicating the theodolite*) Homework?

JOE: (*Setting it down*) In a way.

OFFICER: Say, did you know there's some dead fuckin' animal or something out here?

JOE: That's my daughter.

OFFICER: Sad to fuckin' hear it.

JOE: C'mon inside.

OFFICER: Thanks. I will. (*Entering, he sees Skeeter's body at the table*) This your other kid?

JOE: Skeeter.

OFFICER: Skeeter. That's right. My boy teases him at school.

JOE: Boys'll be boys.

OFFICER: (*To Skeeter*) Hey, old top, glad to see you *back* from the front! (*On the word, he slaps Skeeter on the back, and the body falls to the floor*) Fuckin' shame. Well, ya know, when it rains
. . .

JOE: Don't I fuckin' know it! Can I offer you a beer? Have you had dinner?

OFFICER: Fuck, no, I haven't. My wife's got the cancer, you know.

JOE: Well, sit down. We got plenty left over.

OFFICER: Thanks. I appreciate it. (*He sits and helps himself to casserole*)

JOE: (*Sitting with him*) So . . . how the fuck are things over at OSM? Don't see you in person much anymore.

OFFICER: Oh, you know. The same. Things are looking up, though. Half the town is considered geologically safe from the spreading inferno. Combustion scientists in Pittsburgh some three hundred miles away are experimenting with burnout control, a process by which, instead of dousing the fire, the flames are . . .

JOE: I know, Sam, I know.

OFFICER: You see me on Channel Sixteen?

JOE: No. In the Sunday Supplement.

OFFICER: Yeah, that was a good interview. Smooth. (*Eating*) You got any Tabasco for this?

JOE: Sorry. Wilma does all the shopping and the cooking. She won't have the fuckin' stuff in the house.

OFFICER: That a fact?

JOE: I'm afraid so.

(*The Officer takes a handgun from his jacket and shoots Joe twice in the chest. He then continues to eat for a moment*)

The End

[*NOTE: For curtain call, the actors file onstage through the cellar door to take their bows. The Officer exits, and the actress playing Wilma sprinkles sand on the floor. The four Cernikowskis then perform a soft shoe dance to the tune of "Hard Times, Come Again No More"*]

Jane Nixon Willis

SLAM!

Jane Nixon Willis

In Jane Nixon Willis's *SLAM!* a pair of street-wise high school pals from Queens rap in the men's room of a club on the Bowery of Manhattan's lower east side before rejoining a slam dance group. The *New York Times* reviewer Mel Gussow praised the author for her production in the Ensemble Studio Theatre's Marathon '84: "Miss Willis has her own ear to the wall, capturing the rhythms of male bravado and adolescent behavior. There is an exactitude about her use of the vernacular, with the addition of a kind of David Mamet twist in the transcription."

In addition to *SLAM!* the playwright has also written three full-length plays: *Good Paying Tenants*, a finalist in the 1982 Forrest A. Roberts Playwriting contest; *Triptych*, which was produced at the Nat Horne Theatre in Manhattan in 1984; and a recently completed play, not yet produced. Her film play *Panic City* was produced by Max Film Company.

Ms. Willis's most recent one-act play, *Men Without Dates,* was a hit of the Ensemble Studio Theatre's Marathon '85. This version of *SLAM!* was originally produced in New York by the Ensemble Studio Theatre.

[*AUTHOR'S NOTE*: In September 1983 when *SLAM!* was originally produced at the Nat Horn Theatre, the offstage number used was a trendy instrumental of Michael Jackson's "Billie Jean." This gave Mel and Linc an opportunity to try their hand at Michael Jackson—*Saturday Night Fever*—type break dancing, or in other words, a potpourri of whatever came to mind or body while they recited their song. Using other music is fine with me, as long as it is an appropriate type of danceable rock music that is very different from punk—keeping in mind that the person offstage in the Club put the record on by mistake—and as long as the composer permits its use in the play.

Lastly, any references to present-day personalities may be updated as needed to keep the play immediate. This can be left up to the discretion of the producer.]

Characters:

  LINCOLN (LINC), *twenty-twoish, a sometime high school student; brooding, pensive, but not without a sense of humor;
  from Flushing, Queens; an avid slam-dancer*
  MEL, *nineteenish, a high school student; Linc's classmate; not
  really inarticulate, just confused; he has a kind of Eddie
  Haskell-type savoir faire; he is also from Flushing; an avid
  slam-dancer.*

Setting:

  *The play takes place in a dank, dirty, dark men's room in a
  Bowery punk club on a Tuesday night during the band's set-break.*

At Curtain:

  *As the lights come up, Lincoln staggers in, pinching his nose
  which is bleeding profusely. He has cuts and scrapes on his
  arms as well, his T-shirt is torn and dirty and sweaty. He wears
  jeans and cleat boots. He is out of breath and upset as he
  searches from stall to stall for toilet paper. Music—punk stuff
  offstage.*

  LINC: What. No paper products? Great. Just great. What am
  I, gonna bleed to death here?
  (*Mel enters—he's dressed in similar garb—is equally sweaty,
  but his T-shirt has* BILE *or* SCAB *or* INFECTION *scrawled
  across the front*)
  MEL: Here. Broke the dispenser in the girl's room. (*Pulls a
  couple of maxi-pads from his pockets—pulls the adhesive strip off
  them and tosses them to Linc—who glares at him*) Well, it was the
  best I could do! That's the thanks I get! Bleed to death then. (*Goes
  over and dunks his head in a clogged sinkful of water while Linc
  takes a pad, pinches his nose and tips his head back*) Whoo!
  (*Shakes his head—rejuvenated by the stagnant water*) I got a head-
  ful of concrete on that last one. Whoo! All these memories from
  childhood welled up and flashed before my eyes! Even memories

from the womb! It was intense! (*Sticks his head under hand-dryer*)
Now *that's* what I call slammin'!

LINC: (*Taping pad wrong side to a cut on his arm*) I don't
know. Wasn't too much cooperation in that last one, thanks to you.

MEL: Yo, Nureyev. Takes more'n me to catch you. I figured
you were doin' this ego thing so I didn't wanna interfere.

LINC: Well, you coulda broken my fall, man. A real friend
woulda broken my fall.

MEL: You misjudged. Story is you're responsible for your own
actions out there.

LINC: More like the story is you're shankin' to catch. It's a
jungle out there, pal. Story is group cooperation. Why me? I got a
wimp on my hands.

MEL: Who you callin' a wimp?

LINC: You saw me comin'. I hung in the goddam air for three
or four seconds. Who was gonna catch me? The girls in the corner?

MEL: Tillie the Hun. She's good in a clutch.

LINC: Yeah, I know. She poked me in the eye with her mohawk.

MEL: I wasn't in a position to catch you. If I hadn't'a moved,
my head woulda gotten nailed to the wall by them Florsheim boots
of yours.

LINC: Oh, that's pussy.

MEL: Who's pussy? Who's cryin' and whimpering about a
boo-boo on the nose?

LINC: Boo-boo? I broke it. I think my nose is broken.

MEL: But that's crucial! What are you complainin' about? A
broken nose is crucial! That's like the Purple Heart Award—you'd
have to go to Nam an' back to get the kind of respect you're gonna
get when you go back out there . . .

LINC: Yeah. Right. (*Stands up and looks in the mirror*)

MEL: (*Taking a sip from his paper cup*) Gives you character.

LINC: Character. (*Guffaw*) I got enough character to fill three
people. (*Carefully wipes away some of the blood from his face
—but leaves a little on for effect—then tears off two little pieces of
cotton and sticks them up each nostril*) Know something? It's true.
These *are* more absorbent.

MEL: So. How about last week? When you tried to turn me
into a permanent soprano? Remember? Think it felt good? But did
I complain?

LINC: All right. All right.

MEL: All right then.

LINC: Yeah, yeah, yeah.

MEL: Okay then.

LINC: (*With decorum*) It's a poor sport that holds a grudge. (*Music stops. Mel listens*)

MEL: What are they, breakin' out there?

LINC: (*With a shrug*) Them or me.

MEL: Used to be a time when they'd gig without stoppin' for anything.

LINC: Signa old age, maybe. I think me an' slam dancing are goin' through a passing phrase. It's tough to set a trend and then try an' stick by it.

MEL: You graduatin' this year?

LINC: Got me. You?

MEL: Got me. You?

LINC: Got me.

MEL: You? Like it's no big deal. Longer I stay in school, the longer I stay away from my old man's shop. I don't wanna get locked into a future fulla numerical combinations just yet.

LINC: What's your old man? An accountant or something?

MEL: Nah. He's a locksmith.

LINC: Oh.

MEL: Yeah. Twenty-four hour deal. Snap, snap, there goes my life.

LINC: Yeah, but you might meet a lot of people that way. Get a call from a good-lookin' chick who's just been robbed and plundered. Go over, install a Medico, maybe a window-gate. (*Lifts his eyebrows suggestively*) With a coupla padlocks. Ke-e-eys for the padlocks. I imagine you could meet a lotta humanity that way.

MEL: Yeah. Well. It would still be easier to just not graduate.

LINC: Aw, don't say that.

MEL: I'm saying it. Why, I'm only a quarter of a way through *A Tale of Two Cities*—be a real shame to graduate and never find out if they catch that damn whale or not.

LINC: So who's stoppin' you from gettin' a li-berry card?

MEL: Nobody.

LINC: So get a li-berry card.

MEL: Nah.

LINC: Get a li-berry card.

MEL: Nah. (*Beat*) So what are you doin' for summer vocation? Get it? (*Laughs*) Summer? Season. Vocation? Job.

LINC: Yeah, yeah. Ha-ha, Einstein, I forgot to laugh. I've got a solid gold future ahead of me. I joined the Marines.

MEL: Yeah, yeah. Solid gold. You an' the Bee-gee's.

LINC: No joke. I really did.

MEL: The Marines! What the hell for?

LINC: "The Few, the Proud, the Brave"—the Marines.

MEL: What was wrong with being "The Many, the Silly, and the Scared?"

LINC: I need direction. I need a change.

MEL: But the Marines! Come on! That's like 1940 mentality, man. What're you doin' it for?

LINC: For me.

MEL: To meet girls? Is that how you think you're gonna meet girls? Nobody's gonna notice if you're wearin' a uniform. Certainly not girls.

LINC: I dunno. It's a great deal. I'll get to see the world, meet new an' interesting people, do some exercises, get some definition in my chest . . .

MEL: Yeah, but you got it all here! I mean you got your place in Flushing.

LINC: There's more to life than Flushing, Mel. (*Beat*) What, do I gotta be Bridge an' Tunnel all my life?

MEL: I don't have a problem with that. You have a problem with that?

LINC: Yeah. I'm tired of takin' bridges an' tunnels to get places that I feel spectacular in. I wanna travel an' just be spectacular—I wanna be spectacular twenty-five hours a day.

MEL: What about Bunny?

LINC: What about her?

MEL: You think you're gonna do better than Bunny? Maybe some girl from Ipanema or something? I just don't get it.

LINC: Bunny doesn't know yet.

MEL: I hope at least you're gonna tell her. I know a million guys'd trade places with you.

LINC: I'll tell her.

MEL: Well, I hope so. Your bike. Your Harley. They gonna let you keep that in the barracks?

LINC: Nah.

MEL: Don't say you're gonna sell it.

LINC: I think I'll sell it.

MEL: I think you've fallen off your rocker. I think (*Taps his finger to his temple*) the lights are on but nobody's home.

LINC: I dunno.

MEL: What do you mean you dunno?

LINC: I dunno.

MEL: What you mean you dunno?

LINC: I DUNNO! Want me to spell it for you?

MEL: You're sittin' here tellin' me that you're givin' up your apartment, your girl, selling your bike to go join a bunch of leathernecks. That would lead somebody to believe there's a screw or two loose somewhere. It's like you're leavin' without a trace. It's spooky as hell.

LINC: Maybe.

MEL: Well, then could I have your bike?

LINC: You got it. It's yours.

MEL: Thanks, buddy! My heartfelt thanks!

LINC: (*Shrugs*) Sometimes you gotta lose a lot to get a little.

MEL: Sometimes you gotta lose a lot to get a little.

LINC: I can't find what I want around here. It doesn't interest me anymore.

MEL: But this is the 1980's! There are alternatives!

LINC: Like what?

MEL: Like . . . like how the hell should I know? (*Beat*) Do you have any idea what you're in for? Those dudes are brutal. We're talkin' basic training brutality. You gotta shave your head. Learn how to talk in a monotone. And those that can't cut it get strung up on the end of a bayonet.

LINC: Do the Marines use bayonets still? I thought they just diddled around with nuclear stuff.

MEL: I dunno. Do they?

LINC: Do they?

MEL: I don't know. But I can only say one thing. I hope to God you don't come back a weirdo. They have a hard time adjusting, you know. After being forced to eat milkbones . . .

LINC: Least I won't have to worry about tartar build-up.

MEL: Trying to jerk off in the bunk without anybody hearing, an' pickin' lint off Mrs. Reagan's suits, they come back with a coupla problems.

LINC: Yeah, yeah, so what?

MEL: So what. I'll tell you what. I'd hate to see you come back like Son of Sam and all freaked out. I'd hate to see you a social misfit.

LINC: I won't come back a social misfit.

MEL: And what's more is you come back—decide you want your bike back—you can just forget it.

LINC: Great. Does that sound like something I'd do? Does that sound like me?

MEL: None of this sounds like you. This isn't like you at all.

LINC: How do you know what's like me? (*Beat*) I've seen a lot of humanity from behind that Duane Reade counter. I've seen a lotta those little cheerleaders scamper in and out through the years. Gook on their eyes and crap on their lips—all beautified, and I feel I can say this in all modesty, Mel, because they knew I was working behind that counter. Little chicks with little rosebud titties—buying banana perfume and Tampaxes, white shoe polish for the Capezios and pineapple shampoo. I've seen a lot. Crap to take the hair off their legs and crap to put more hair on their heads—I've seen 'em on Prom Night, last minute stop to buy plastic earrings to match their dress and rolling papers for the pot in their clutch bags. And after the prom, creepin' in to buy those home pregnancy kits. I've been privy to some amazing secrets, Mel. But it has its setbacks.

MEL: Yeah. But I've come to the conclusions that almost everything has it setbacks. It's part of nature.

LINC: Yeah. Well. By the time they're seniors, they don't get doodied up anymore to come into the Duane Reade. By then, they've either met some college asshole or Hell's Angel who makes their hearts go pitter-patter.

MEL: Pitter-patter.

LINC: I know everything about them and there's no mystery left. My sensitive and giving heart, Mel, my sexual prowess, nipped in the bud. An unfortunate situation, Mel. But it starts all over again with the incoming freshman. But hell, I'm getting too old for this! I had this nightmare, Mel, me standing behind the counter with all these little Annette Funicellos swarming around me . . .

MEL: Were they wearing bikinis?

LINC: Yeah and swarming around me like horny, little virgin bees . . .

MEL: (*Nodding*) Yo. The Killer Virgin Bees.

LINC: And they're waving bottles of shampoo and boxes of Miss Clairol and they begin to close in on me—until I can't breathe and it's like I got two choices, Mel. I can either be a dirty old man or a flaming faggot, and if I can't figure out which one, people will figure it out for me. I gotta get outta here. I can't go back to high school.

MEL: Looks pretty dreary. Dreary. Maybe we should go for our equality tests, instead.

LINC: Equivalency, Mel. You'll never get it if you don't know what it is.

MEL: "You'll never get it if you don't know what it is." How true. How true. Truth. "You'll never get it if you don't know what it . . ."

LINC: I'm beginning to feel like a artifact. Like the Sphinx or a druid or something.

MEL: I know exactly what you mean.

LINC: Yeah?

MEL: It's goin' through the motions. You wake up, have a relationship with somebody. Hello, goodbye—it's over before it began.

LINC: Slam, bam.

MEL: Thank you, ma'am. You eat. Listen to other people talk. Pop some brown-haired, grey-eyed chick on Saturday night. Make a point of askin' her her name. Maybe write down her phone number . . . and you look at yourself a year later, and all you've got are a bunch of dirty little slips of paper in your coat pocket. A goddamn atlas of pencil-scratched phone numbers. What could of been. But you forgot to write the fuckin' names down above the numbers! And not only that, but you look around you and it seems like EVERYBODY you know is slippin' away from you and suddenly you've got nobody to reflect you, good or bad on the outside an' inside. You're slippin' away from yourself because you just can't keep up! You can't keep up! You honestly can't remember what you said you wanted to be when you grew up. (*Stabs his knife in the stall*) But you can't go around bein' hurt and confused all the time, so you lock yourself up a little bit—'til you start to feel like somethin' outta *The Invasion of the Body Snatchers* . The only time you get to release is here—when you and a bunch of other guys can knock themselves numb. MAKE IT ALL GO AWAY. The thing I love about this place isn't the music—or ramming heads or throwin' myself off the stage—the thing I love here is knowing that everybody else came here for the same reason as me. TO GET OUT OF THEMSELVES! It makes me feel . . . close. But, as for tomorrow, and the rest of the week, I'll go back to being a robot. A zombie. A clone. I feel the exact same way you do, Linc. Like a Droid.

LINC: (*Gently and quietly*) Mel—not a Droid. A druid.

MEL: Oh. Then forget what I just said. (*After a moment*) A what?

LINC: Druid.

MEL: What the hell's that?

LINC: Druid. "D-R-U-I-D." An ancient priest. Soothsayer. Druid.

MEL: How come you're talkin' so funny?

LINC: Because I got cotton up my nose.

MEL: All right smart guy. Use it in a sentence.

LINC: (*Thinks a moment*) The druids of Anglo Saxia employeth herbal teas an' natural remedies to foretell the future and to cureth the ills of the human condition.

MEL: (*Pulling out a switchblade, carves his initials on one of the stalls*) Oh. Very nice. Very nice. I don't know why you have to go

off and see the world. You know so much already. You have such
tremendous breadth of brainth.

LINC: You could too. Have breadth of brainth.

MEL: Maybe I don't want it.

LINC: Get a li-berry card.

MEL: Nah.

LINC: Get a li-berry card.

MEL: No way.

LINC: I'm serious Mel—get out of here. Get out while you still
can. No joke.

MEL: (*Slowly, quietly turns to Linc*) Well I don't need your advice, pal, so keep it to yourself. No joke. (*Points the knife at Linc
in emphasis. Brief silence*)

LINC: Sorry. Didn't mean to get personal.

MEL: Well don't worry. You didn't. *Nobody* gets personal
with me. *Nobody*. (*Linc spits an ice cube at Mel—who catches it*)
What's this?

LINC: An ice cube.

MEL: Thank you, Professor Druid, and what am I s'posed to do
with it?

LINC: A little natural remedy. For your boo-boos. (*Mel takes
the ice cube, rubs it over his cuts and scrapes, then tosses it back to
Linc who puts it back in his mouth and sucks on it. Mel watches
with interest. Linc is humming to the tune of Campbell's soup
commercial*) Mmmm-mmm-good.

MEL: (*To same tune*) Mmmm-mmm-good.

MEL *and* LINC: (*Singing*) That's what Campbell's soup is . . .
mmm-mmm-gooood!

LINC: Boy. Am I gonna miss these Tuesday nights. These are
going to be one thing I definitely miss. Never to be had again.

MEL: You gonna be stationed someplace?

LINC: Yeah. Maybe Lebanon.

MEL: Lebanon! I remember Lebanon. Like the old man says
. . . (*Imitating his father*) "Lebanon bologna an' cheese on rye.
The Brooklyn Dodgers an' a three-cent cigar—when Castro meant
convertible."

LINC: But where I really wanna go is Knockwurst. I'd knock
up for knockwurst. Knockwurst street in Gay Paree.

MEL: Lovely place, Knockwurst. Akin to Hard-on, Arkansas
and Boobieville, Vermont. Though neither are as near and dear as
Brussels Sprouts.

LINC: I take a fancy to Turkey when I'm Hungary!

MEL: Mon Dieu! Parlez-vous! Chevrolet! They put too much
Greece in Turkey!

LINC: Seriously, Bruce. What did Mississippi wear?

MEL: I don't know. Alaska. What did you wear, Ms. Sisippi?

LINC: Fool! Wench! Hand Maiden! Hand job! Silly Goose! She wore her New Jersey!

MEL: Well!

LINC: Well!

MEL: Well.

LINC: Well, that was good for a minute or so.

MEL: You want a party or something?

LINC: For what? My birthday?

MEL: For goin' away.

LINC: Yeah, sure!

MEL: Want me to throw you a surprise party or something?

LINC: Yeah. A surprise party would be nice. And surprising too. But where?

MEL: Where is the question.

LINC: How 'bout your place?

MEL: Who should I invite?

LINC: No problema. I know scads. The Vanderbilts, the Rockefellers, Christie Binkey (*Eyebrow wiggle*) Prince Charles, Yogi and Boo-Boo . . . Tillie the Hun, and Miss Burke would never forgive me if I left without saying goodbye after five years. I'd like to see her in something strapless with chalk on her face.

MEL: How about Bunny? Want me to invite Bunny?

LINC: Bunny honey Bunny-buns. Bunny the honey?

MEL: Should I invite her?

LINC: We're kind of on the out and out.

MEL: How come?

LINC: She's sort of upset with me because I didn't go visit her after her appendix thing. Well, actually I did visit her. I peeked in her room the day after she got it out. But she was hooked up to this stand that was holding plastic bags full of this white liquid—it was plugged into her arm, pumpin' this crap that looked like baby's throw up, and it had wheels and, frankly, it was real unnatural, real embarrassing. She was not the same girl I'd known the week before. So I left.

MEL: Funny, but if I didn't know you better, I'd say you were a fair-weather kind of friend.

LINC: Yeah. I thought of that too. But then again, I'm your pal, an' you're a pretty dreary guy.

MEL: Thanks. Well. If you change your mind, I'll invite Bunny. Bunny's A-okay. A wonderful human being.

LINC: Well I think the whole thing's kind of over. I mean, what am I gonna do with her? Have her come to port and throw roses at my destroyer? Us callin' to each other—"WRITE!" (*Imitates Bunny*) "You write! I'll write when you write!" (*Imitates himself*) "I'll only write if you write me back, baby." (*Bunny*) "Okay! I will!" (*Himself*) "Okay! I will!" Nobody writes. They say they will, but they don't. No. I'll just be one of those lone guys on the deck they make movies about.

MEL: Oh. Okay. Too bad. Your party.

LINC: Nah. It's just this thing with me. I don't know. I think that most of my life, I knew I was going to leave. I didn't want to leave somebody behind.

MEL: Yeah. Well. Don't worry about that.

LINC: But I'll tell you something, while I'm over there in Bologna land . . . I'll miss ya.

MEL: I'll miss ya back.

LINC: Multiply that by three, that's how much I'll miss ya.

MEL: Multiply that by six, divide by two, add six and subtract . . .

LINC: You lost me.

MEL: Just come back, asshole, all right? Do me a favor an' just come back in one piece.

LINC: (*With eloquence*) Sit on my face.

MEL: Eat me, Pal, eat me.

LINC: Which reminds me.

MEL: Yo.

LINC: Besides taking care of my Harley Davidson, I'd appreciate it if you'd keep an eye on Bunny.

MEL: Sure, no problem.

LINC: Nothing big, just a lube job an' tighten her seat.

MEL: Yeah, but what about the Harley Davidson? (*Finds this real funny*)

LINC: As for Bunny—she's smart, and savvy, but a woman all the same.

MEL: (*Making a mental note of this*) Smart and savvy, but a woman all the same.

LINC: If maybe you could call her occasionally. (*Scribbles her phone number down on a piece of cotton—hands it to Mel*) She works in Redhook someplace. This is her home number.

MEL: Where's her phone?

LINC: In the kitchen. Why?

MEL: I wanna be able to picture where she is when I call her. What kind of phone is it?

LINC: I don't know. One of those wall deals.

MEL: Okay. I just wanna . . .

MEL *and* LINC: Be able to picture what kind of phone she's talking on when I call her.

MEL: Hey, buddy. What can I say?

LINC: I realize it would be infringin' on your Saturday nights and Sunday mornings.

MEL: No problem. Have no fear. Big Mel is here. (*Thinks*) Oh! What an asshole! I forgot to write her name above the number . . .

LINC: I already wrote it down for you. Her middle name is Phyllis. That's what the "P" stands for.

MEL: Bunny Phyllis Baxter. Hey. Think she'll go for it? For me?

LINC: Melvin, baby—if there's anybody who wouldn't go for you, I myself wouldn't wanna be on a first name basis with them.

MEL: Yeah, yeah, yeah. Just remember you got your friends. (*Gives Linc an awkward hug*)

LINC: Shankin' to catch old man?

MEL: Shankin', shankin'.

LINC: Crucial Boss or what?

MEL: Crucial Boss!

(*Instrumental starts up—offstage*)

LINC: (*Listening to walls*) What's this pussy music they're playin'? What is this? The fuckin' Jackson Five?

MEL: Sounds like the Jackson Five to me.

LINC: (*Pounding the walls*) What is this? The junior prom? HEY!

MEL: Sounds like the junior prom to me! (*Pounds on the wall*)

LINC: HEY! WHY DON'T YA JUST BRING OUT *A HUNDRED AN' ONE POLKAS* WHILE YOU'RE AT IT!

MEL: YEAH, WHAT IS THIS? *A HUNDRED AN' ONE POLKAS*?!

LINC: PUSSY STUFF!

MEL: Yeah! Pussy stuff!

LINC: What is this!

MEL: WHERE ARE WE, ANYWAY?

LINC: I MEAN WHERE THE HELL ARE WE?

MEL: WHAT IS THIS CRAP?

LINC: WHAT ON GOD'S EARTH IS GOING ON HERE ANYWAY?!

MEL: IT'S SLOW CRAP!

LINC: TOO SLOW FOR US!

MEL: TOO SLOW FOR DANCING! Slow dancin's dead cause slam is great . . .

LINC: . . . A boot to the face is all it takes.

MEL: Charisma is out, we got strength and might.

LINC: 'Cause we are the warriors of the night—yeah we are . . .

MEL: . . . The warriors of the night . . .

LINC: Yeah, the thing that works is a kick in the gut . . .

MEL: Bein' close it hurts too much, yeah, bein' close it . . .

LINC: Second verse, same as the first. Ready, Teddy?

MEL: (*Offering his arm*) We're on, Don.

LINC: We got a show to attend!

MEL: We got a dance to slam!

LINC: WE GOT WORLDS TO CONQUER! (*Misses the door, slams into something offstage*)

MEL: Sorry, Linc. I underestimated.

LINC: (*Re-entering with bloody nose. Then feebly*) And on that note.

MEL: And on that note!

LINC: (*Righting himself*) They slipped away from what they knew—the powder room dependable and true . . .

MEL: Unto the twilight! The darkening night!

LINC: Of which held! . . .

MEL: That which they did not know!

LINC: (*Offstage*) Yeah, yeah, yeah.

MEL: (*Offstage*) Hey—do me a favor—take the cotton outta your nose—you look fuckin' retarded.

LINC: (*Offstage*) Yeah, yeah, yeah.

(*Blackout*)

The End

Romulus Linney

THE LOVE SUICIDE
AT SCHOFIELD BARRACKS

Romulus Linney

Romulus Linney makes his third appearance in the *Best Short Plays* series with the recent one-act adaptation of his full-length play *The Love Suicide at Schofield Barracks*. The earlier full-length version was first produced in 1971 by Herbert Berghof at the H.B. Playwrights Foundation in Manhattan and on Broadway in 1972 by Cheryl Crawford at the ANTA Theatre.

This short edition of *The Love Suicide at Schofield Barracks* was originally commissioned by Actors Theatre of Louisville and presented in their '84 SHORTS Festival. The play traces the inquiry on a major general and his wife who have carried out a murder-suicide pact. As testimony unfolds, a portrait emerges, of both individuals as well as the social circumstances that could produce such extreme behavior. The Louisville premiere was praised by *Louisville Times* drama critic Dudley Saunders for its "searing, well-detailed dialogue" and "well-rounded characters." Responding to a subsequent production at the Fifth Annual Play Festival of the People's Light and Theatre Company in Malvern, Pennsylvania in the fall of 1985, *Reading Eagle* reviewer George Hatza called the play "an indelible theatrical experience that any thinking person should run to see. It excites and enriches our hearts and minds, and cogently reawakens a political debate our current leaders have tried to suppress." The two earlier plays in this series from Mr. Linney are *F.M.*, published in the 1984 edition, and the Obie winner *Tennessee*, which appeared in the 1980 edition.

Mr. Linney's earlier short play *F.M.* was also well received. When it premiered in May, 1982, at the Philadelphia Festival Theatre in a production which he also directed, Nels Nelson of the *Philadelphia Daily News* hailed Mr. Linney as "a luminous creative spirit touched by so superior a gift that we would cheerfully knight him on the spot." The Philadelphia audience responded with a standing ovation for the tale about the discovery of a Faulknerian talent in a college creative writing course where two Southern women students of antagonistic dispositions abandon the class to the delight of the teacher and her Gothic protege. A subsequent production of *F.M.* in Manhattan in 1984 also received critical acclaim.

His most widely produced play, *The Sorrows of Frederick* , is a psychological drama about Frederick the Great. Its many stage productions include the 1967 premiere at the Mark Taper Forum in Los Angeles with Fritz weaver in the title role. Subsequent productions were presented in New York with Austin Pendleton, in Canada with

Donald Davis, in Great Britain with John Wood, and later, Tom Conti. It also was performed at the Dusseldorf Schauspielhaus in Germany and at the Burgtheater in Vienna, where it successfully played in classical repertory through the season of 1969-70 in a production that won two Austrian theatre awards.

Born in Philadelphia, Pennsylvania, in 1930, Romulus Linney grew up in Madison, Tennessee, and spent his summers in North Carolina. He was educated at Oberlin College, where he received his B.A. in 1953, and the Yale School of Drama, earning an M.F.A. there in 1958. He has taught playwriting at many schools, including Columbia University, Brooklyn College, the University of Pennsylvania, Connecticut College, and currently, the University of Pennsylvania and Princeton.

He received two fellowships from the National Endowment for the Arts, and from 1976 until 1979 served on its literary panel. In 1980 he was awarded a fellowship from the Guggenheim Foundation, and in 1984 he received the Award in Literature from the American Academy and Institute of Arts and Letters.

Mr. Linney is the author of two highly regarded novels, *Heathen Valley* and *Slowly, by Thy Hand Unfurled*, and numerous other plays, including *Democracy, Holy Ghosts*, and *Old Man Joseph and His Family*. Mr. Linney also has written extensively for television, had an opera made from a short play, *The Death of King Phillip*, and has published a number of short plays and fiction in numerous literary magazines. As a director, Mr. Linney recently staged his own plays for the Philadelphia Festival of New Plays, the Actors Studio, the Alley Theatre in Houston, and the Bay Area Playwrights Festival in California.

His most recent plays include *Childe Byron*, produced in New York by the Circle Repertory Company, in Louisville by the Actors Theatre, in Costa Mesa, California by the South Coast Repertory, and in London by the Young Vic; *The Captivity of Pixie Shedman*, at the New York Phoenix Theatre and the Detroit Repertory Theatre; *El Hermano* and *Goodbye, Howard* at The Ensemble Studio Theatre in New York; *April Snow* at the South Coast Repertory; *A Woman Without A Name* at the Empire State Theatre in Albany, New York and at the Denver Center Theatre Company; *Sand Mountain* at the Philadelphia Festival for New Plays and the Whole Theatre in Montclair, New Jersey; and *Pops* at the Bay Area Playwrights Festival in California.

Characters:

THE COMMANDING OFFICER
CAPTAIN MARTIN
SERGEANT BATES
KATHERINE NOMURA
SERGEANT MAJOR RUGGLES
LUCY LAKE
COLONEL MOORE
LORNA ANN BATES
EDWARD ROUNDHOUSE

Place:

Schofield Barracks, Oahu, Hawaii.

Time:

Just after Halloween, 1970.

Scene:

The ballroom of the Officers' Club, Schofield Barracks, Hawaii. Monday morning, November, 1970.
    Around the wooden dance floor sit Officers' Club tables and chairs, arranged for an improvised inquiry. Two tables sit on either side of the dance floor, one for Captain Martin and the other for the Commanding Officer. On Martin's table are two wooden Japanese boxes and some papers. Seven chairs sit to one side, and on the other, four antique armchairs facing the dance floor, each with a large RESERVED sign on it.
    Lights come up on Captain Martin, a young career officer, pushing a comfortable desk chair, on rollers, to the center of the dance floor. He sets by it a small table and on that he puts a pitcher of water and several glasses.
    He double checks the room. Then he opens the ballroom door and speaks to people outside it.

MARTIN: Please come in. *(Enter Sergeant Bates, Lorna Ann Bates, Colonel Moore, Katherine Nomura, Sergeant Major Ruggles, and Lucy Lake)* Good morning. Thank you for coming. Please take a seat. As soon as the Commanding Officer arrives, we'll begin. *(They sit in the chairs. Martin checks them off the list. Enter the CO. He is a Brigadier General in his forties. Martin rises)* The Commanding Officer of Schofield Barracks. *(The military personnel rises)*

CO: Please be seated. And thank you for coming. *(To Martin)* Are they all here?

MARTIN: Sir, all but one. A Mr. Edward Roundhouse.

CO: Who's he?

MARTIN: He owns several restaurants on Oahu.

CO: All right. We'll start. *(He addresses the people)* Ladies and gentlemen, this is an unusual and preliminary inquiry. It is authorized not by the Code of Military Justice, or by the Provist Marshall, but by a United States Army General Order, issued to me by my superior officer, the former Commanding General of Schofield Barracks, while he was alive. I will ask you some questions. You may answer or not. You may add whatever you wish. We thank you very much for whatever you have to say. Captain. *(He sits at his table)*

MARTIN: Master Sergeant Norvel T. Bates, please. *(He indicates the desk chair. Sergeant Bates sits in it)* Sergeant, you understand you are not required to answer under oath, or against your wishes?

BATES: I understand, sir.

MARTIN: You are on the General's staff?

BATES: I am the General's Enlisted Aide.

MARTIN: We have a note here, from the General, speaking of you very highly. You were aware of his esteem?

BATES: *(In sorrow)* We knew each other pretty well.

MARTIN: You played a large part in his preparations. Can you describe that for us?

BATES: I'll do my best. Late Saturday morning, I was summoned to his quarters. He handed me a sealed manila envelope. In it was a General Order he had written out by hand and signed. I was ordered to process it. *(To the CO)* I did, and that was the order you received, sir, to hold this inquiry.

CO: Right, Sergeant. Go ahead.

BATES: Then he asked me to sit down. He made me a drink. His wife joined us. Then he said something that surprised me. He told me he and his wife were writing a play. For two people, with masks. To do at the Officers' Club. I tried to show polite interest. But then they asked me to help them.

MARTIN: Write the play?

BATES: No, sir. Be in it. They wanted me to read part of it aloud at the Officers' Club Halloween party. They said, "Here it is, look at it."

MARTIN: What did you think of it?

BATES: I thought it was silly. I didn't understand it. When I saw one of the last lines, "I will wait for you in heaven, my noble husband," I thought, oh, Lord. But, sir, I can't tell you how much I admired the General and his wife. And if what they wanted to do was make fools of themselves at a Halloween party, I was glad to help out.

MARTIN: What else were you asked to do?

BATES: On the porch, as I was leaving, the General gave some verbal instructions. He told me no matter what happened Saturday night, I was to return to his quarters directly after the party and take possession of papers I would find on a card table in the living room. And I did that. In shock, but I did it.

MARTIN: Describe the papers.

BATES: First, the will. The General and his wife liquidated their estate. It was a lot of money, and they left it all to an Oriental-American orphanage in Honolulu. There is a certified check already in the mail to that orphanage now. I put it there, by his order.

MARTIN: How much was it?

BATES: Three hundred and fifty-five thousand dollars. They gave that orphanage everything they had.

MARTIN: What else did you find?

BATES: All kinds of resignations, from all sorts of things he belonged to. On top, his resignation from the American Archery Association, and from the Army of the United States. I was to mail those, too. And then—of course, their bodies.

MARTIN: Explain.

BATES: Notarized document, donating their bodies to a civilian research hospital in Honolulu.

MARTIN: Thank you, Sergeant. Anything else?

BATES: Yes, sir. This envelope, sealed. It says on the front that I am to open it and read its contents at the end of this inquiry, if as the General directed, it is held here. If not, I am to destroy it. His signature is on it, there.

CO: Let me see that, please. *(Martin takes the envelope quickly to the CO. He looks at it carefully, and gives it back)* That's what you'll do, Sergeant. As ordered.

BATES: Yes, Sir.

CO: Thank you very much. Is there anything you yourself would like to add?

BATES: Yes, sir. I want to say I still admire the General. He was the best soldier I ever saw.

MARTIN: Thank you. Please stay in the room. Miss Katherine Nomura, please. *(Bates goes to his seat. A Japanese woman takes the chair)* Miss Nomura, this is an informal inquiry, conducted along lines suggested by the General in his order. You may answer or not and we are obliged for your help. Do you understand?

MISS NOMURA: Oh, yes.

MARTIN: How long have you been in the service of the General?

MISS NOMURA: Four days.

MARTIN: How did you come to work for him?

MISS NOMURA: I was sent to him from a commercial bureau. I fitted his requirements.

MARTIN: What were your duties?

MISS NOMURA: Very light secretarial work, for his wife. I know now, of course, it was to read the play. Which also explains his requirements.

MARTIN: What were they?

MISS NOMURA: They were for a female with a fondness for Japanese plays and some knowledge of them. Who should have one other qualification I prefer not to mention. He had trouble finding me.

MARTIN: And you read the play aloud, with Sergeant Bates, on Saturday night?

MISS NOMURA: Yes.

MARTIN: What did you think of it?

MISS NOMURA: I thought it was very beautiful.

MARTIN: Why?

MISS NOMURA: I knew what it was they had written. It is an old Japanese story.

MARTIN: What is?

MISS NOMURA: Their play. It is a shinju.

MARTIN: And what is that?

MISS NOMURA: A love suicide. A kind of play, in which lovers, who cannot live together any longer, commit suicide together. There have been a great many of them.

MARTIN: Do you mean plays, or love suicides?

MISS NOMURA: Both.

MARTIN: I see. Now Miss Nomura . . .

MISS NOMURA: Please. One other thing. It is not a sin, or a disgrace. It is not an act of psychological self-hatred. It is release from illusion. It is embrace of eternal truth. Their life then become a poem they leave behind, and is considered a great achievement. They are taken directly into heaven and are reborn on lotus leaves. Thank you.

MARTIN: I see. Now, Miss Nomura . . .

CO: *(Breaking in)* Miss Nomura, did you therefore have some idea of the actual purpose of the play?

MISS NOMURA: Oh, yes.

CO: You *did?*

MISS NOMURA: I said yes.

CO: You mean you knew Saturday night they were going to kill themselves on this dance floor?

MISS NOMURA: I knew they were going to act out a shinju on this dance floor. It did occur to me they might be in earnest.

CO: Then pardon me, Miss Nomura, why didn't you tell anyone?

MISS NOMURA: That would have spoiled a shinju. *(Pause)* And who would have believed me? Would you? If I had informed you that the Commanding General of Schofield Barracks intended to kill himself in a play at a Halloween party?

CO: I see what you mean. What else did they tell you about the performance they had planned?

MISS NOMURA: Nothing. I was to meet with Sergeant Bates at the Officers' Club at about ten o'clock. We were to read our parts while they acted out the play on the dance floor.

CO: And you understood what they might really do?

MISS NOMURA: I said yes. *(Pause)* If a man and his wife decide the home they loved has become ugly, and seek a better one, is that impossible to understand?

CO: Thank you very much.

MARTIN: Is there anything you wish to add?

MISS NOMURA: Oh, yes. I am glad I saw what I saw.

(She gets up and sits again in her chair. The CO stares at her for a moment, then nods to Captain Martin)

CO: Who's next?

MARTIN: Sergeant Major Reuben H. Ruggles, please. *(A calm, quietly arrogant soldier in his forties takes the chair. He carries a handsome swagger stick, with an American eagle on one end)* Sergeant Major, do you understand the informal nature of these proceedings? That you don't have to answer a question if you don't want to?

RUGGLES: I do, sir.

MARTIN: The General tells us here that you first served under him in Korea. As a platoon sergeant in a line company.

RUGGLES: That's right.

MARTIN: His directive characterizes you as an outstanding combat NCO.

CO: And I can certainly agree with that. Sergeant Major Ruggles' long career since Korea, and his top to bottom knowledge of the Army is well known.

RUGGLES: I thank you, sir.

MARTIN: After giving us his opinion of you, Sergeant Major, what the General asks for now, is your opinion of him.

RUGGLES: Yes, sir. *(Quickly)* He was a great General, it was my privilege to serve under him.

MARTIN: There's a note here that you had a conversation with him, in his office, last week. Is that correct? *(Ruggles, surprised, pauses then nods)* Can you tell us about that?

RUGGLES: *(Slowly)* If I have to.

MARTIN: You don't have to. The General asks you to.

RUGGLES: Oh, he does, does he?

MARTIN: Can you tell us about your conversation with him?

RUGGLES: To some degree, Lieutenant, sir. A private, D Company, 19th Infantry Brigade, a black man, had a nervous breakdown on the rifle range Friday morning. Live rounds. It was dangerous. He was disarmed by a big Georgia Sergeant with a big red neck, who fractured the black man's skull. There was going to be real trouble. The General took action.

MARTIN: What did he do?

RUGGLES: Several ineffective things. Then he consulted me.

MARTIN: And what did you do?

RUGGLES: I figured the race riot, or whatever was going to happen, was going to happen on Saturday, the next morning, at the full Division parade. It had to. The General sent his black cadre around Friday night and posted all his bulletins. Saturday morning, at the parade, we'd see. Now, in two months, a black Sergeant, 12th Artillery, after his twenty years, was supposed to get out. Slated for a little parade. Two horns and a drum outside a quadrangle, where some Major would shake his hand, and that would be that. So, on Friday night, I had a chat with a Personnel Specialist and then another one with our black Artillery Sergeant. I told him he was going to retire the next morning. He really didn't want to retire the next morning, but I convinced him.

MARTIN: *(Puzzled)* Of what?

RUGGLES: To go home when he was told. Saturday morning, this Division massed for parade. Band started, flags unfurled and when seven thousand combat ready troops thundered past the reviewing stand, with tanks and artillery and choppers whirling in the air—wind, flags, the great army in all its glory—who do you think was standing up there to receive all those salutes? The General and his black Sergeant, honored on the day of his retirement. Whose name, by the way is Remus. That's right. Reginald O. Remus. Well, everybody saluted the colors and the colors saluted everybody and it was all just one big happy family.

MARTIN: In other words, Sergeant Major, what you did was put a black man in a window. Is that what you're so proud of?

(Ruggles stops laughing, looks mildly but dangerously at Captain Martin)

RUGGLES: You best not talk to me like that, son, sir. I am nearing the end of a long and honorable career. You ain't, not yet.

MARTIN: After the parade, the General had a talk with you. What did you say to each other? If you please. *(Ignoring Martin, Ruggles speaks directly to the CO)*

RUGGLES: General, sir, what do I have to do here? Six weeks before I retire! I am only an enlisted man. I respectfully ask you to direct me.

CO: Follow your conscience and say what you please. Whatever you say will be to your credit.

RUGGLES: *(Doubtfully)* Yeah. Thank you, sir. If that's what you want.

CO: That's what we want.

RUGGLES: After the parade, he took me into his office, closed the door, pulled out a bottle of Jack Daniels. And we had a drink together.

MARTIN: And that was all?

RUGGLES: No, that wasn't all. He thanked me for the saving of his ass. Because putting Remus up there with him probably stopped a race riot, and certainly saved his ass. He was grateful, or something. Anyway, he wanted to talk. Like we was chums.

MARTIN: What did he say?

RUGGLES: Lots of dumb things nobody knows the answer to. If I really thought the new all-professional Army could become a black dumping ground. If I'd wondered if the Army was getting like a big corporation that could plan but couldn't fight. Things like that.

MARTIN: What did you say?

RUGGLES: I said I didn't know, what else? I reckoned a mostly black Army would have mostly black officers and mostly black parades, like in Haiti, and I reckoned men would always fight but I wasn't sure about officers. He didn't like any of that, and changed the subject.

MARTIN: To what?

RUGGLES: Remus. Asked me if I knew why old Sergeant Remus kept his name. Why he never changed it. "Maybe he liked it," I said. "Remus ain't just a slave name. I read a book or two, now and then. Remus was one of the founders of Rome. Didn't you know that, General?" "I guess I did, but I forgot," he said. "What happened to Remus?" "Got killed," I said, "founding Rome. By his brother. But she gave him his name, and he kept it, and so did Sergeant Remus, and so have I. We all made our deal with Rome. We keep it for twenty years and Rome keeps it for twenty years, and we both got it made." "I don't understand," he said. "Well, General," I said, "maybe that's because you're not a Roman, really, and Remus is. And I am. And if you're not, then I pity you."

CO: Sergeant Major, you spoke that way to your Commanding General?

RUGGLES: Why not, sir? I'd just saved his dammed ass for him, hadn't I? One chance in twenty years to talk turkey to a General? Shit, I let go. I told him the Army he believed in didn't exist. That it was a god damned fairy tale he was told at West Point. That I found out what the Army really was, in Korea. "Korea?" he said, politely as if remembering the country was all I'd meant. "Yes, sir, Korea," I said. "When you and me was young, General, and made our bargains with Rome." "I don't know what your bargain was, Sergeant," he said. "But mine was to serve my country." "Mine was to be a killer," I said, "and serve myself. To do what I was told to do, so my country would serve me. The trouble with you is, General, you just don't like what your country wants you to do." He didn't like that idea, neither, and changed the subject again.

CO: To?

RUGGLES: Nostalgia. Maybe he thought that would be safe. "What I remember about Korea," he said, "is great long lines of marching men, ice cold nights, bleak Asian skies, and the hard, lonely task of doing your duty, and serving your country." "What I remember," I said, "is a damn good Roman soldier staying alive. White men, black men, Rome gives us all our names. Then murders us, if it thinks it has to. But if we survive, we keep that name and are honorably retired with it." "Fair enough," I said, "twenty years ago, and so did old Remus. Duty, honor, country, like they say at West Point. But hell fire, for me and Remus, it wasn't to die for our god damn duty, it was to kill for the god damn Army! Kill for it and live! Tell me it's hard? You think I don't know that, General? I've seen a few people die in the war. My SON, my own SON, HE died in the god damn war, General! But not me. I'm alive, and I kill for this Army and live! Make money off the fucking P.X. for it, and live! Serve up slant-eyed pussy to

Generals like you for it, and live! You don't have to tell me my duty, General. I know all about it. You give it to me and I done it, and so did my boy, whatever it was. He didn't live, but I did, to my honorable old age, and by God, I expect Rome to keep its bargain! I understand," I said, "what the real Army is, and I would rather have the common virtue of a down-in-the-dirt, dog-face soldier, than the glory of a fake like you!" *(Pause. Ruggles stands)* And that was the end of the interview. Well, sir?

CO: All right, Sergeant Major. Anything else you have to say?

RUGGLES: As a matter of fact, there is. When the General took over this Division, he gave me and the two other Sergeants Major a swagger stick. This one here. He said he wasn't the smartest man in the world but he was smart enough to know who understood the Army: old time Regimental Sergeants Major. He was always going to depend on us to tell him the truth when no one else would. Well, that's exactly what I did.

CO: Thank you, that's all. Please remain in the room.

RUGGLES: Thank you, sir. I prefer not to.

(He walks deliberately out of the room)

CO: Next.

MARTIN: Sir, next on the General's list is Lucy Lake.

CO: Is she here?

LUCY LAKE: Yes, I'm here.

(An extremely plain, blunt, white-haired, down-to-earth old New England woman takes the stand)

CO: *(With charm and courtesy, truly impressed)* Miss Lake, in his directive, the General tenders you an apology for taking up more of your valuable time. And speaking for the rest of us, allow me to thank you very much for coming here today.

LUCY LAKE: All right.

CO: Poets are not usually close friends with Generals. Am I right about that?

LUCY LAKE: No. I knew Archie Wavell in World War II very well. He loved poets.

CO: A British General, I believe. In America, however?

LUCY LAKE: America however, nope. Rare.

CO: You understand, Miss Lake, the nature of these proceedings?

LUCY LAKE: I get the idea.

CO: How did you come to meet the General?

LUCY LAKE: I didn't. He came to meet me.

CO: When?

LUCY LAKE: Last summer.

CO: Can you tell us about this meeting please?

LUCY LAKE: Breadloaf Conference, Middlebury, Vermont. Writers meet would-be writers, who pay to come, listen, and have their material read.

CO: *(Surprised, breaking)* Mike had been writing poetry?

LUCY LAKE: Yep.

CO: And he went there on his leave? His vacation?

LUCY LAKE: Yep.

CO: Go on.

LUCY LAKE: That's it. John Ciardi and I were working with the poets. We all met.

MARTIN: What was your opinion of the General's poetry?

LUCY LAKE: Not just his. His wife's too.

MARTIN: Their poetry, then.

CO: What did you and Mr. Ciardi think of it?

LUCY LAKE: Oh, they were dilettantes, but not impossible. Bad, but not always completely. But, poets, you see, love very specific things, the concrete particulars of life, while Generals can be—well, general. You could see that wrong with him. He didn't understand it at first, but he learned. And he did have a feeling for building, making a poem. Bringing disparate elements together. Yet I felt it was his wife who was truly remarkable.

CO: As a person, or a poet?

LUCY LAKE: Both. Poets are people, General, even when they may seem at times mysterious to you as generals do to me. She was a lovely woman, sprightly, with a sharp eye. It was my pleasure to know her.

MARTIN: Did they say or do anything unusual at this writers' conference?

LUCY LAKE: No. He was very self-conscious. Said he was retired. He and his wife seldom came to the parties with everybody else. They worked on their poems. Took long walks. Looked at Vermont, the mountains and the stars. They had a quiet, enriching cultural experience, just like it says in the brochure.

MARTIN: How about you, may I ask?

LUCY LAKE: I was drunk most of the time. It's a fun two weeks.

CO: When did you hear from them again?

LUCY LAKE: Just a month ago. Three lectures on American Poetry, University of Hawaii. Money. I was in the newspaper, and the General called. So I spent the last two weeks with them, in a little beach cottage they'd rented for me. Patrons, almost. Too bad they're dead.

CO: Miss Lake, you have been seeing them for the past two weeks?

LUCY LAKE: Yep.

CO: Well?

LUCY LAKE: Well?

MARTIN: Miss Lake, the General and his wife committed suicide Saturday night!

LUCY LAKE: I know it.

MARTIN: Well, haven't you any—didn't you notice . . .

LUCY LAKE: I noticed! Some of it I may tell you about, and some of it I may not. You ask the questions, and I'll make up my mind as we go along.

CO: Certainly. But the first question is this: you're hostile to everything here, aren't you?

LUCY LAKE: Yep.

CO: Understood. In your meetings and conversations with the General and his wife, did they ever indicate anything unusual about themselves?

LUCY LAKE: General, you are going to have to be more specific.

CO: I'll do my best. Did they talk about suicide?

LUCY LAKE: Nope.

MARTIN: Criticize the Army? The country?

LUCY LAKE: Never.

MARTIN: Did they exhibit psychological peculiarities? Show nervous strain? Act or think in strange ways?

LUCY LAKE: No. I did all that. They were fine, always quite composed. We simply talked about poetry and watched the sea. They drank a little, I drank a lot, and exhibited psychological peculiarities.

MARTIN: I see.

LUCY LAKE: Good.

CO: But Miss Lake, didn't anything about the General say anything to you—about his despair, his impending suicide?

LUCY LAKE: Nope.

CO: *(Angrily)* Well, perhaps the man was trying, Miss Lake, and you were too drunk to pay him any attention! Is that a possibility?

LUCY LAKE: *(A long pause)* They talked about writing a play. Something Japanese, using poetry and masks. I said I didn't think anybody did that anymore, but they wanted to. I suggested some plays to look up. They'd never read Chickamatsu, a good eighteenth century Japanese playwright. They liked one of his plays in particular. From what I hear, their own was a copy of it.

CO: What play is that?

LUCY LAKE: *The Love Suicides at Sonezaki.* Famous, in Japan. *(Pause)* That was their last visit.

CO: Miss Lake, what did you think about an American Army General and his wife, doing all this?

LUCY LAKE: I thought it unutterably sad. Sobering. At their age, watching them try to find a life in poetry. They began like good children, slightly worshipful. Stealing quietly into the world of art, a magic forest they thought filled with mossy groves and dappled pastures and innocent living things. Finding instead the pits and swamps and the true difficulties of the animals within. Sheila— oh, I tried to tell her—ahh!

CO: Please take your time.

LUCY LAKE: Well, what a waste! She must have been such a cheerful girl! Not beautiful, but—radiant, whole, a good American girl! A Navy nurse, picked up by a young Army Captain, as they stood wondering in front of the great golden Buddha at Kamakura. They had just conquered Japan. So they shacked up, took a trip. Nikko, Nara, Fuji, the Inland Sea, everywhere. Then they married. They loved each other, Japan, and the Army. In twenty years, they managed to spend only seven west of Hawaii. And then it all— well.

CO: And then?

LUCY LAKE: Oh, Jesus, General. If you don't know, how can I tell you? Ask me another!

CO: Well, *(Swiftly)* I don't know, Miss Lake! And, yes, I certainly will ask you another. Which I hope you might answer without this attitude that bores me as much as I bore you. The General and his wife committed suicide. Do you know why?

LUCY LAKE: *(Swiftly)* And if I do, and if I tell you, do you suppose I'd believe you would ever take me seriously?

CO: Well. why do you think you were asked to come here?

LUCY LAKE: Oh, because my name was on that list. For the recording session.

CO: The what?

LUCY LAKE: Recording session. That's all this is. We're his secretaries, scribes! The General has us here writing it all down for him, what he made happen through us. We were all used. Somehow. Still are. *(Pause)* Bringing his disparate elements together.

CO: That may be.

LUCY LAKE: Has to be. Why weren't you there, by the way?

CO: At the Halloween party?

LUCY LAKE: Sure. You were second in command. Number two, right?

CO: Yes.

LUCY LAKE: Well, where were you?

CO: In the field. Inspecting a supply base on another island.

LUCY LAKE: And who sent you there?

CO: The General.

LUCY LAKE: Sure.

CO: In any case, Miss Lake, believe me, whatever you have to say, I will take it seriously.

LUCY LAKE: *(Smiling)* Promise?

CO: Promise.

LUCY LAKE: Okay. Ask.

CO: The General and his wife committed suicide in this room. Why? *(Pause)*

LUCY LAKE: Because he came to believe, literally now, something dreadful. And his wife had the courage to agree with him.

CO: And what was that?

LUCY LAKE: That he was a sort of child murderer. That he had murdered his son. *(A pause)*

CO: Miss Lake, the General's son was a grown man. A combat Marine. He was killed in action in 1965, near Danang.

LUCY LAKE: Precisely. *(A pause. The CO smiles)*

CO: Well, my dear Miss Lake. *(A pause. Lucy Lake does not smile)*

LUCY LAKE: Well, my dear General. *(A pause again. The CO laughs, throws up his hands)* Yeah, you see?

CO: What?

LUCY LAKE: You were going to take me seriously, remember?

CO: Well, I'm very sorry, but I certainly expected something more worthy of Lucy Lake.

LUCY LAKE: *(Coldly)* And I expected you to keep your word.

CO: *(Coldly)* I beg your pardon. You say the General believed he'd murdered his son. How? And now let me ask you to be very specific.

LUCY LAKE: He believed he had done his duty. He believed his duty led to the useless death of his son. He questioned his duty. He decided he had become a moral lunatic.

CO: A what?

LUCY LAKE: Mo—ral lun—a—tic.

CO: This is ridiculous. What did doing his duty have to do with the death of his son?

LUCY LAKE: It was the murder weapon. The instrument of homocide.

CO: You don't make sense.

LUCY LAKE: Call it poison. He had poisoned his son. That help?

(The CO sits back in his chair, and looks at Martin)

MARTIN: *(Tersely)* Did the General ever say he'd murdered his son?

LUCY LAKE: Not in words.

MARTIN: Did his wife?

LUCY LAKE: No.

MARTIN: You never overheard them say that?

LUCY LAKE: No.

MARTIN: And you still . . .

LUCY LAKE: Insist the General believed he had murdered his son. And his wife did, too. Yes.

(The CO, angry in spite of himself, stands)

CO: Are you married, Ma'am? Do you have any children?

LUCY LAKE: Not any more, thank God.

CO: Then what do you know about it? How dare you—with your book review platitudes—insult a good servant of his country, a wonderful father to his son? Mike never pushed his boy to the service. He ran to it! He embraced it! Mike and his son, my boy and I, we were all proud of *any* life, given for our country! And your pompous scorn here, is obscene!

LUCY LAKE: Bullshit, General! Don't talk to me about dead children! Pompous am I? What's an enlisted man's tour of duty in Vietnam? What's an officer's? You make those boys serve one solid year in that deathtrap, and how long do you serve? How long, you son of a bitch? Six months, that's how long! You watch them die from your helicopters, and then fly home to your bloody promotions! Don't call *me* obscene!

CO: But what kind of a woman are you? To say such things to people who give their lives for your comfort and safety? What do you know about the real difficulties of military life? Who are you? Not married. No children. And it's Sheila you keep talking about. Just why were you here, messing about in her life? Just what kind of a creature are you anyway?

LUCY LAKE: Just an old fashioned literary dike, General! Who's been through wars you would never survive! *(She holds up one hand)* But. You seem like a decent man. I'm sorry about your son. We should speak to each other with respect. Mike and I did.

CO: So we should. I beg your pardon. *(He sits down again)*

LUCY LAKE: And of course you're right. I did stay to be with Sheila. I don't often find someone I like as much as I like her. We became good friends. On those afternoons by the sea, we knitted, Sheila and I, and talked about poetry and children.

CO: I can't understand that. I knew them longer and better than you did. They grieved. But they knew why their son died. They

loved their country as well as their child. They wouldn't write ama-
teur romantic poetry about that.
(Lucy Lake opens her purse, takes out a piece of paper)
LUCY LAKE: This is a sonnet. Written together. Shall I?
CO: Yes.
LUCY LAKE: *(Reading)*
On Making Love Again

But for this night and rain we wouldn't weep,
As that dear face fades slowly from our keep.
And we drink gallons, press our souls to sleep,
And in this world alone no harvest reap.
Backs again should bend, old fists be furled
As if from sperm and womb we'd simply hurled
His being, so deep in our ambition curled,
Away! Right now! Into some better world.
It's dry, my love, to bear these dreams we seek,
And tears at night fit best the treacherous meek:
I've watched my heart, I know the blood-sharp beak
Run through it is my own: It mends next week.
But wet and heedless rain undoes the national spite,
And my corrupted love is yours through rain and night.
(Pause. Lucy Lake shrugs) Romantic poets today are all in the
Army.
CO: Is there anything else you'd like to say?
LUCY LAKE: I'd like to tell you something.
CO: Fire.
LUCY LAKE: I was married, General. Three times, years ago.
Before I learned what I know about myself now, that I destroy as
much as I create. I, too, had a son who died. In an Ivy League
University, where he should never have been. A battlefield where
he wanted to please me. Where he perished.
CO: I'm truly sorry. But that's more like it. It's your son
you've been talking about here. I understand.
LUCY LAKE: My son and yours, General. And Mike's. Ours.
(Pause. She looks around) Wait a minute. Has anyone else—called
here today—lost a son—or a child—in any way . . .
MISS NOMURA: That was the General's other qualification for
his private secretary.
BATES: Yes.
MRS. BATES: Our firstborn.
MOORE: Me, too. And Sergeant Ruggles.
LUCY LAKE: I told you that man had a feeling for building a
poem.

CO: Thank you very much. Please stay.

LUCY LAKE: Sure. It's my story, too.

CO: Next.

MARTIN: Colonel Robertson H. Moore, please.

(Colonel Moore, a thin, healthy, sardonic man, gets up and goes to the witness chair)

MOORE: And I do understand the nature of this inquiry, et cetera, et cetera, and I am Robertson H. Moore, Colonel U.S. Army, Chief of Staff, this Division, and I know exactly why the General got me down on his little list and why I'm here and what I'm supposed to say and I'll be just delighted to say it.

CO: *(Smiling)* All right, Robie. Go ahead.

ⵏ MOORE: A pleasure. I suppose I'm here to give the minority report, my usual function. I really don't mean to dance on the man's grave, but I disagreed with the General on just about every idea he ever had. The only thing I approved was the way he played poker. That he knew how to do. And his archery, of course. But tennis, his mind collapsed every second set. And golf, a game of fidelity and endurance, well, to watch him go to pieces inside a constant framework, under stern and unchanging rules, well, it was to realize that he was a profoundly childish man. It sometimes passes for intelligence. Sorry, ladies and gentlemen, but that's the freezing truth.

CO: And just what we want you to say, Robie, go on.

MOORE: You really don't have to call me "Robie." Little telegrams are no doubt replacing both of us at this moment: you as executive officer and heir apparent, and me as his ridiculous chief of staff. He appointed me above my time in rank, and kept me there against my wishes. He also started calling me "Robie," with nauseating condescension.

CO: I beg your pardon, Colonel. Your record speaks for itself. You've been very effective.

MOORE: Well, I do have my passion for details. Okay. But that isn't why he kept me there, over the heads of at least five other officers. He made me his chief of staff because I was a thorn in his side. Due to the chemistry of our personalities, or whatever, I could never lie to him. Or flatter him. He kept me with him because I always told him what I thought of his decisions, and him. And I disapproved of that more than anything.

CO: You disapproved of a superior officer who allowed you to speak honestly to him?

MOORE: Of course! That isn't the way this Army or any other army works, and you know it and I know it and he knew it! As a matter of fact, it isn't the way anything works, as everybody knows! But it was his perverse nature to be—well, illustration, please. May I? I mean, I won't be sued for slander, will I?

CO: You won't be sued for slander, Colonel.

MOORE: Fine. That Italian place down the pike, you know, was his favorite off-post restaurant. It's pretty dependent on the military, so of course the waiters all peed in their britches every time he walked in the door. Okay, fine. But you see, he made them play it the other way around. They had to joke with him—ha, ha—and pick on him and kid him and bully him a little, you know—ho, ho— so he could just be one of the boys there. Another good fellow, who belongs, and who'd get it, just like anybody else, if he stepped out of line. Christ, you half expected him to go out and lay some bricks with them on weekends. Pals, real sports, and it was pathetic to watch him. Sickening. You might have respected the man if he'd made those flunkies bang their heads on the floor and run their tails off when they brought him his Chateaubriand—I think he hated Italian food—but watching him play that game with them made me want to vomit. Because that's what I was! Honest, outspoken, independent. Chief of Staff, nothing. I was his flunky Italian waiter, and I hated it, and him.

CO: All right, Colonel Moore. You've filed your minority report. Did you have any specific confrontation with him just before the incident?

MOORE: Well, I fought him damn near every day, you know, so I hold out to you an embarrassment of riches. But the biggest fight we had, and the gem, was, of course, about the President.

CO: President?

MOORE: Yes. Of the United States. Yes.

CO: Ah. You mean the conference?

MOORE: That's right. That was called off. That's right.

CO: Well, what about it?

MOORE: As everybody knows, on September 15th, the President of the United States announced another Hawaiian conference with the president of our noble allies in Indochina. Word had come down to the General almost six weeks ago. September 25th. Same old thing. Three days of the President in Hawaii. The General had a fit.

CO: Why?

MOORE: Oh, God knows. He was full of little explosions, you know. He bitched and raved about the preparations involved, when of course the President would never come within thirty miles of Schofield. Then he said the hell with it, and left the paperwork to me. Okay. Five days later, with steam coming out of his ears, he wanted to know why the hell our contingency plans for the arrival in

Hawaii of the Commander in Chief weren't smoldering red-hot on his desk. "Because you said the hell with it," I said. So he hopped all over me, and I hopped and we both hopped.

CO: Why the sudden change in attitude? Duty?

MOORE: Hardly. The General's idea of his military duty was much too sophisticated to include anything as simple as obedience. No, what happened was brand-new. Army Headquarters had now scheduled the President, if he felt like it on Saturday night, to visit Schofield Barracks and attend the Annual Officers' Club Halloween Party. Now, the General thought that was just dandy, so we worked like hell.

CO: But that conference was called off.

MOORE: Right. Poof. Fini. No Hawaii conference with Indochina. No Halloween with the President. The General, surprise, after all that work, wasn't angry. No, he had a strange, dippy, far-off look in his eyes, as if he was dreaming about something impossible, and he said, "Well, we'll just pretend he came. We'll have chairs marked RESERVED for him, and for me, pretend he came, and have the party anyway." And that was that. *(Pause)*

CO: Interesting.

MOORE: Yes, isn't it.

CO: Well, Colonel, were there any other confrontations you wanted to tell us about?

MOORE: You don't get it, do you?

CO: Get what, Colonel?

MOORE: Never mind. Neither do I. But it's here, somewhere. Yes, there was another confrontation, of sorts. A day or so later. He came into my office and put a photograph from a newspaper on my desk. Of a Buddhist monk in flames. You saw the gasoline all over him, burning. You could still see the man in the fire, looking out at you. "How about that?" said the General. I was mad at him. "Barbecued gook," I said. "So what?"

CO: Colonel Moore!

MOORE: Sure I did. He looked at me with profound distaste, while I so regarded him. And I thought, to hell with this. "It is a pathetic, useless gesture," I said. "It is utterly un-American. What does it accomplish?" And he just looked at me a minute, and then, by God, he slapped me on the back. "You're absolutely right," he said. "There has to be something more. And now I know what it is. Thank you, Colonel." And he walked out of the room.

CO: What did he mean?

MOORE: Who knows? Maybe his kamikaze act. Maybe something we haven't got yet. Anyway, nothing more from me, except I was here Saturday night, and I find most extraordinary the justice of it. I still can't believe he did it, but the man gave himself exactly what he deserved.

CO: Now, Robie!

MOORE: *(Quickly)* Sorry! I didn't mean that. *(Pause)* Oh, hell yes, I did. You see? It's hard being a United States Army Colonel and an Italian waiter at the same time. Sorry. *(He steps down)*

MARTIN: Mrs. Norvel T. Bates, please. *(A woman in her late thirties takes the chair. She is very decorous and proper, dressed in a simple ladies suit)* Mrs. Bates, this inquiry does not require you to answer if you don't want to. Is that clear?

MRS. BATES: Yes, sir.

MARTIN: You are Lorna Ann Bates, married to Sergeant Norvel T. Bates, Headquarters Company, this Division?

MRS. BATES: Yes, sir.

MARTIN: You live here at Schofield, in Army housing, with your husband and three children?

MRS. BATES: Yes, sir.

MARTIN: Mrs. Bates, you are also in charge of the Schofield Day Care Center?

MRS. BATES: Yes, sir.

(Enter Edward Roundhouse, a large man, with a tortured look, wearing casual, comfortable clothes)

ROUNDHOUSE: I beg your pardon. I am looking for a Captain Martin.

MARTIN: I am Captain Martin. Please have a seat. I'll be with you in just a moment. *(He indicates a seat with the others, turns back to Mrs. Bates. Roundhouse sits down)* Mrs. Bates, is it true that the expansion of the Children's Day Care Center was the General's idea?

MRS. BATES: Oh, yes. His wife's. There wasn't much to it until they came.

CO: *(Smiling)* And brought you.

MRS. BATES: And brought me, yes, sir.

MARTIN: Mrs. Bates, we have no particular questions here to ask you. By your name the General noted that you would know what to tell us, and that he hoped you would. Do you understand what he meant?

MRS. BATES: Yes, I'm afraid I do.

MARTIN: Are you willing then, to talk about it?

MRS. BATES: I guess I have to. If that's what he wanted. Like I say, everything at the Children's Center was just wonderful until about three weeks ago. Then they took to coming to the playground together, every day. Something was different about them. I don't know how to describe it. They just stood there by the fence, watching. Then, about ten days ago, they told me they wanted a child.

MARTIN: I beg your pardon?

MRS. BATES: They said they wanted a child, for the Halloween party. A little boy who could be in a play.

MARTIN: What was your answer?

MRS. BATES: To them? We have twelve children four afternoons a week. Mostly Eurasians, GI fathers, abandoned by both parents. They're sent here to us for the chance to mix and play with other children. So I called.

MARTIN: Called who?

MRS. BATES: The orphanage. They said as long as the General and his wife were responsible, of course. So I introduced them to a new little friend we have: Yoshida Robinson. Yoshi is six and a half.

CO: Mrs. Bates, are you telling us that a child, from an orphanage, was being prepared by the General and his wife to take some part in a play that became an act of violence? A part in their deaths?

MRS. BATES: No, of course they wouldn't do anything like that! No! But, Yoshi was supposed to have been there, and was, except for me . . .

CO: Except for you, Mrs. Bates?

MRS. BATES: Yes. Me. I let them down, you see. I took Yoshi away from there before it happened. When they came out with those masks on, acting so strange, I just took him home.

CO: Be glad you did.

MRS. BATES: Yes, but after all they had done for me, I . . .

MOORE: All they did for you, Mrs. Bates, was use you. Can't you see that?

MRS. BATES: *(Very upset)* That's not true!

CO: Well, Mrs. Bates, they did in fact involve you, and through you, a child, in an act of violence. Why?

MRS. BATES: I don't know why! But this is all wrong, me making them look so bad! And after I let them down, let them down!

CO: Mrs Bates, you didn't let anybody down. You prevented what looks like some wanton act of cruelty.

MRS. BATES: *(Horrified)* Cruel? Them? *(She breaks down)* Aw, shit! *(There is a shocked silence. She jumps out of her chair, goes to her husband, Sergeant Bates, and put her hands on his shoulders)* Oh, Norvel.

BATES: Lorna, go on and say what you want to say.

MRS. BATES: It ain't going to do no good.

BATES: That's all right. Say it.

CO: Mrs. Bates, you have absolutely everybody's respect. Nothing you can say will change that.
(She looks at him and at the people, her attitude and personality shifting. She takes her seat again, staring at everyone, something in her now quite coarse and tough)
MRS. BATES: You think so? We'll see.
CO: Please.
MRS. BATES: I met them first outside Miami, at a place called Slim's, on Route One. Dinah Shore and Jerry Lewis don't play Slim's, but I did. That was in the summer of 1966. I was thirty-five long American years old, and I thought I had seen all the ugly, low-down American things a girl like me could see. I wrote a song about that. Used to sing it, with my Star-Spangled Garter-Belt Guitar: "I'm highway born and highway bred, I'll be highway shed, and highway dead." I'll sing it for you sometime, at the Ladies' Club. Well, that night, I was just back from the Dominican Republic, where I'd been for a while, with a real nice man I knew. Brought back an act with a snake, and a few other things. Like smashing customers' beer bottles in a big towel and rolling around stripping in the broken glass, and not getting cut. "Not one little bit, on one pretty tit! No, sir, not even one cut, on this big bouncing butt!" Things like that I learned for a living, and playing with snakes, and men. I didn't even see them come in. They were just there, sitting at the piano bar, when I came back out, dressed. They were wearing just plain old clothes, of course, and just wanted a quiet, relaxing, low-down bar sort of a drink. They could get awful tired, you know, of officers' clubs and official parties they had to go to. *(She smiles, fondly)* Oh, we had a time that night. They stayed; and we sang a lot, and drank a lot, and had the best time together. They even sent me a Christmas card that winter, and we wrote now and then, and about two years ago they wrote asking where I'd be that summer, and they came to see me. "Hello," they said. They didn't ask why I was at Freedom Ranch, in Calcutta, California, which is a western-style mental encounter group-type whorehouse, because they knew. I was working, like before. This time I was the house masseuse. I had aged, you see, just slightly. "Say, friends, if anybody feels like an informal massage therapy, just call the house girl, Lorna, the prostate professional. Give you a spurt that sure can't hurt." "Hello," they said. "Hello," I said. "You're looking fine," they said. "Oh, yes," I said, "I've come up in the world. High society, now." "Any different?" they asked. "No," I said. "Same old highway trash. Better clothes, and the pimps have Ph.D.'s." And they laughed, and that was the night, because of so many things, I don't know, it came to an end for me,

and I swallowed everything I had in the medicine cabinet, and went to sleep dreaming of my first husband, my childhood sweetheart I married in Plainfield, Kansas, who when he got mad at me used to fry my brassiere and panties in the oven, and I did sleep, and I was gone away from it all, a free American at last, at peace, and the, oh, God, I woke up in the hospital, with the General and his wife, who'd got worried about me, and come back that night, and saved my life. "WHY?" I asked them, when I saw them at my bedside. He was dressed right then. It was the first time I'd seen him in his uniform, looking so—strong. "Because, Lorna," he said, "you are a good decent woman, and we know that, and we're your friends." And they did what they'd come to see me about. They got me and Norvel together. Norvel was alone then, his first wife'd left him, with two children to care for, and so, after a while, we was married. After almost forty years, I was saved. Saved from the ditch, from the rock-bottom highway trash of these United States! *(She looks about. Filled with anger and anguish, she stands up)* And now they've gone and done what they saved me from! They have killed themselves, like I tried to do. And everybody wonders why. Well, Jesus Christ on the Cross, I'll tell you why! They were too god dammed good for their own stinking country, that's why! And after fifty years of believing in it, they found that out! *(She weeps)* I could have told them that! They didn't have to die for that, god damn it! The good life they gave me, they couldn't keep for themselves. *(She stares at everyone with defiance)* Because it is the Army that is the most decent thing about this country. Everything else I ever seen in it is shit. And the General, except for the husband he found for me, is the only top-to-bottom real man I ever met. *(She smiles, bitterly)* I would be happy to work forever at the Day Care Center. I am proud of what I done there. My husband, and his children, and me, we will be all right. What the General and the Army gave to me, this country cannot never take back away from me again. That's what they mean to me, the General and his wife.

(She goes to her seat, and the military personnel all stand while she does)

CO: Next.

MARTIN: Are you Mr. Roundhouse?

ROUNDHOUSE: Roundhouse, Edward E. I wasn't coming, but I had a drink and changed my mind. You want me to sit there?

MARTIN: Please. *(Roundhouse goes to the chair, stands by it)* This is an informal and preliminary inquiry, and we thank you for coming. The General left us notes, one saying you were an old and valued friend. That you would have something to tell us.

ROUNDHOUSE: I want to see the note. *(Martin looks at the CO, who nods. Martin gives Roundhouse the note. He reads it, hands it back)* All right. *(He sits in the witness chair)*

MARTIN: You are the owner of a restaurant on the island?

ROUNDHOUSE: Several now. Because Michael got me the first one, when he was a major, stationed briefly here. Its title was Michael's idea, The Breeze and I. He found it for me, helped me buy into the place, where I washed the dishes and swept the floors until it became a lunch stop for tour buses from Waikiki. Now you must ask me what I did before sweeping the floors of The Breeze and I. *(Pause)*

MARTIN: What did you do before sweeping the floors of the Breeze and I?

ROUNDHOUSE: I was President of two American universities. After a scholar's education in classical studies—my doctoral thesis was the superiority of Xenophon over Plato as a gauge to the true character of Socrates, I graced several advanced faculties, and in due process, bored finally with Socrates and Plato, turned my hand to university administration. Then, in 1945, I became President of Triton College, in Ohio. In 1951, President of the University of the Southwest. In 1952, I began sweeping the floors of The Breeze and I. Follow me?

MARTIN: Well, I . . .

ROUNDHOUSE: Never mind, don't try, just listen. In those lost days of my academic glory, I traveled often, up to my neck in liberal crusades. In the summer of 1952, I brought about the publication of a novel, in seven western countries and Japan, simultaneously, by the proscribed Baltic poet, Kaslaus Regler. Well. Salutations from Schweitzer, retreats with Russell, cocktails with Camus and supper with Sartre. I met Michael and Sheila in August of that same summer, on the great sweeping porch of the Zen temple that over-looks the Ryuanji Stone Garden, outside Kyoto. They were on a vacation, and we liked each other at once. On my way home, I stayed with them a week, here. We became good friends. I enjoyed their sturdy common sense, and respected their intelligent patriot-ism. They loved to hear all about the great figures in the wide world I journeyed in so freely. Then, time up, I returned home, to give my incoming freshman class my most stirring speech on the advan-tages of being an American, how lucky we were, of the endless possibilities thereunto appertaining, of their duty to the very best in themselves, and after that, there was a business trip to New York, where, in a perfectly respectable hotel bar, over a glass of sherry, I met a young man who thought me equally charming. We adjourned to my room, where he turned out to be cruising for the vice squad.

He arrested me, that little Benedict Arnold, whose legs, O Perversity of Memory, I can still remember. Those were the days of terror, you recall, when you were probably not merely a homosexual, debauching a poor, innocent policeman, but also most likely a Communist, since both vices were obviously intimately connected. When I got out of jail, what the Hearst papers in Chicago didn't do to me, the faculty and Board of Trustees of the University of the Southwest did. Never mind the honors and the service now, the friendships and acclaim in Europe. As far as my country, which I loved, was concerned—just another fairy. *(Pause)* All a kind of hideous joke now, except that it killed my mother. Contrary to what you are told in the Dell edition of Freud, I was very fond of her. But there I was, Mama dead as mutton, and with her my distinguished career in higher education, which had educated in bitterness, alas, only myself. I vaguely supposed I would go to Paris, call myself Sebastian Melmoth, and die there like Oscar Wilde. But my little Major Michael from the summer contacted me, and said, "I have a better idea. Come here." With Michael's help I bought my little restaurant by the sea. And as Michael foresaw, a tidal wave of tourists rolled over me. So here I am, better off than ever, a closet queen midwestern college president, turned into a rich, free comber of Somerset Maugham beaches, and boys. I am even a force in the economics of this state now, and believe me, nobody says a word. *(Pause)* Michael didn't do it just for me. We made a deal. "Take this place, and save yourself with it," he said. And in return, I was to make The Breeze and I, in the evenings only, a place for certain soldiers of the Army this young Major loved. "They can be good men, too," Michael said. "The Army should help them. You should help them." "Deal!" I said. So I put Offenbach in my jukebox, draped with fiendish cunning fish nets and sailcloth on the walls and ceilings, arranged booths for dignified semi-privacy, and created what Michael had wanted. At noon, of course, I made a killing, the place jammed with Los Angeles dentists and their fat wives, bedlam but profitable, and at night, under an Oahu moon, something else. *(Pause)* It's been that way now twenty years. Major Michael left Schofield for other assignments, passing through now and again. He would call me on my birthday, and at Christmas, like a good son. He wrote me letters from his battlefields in Korea and Vietnam. Then he returned to Schofield Barracks. Major General Michael, commanding. And once again, as it was in 1952, one night a week The Breeze and I was closed. Only two men drank the coconut rum, ate the bonito, listened to Offenbach and looked at the moon together. But now it was the war he talked about, and what happened to him in it. About the quicksand and the folly. About the jealousy of generals, the panic over their careers, the ugly personal maneuvers that turned what should have been counsels of war into blind tangles of vipers. About a President of the United States who so skillfully invited his generals to lie to him, they finally didn't care when they were lying and when they weren't and neither did he. *(Pause)* On the last night we spent together, he told me he understood now, what my country had done to me. "Me, too," he said, his face like slate. "We are going to lose this war. No matter what else we call it, this Army of the United States will be the scorn of history and rightly." He looked at his watch then, and my telephone rang. "I've had someone call me here," he said. "Is that all right?" I said yes. He talked briefly to the leader of a Washington protest march, told him to use his name and hung up. *(Pause)* And there we were. A disgraced college president and a defeated Army General. "I won't see you again," he said. "But let's kill the bottle first." And we did. We embraced. And that was the end of us. I had watched him turn, warrior into priest. Religions come and go, conversion remains. I saw it touch him, burning away the soldier he had always been. I loved him. I admired him. In an age where everyone else is innocent, Michael chose the terrible right to be guilty! *(Pause)*

MARTIN: *(Coldly)* And to betray his country, sir.

ROUNDHOUSE: His country, young man, betrayed him. *(He looks about)* Did he do it here?

MARTIN: Right here. Thank you, Mr. Roundhouse. *(To CO)* Sir, that's the last of the witnesses.

CO: Right. Ladies and gentlemen, the last request the General makes is for a simple review of what they did. Captain Martin. *(Martin gives Bates and Nomura a page of the play)* Mr. Roundhouse, please stay with us. *(He goes back to his seat)* Sergeant Bates, Miss Nomura, would you please read what you did Saturday night? And Captain Martin, do we have the masks they wore?

MARTIN: Yes, sir.

CO: Let's see them, please.

(Martin moves the table holding the masks to center. He opens the wooden boxes and sets the masks out, on wire stands. We see their faces, a suffering Japanese warrior and a beautiful woman, staring, with an Army 25th Division flag on one side of them and an American flag on the other. The CO nods to Sergeant Bates)

BATES: *(Reading)*
    The sky is lit
    with fires of war

MISS NOMURA: *(Reading)*

The smell of death infects the world
and blood rains down from heaven
(Lights change, dimming slightly, while a circle of light comes
up on the two masks)
BATES:
But today I leave the field
And with my wife
I make this pilgrimage
Evening falls
Night comes upon us
MISS NOMURA:
Birds fly up and vanish
in the darkening sky
BATES:
We have reached the river
that leads to the mountain we seek
We step into our boat
to cross the swift waters
MISS NOMURA:
And I remember
when long ago
down these same rivers
once we sailed
BATES:
Now they stream with blood
choked on the bodies of the young
my soldiers dead in the war
MISS NOMURA:
And I see in the currents below
beneath my child
beneath his hanging arms
and drifting hair
my husband's face
and mine
BATES:
Now we have come
to the Mountain of Death
MISS NOMURA:
Where young lovers come to die
a grove of pines
a bed of stones
BATES:
It is hard to think of ourselves
climbing this mountain

as a suicide of lovers

MISS NOMURA:

For happiness and youth were ours
We married in joy and pleasure
We had many victories
and great powers
but now we are here

BATES:

O my country farewell
You once were all the world to me
what you taught me I became
and served you far too well
I am yours no longer

MISS NOMURA:

O great compassionate Buddha
before your beautiful face
shining down upon us
I met my brave young husband
years ago
Husband!
Now!

BATES:

The knife may part the flesh
but miss the heart
I must use my bow

MISS NOMURA:

Use your bow
and your arrow tipped in steel
Kill me! Kill me!
I will wait for you in heaven
my noble husband!

(Pause)

Wait! Look there!
Ah!
Look there!

(Pause. The light on the masks fades)

MARTIN: And that was it. They waited a minute and—did it.
With the General's wife pointing—where, Sergeant Bates?

(Bates points toward the door of the ballroom)

BATES: There.

CO: What was she pointing at?

MARTIN: Nobody knew.

LUCY LAKE: I know. The child.

CO: You mean the orphan?

LUCY LAKE: Yoshida Robinson. Yes.

MRS. BATES: No! I'd sent him home!

LUCY LAKE: But they expected him.

MRS. BATES: That's right.

LUCY LAKE: Then the General meant to do something with the child.

MOORE: I know what we've forgotten! Those chairs! *(He points to the four antique armchairs with their* RESERVED *signs pinned to them)* Here! RESERVED! For who? The man who didn't come, but who damn near did, and who almost sat right here in this chair Saturday night. The man that lunatic general pretended HAD come! The President of the United States, that's who! I don't know why that man committed suicide, but I do know what he really wanted to do! Shoot the President!

LUCY LAKE: No, that's not it!

MRS. BATES: Never!

MOORE: The President of the United States, shot to death, right here!

LUCY LAKE: No. You're forgetting the child. Yoshida Robinson. A bequest to an orphanage. That was the heart of it. *(Lucy Lake steps forward)* The President? Where would he have been?

MOORE: There! Right there!

LUCY LAKE: The General and his wife, at the end of the pay?

MARTIN: There!

LUCY LAKE: And the little boy would have come in . . .

MRS. BATES: There! To them!

(She points out the spot where the child would have entered. It is right in front of a chair marked RESERVED*)*

LUCY LAKE: The General was going to kill the child.

MRS. BATES: Do WHAT to the child?

(They all react, in a quick explosion)

MOORE: *(Simultaneous)* No, the President was the target! That's who he wanted to kill!

MISS NOMURA: *(Simultaneous)* It was a shinju! You don't understand!

LUCY LAKE: *(Simultaneous)* The child! That was the poem! The child!

BATES: *(Simultaneous)* Lorna, please. Calm down.

MRS. BATES: No! No! It's wrong! They're all wrong!

(The CO stands up)

CO: That will do! *(Pause)* We have not finished. Sergeant Bates, you have a sealed envelope from the General?

BATES: Yes, sir.

CO: Open it and read it. Let him speak for himself.

(Sergeant Bates opens the envelope, takes out a sheet of paper and reads from it)

BATES: *(Reading)* General. Plan A. To cut the throat of an Oriental-American child, and throw his blood on the President of the United States. Plan B. To make that intention known to you, to others, and if possible, to public record. Goodbye.

(Bates gives the paper to the CO. The CO stares at it a moment)

CO: Is there a medical report?

MARTIN: Yes, sir.

CO: Read that.

MARTIN: *(Reading)* The General's wife died, unresisting, from the intrusion into her throat of a steel-tipped archer's arrow, shot from a sixty-pound bow. It severed the right carotid artery. She herself grasped the arrow in both hands, wrenched it back and forth in her throat. The General then took off his mask, drew his Army automatic pistol, placed it against his ear and pulled the trigger. The force of the explosion, at that range, removed the entire cranial vault. Both deaths were suicide.

(Pause. The CO looks at the people)

CO: Thank you.

(Captain Martin goes to the door. They all go out. The CO sits down. He looks at the masks. Lights fade on the masks, staring)

The End

David Kranes

GOING IN

David Kranes

David Kranes makes his debut in *Best Short Plays* with *Going In*, a sensitive study of a physician's mid-life crisis involving his wife and son. The play appears in print for the first time in this anthology. An earlier play, *Drive In*, was published in the *Playwrights for Tomorrow*, edited by Arthur Ballet.

Mr. Kranes is a graduate of the Yale School of Drama, where he studied playwriting with the late John Gassner, noted anthologist and theatre critic. Mr. Kranes' full-length play *The Salmon Run* was the co-recipient of the 1985 National Repertory Theatre Award, and the Manhattan Theatre Club has scheduled one of his plays for their 1986-87 season.

The playwright also writes novels and screenplays. His novel, *The Hunting Years* (1984), received a laudatory review in the *New York Times*, and a new book of fiction, *Keno Runner,* is scheduled for publication in the fall of 1986. Also during this year his screenplay *Truants* goes into production.

A Distinguished Teaching Award has been given to Mr. Kranes by the University of Utah, where he teaches playwriting, dramatic literature, and theatre history. In addition to his position as professor, Mr. Kranes is the artistic director of the Playwrights Conference at the Sundance Resort in Provo Canyon, Utah. This Center for Performing Arts at Sundance offers selected playwrights the opportunity to develop their skills and artistry. Ideas and concepts are explored in depth at the conference without the financial and critical pressures of the commercial theatre.

Mr. Kranes lives in Salt Lake City with his wife and two sons, and continues to write for the stage, the cinema, and the reading public.

This play Mr. Kranes dedicates, "For Jon."

Characters:

> JONAS WALTER, *forty-two*
> RICH AMBLER, *a physician/colleague, thirty-eight*
> POLLY AMBLER, *Rich's wife, thirty-six*
> MEG WALTER, *Jonas's wife, forty*
> CARTER WALTER, *Jonas's son, seventeen*

Place:

> Jonas's den. Bookcases crammed mostly with medical books and journals. A built-in television. Leather couch and chairs. A bar/cabinet in an old dry sink. Three colorful and lit older juke boxes in the two back corners and front left.

Time:

> *Before we realize.*

Before the Curtain:

> *Music from one of the juke boxes. Joined (five seconds later) by music from the second jukebox. Joined (five seconds later) by music from the third jukebox. All the songs are fifteen to twenty years ago. The level of the music—after the initial surprise of three braided songs at once—becomes accommodated by the listener.*

At Curtain:

> *Jonas and Rich are in the room and are picked up in the middle of a late, friendly, tired, somewhat drunken argument.*

JONAS: You go *in*.
RICH: Oh, come on! Why would you. . .
JONAS: *(Slow, deliberate, instructional)* You . . . go . . . in, Rich.

RICH: Jonas, you don't go in. You don't *need* to go in.

JONAS: Well, I say: You go in! What *else're* you going to do?! Radiate?!

RICH: Why is that such a . . .?

JONAS: You can't radiate in that situation!

RICH: Some people would radiate.

(One of the songs will end somewhere in the midst of this argument. Jonas, who is on his feet anyway, will take some quarters from a mound he has on the bar and—without losing a beat in the discussion or shifting focus from Rich—make his next set of plays.

The three jukes will run down on their last song about a second or two of each other . . . which keep Jonas in motion, circling)

JONAS: Really?

RICH: Yes, really.

JONAS: Who?!

RICH: Well . . .

JONAS: Who's radiates when you've got a . . .!

RICH: *Fitzer's* radiated patients who've had . . .!

JONAS: Oh, Jesus. Fitzer!

RICH: Yes! Fitzer! Fitzer's no . . .!

JONAS: Fitzer's a cretin! Fitzer uses leeches! Fitzer pays more in malpractice insurance than you and I declare in taxes! Listen, how did that computer graphics new issue, that I told you about, work out for you?

RICH: Made a triple in seven months.

JONAS: "Thank you for the tip, Jonas."

RICH: "Thank you for the tip, Jonas." Jonas, look, Fitzer was only Chief of *Neuro* — when he was at . . .

JONAS: Right! Salmon Idaho Regional Hospital! Salmon, Idaho Regional, Dr. Ambler! Where's that?! What's that?! Practically Canada!

RICH: Oh! I love this! Now we're going to eliminate Canada!

JONAS: Are you going to say that you think Canadian medicine even *compares* to . . . ?!

RICH: Well, the NIH certainly seems to think that what Fitzer is doing is . . .

JONAS: Rich, look, I don't need to be instructed about the NIH. I've been given any *number* of grants by the NIH.

RICH: But not the last one you applied for. And Fitzer . . . !

JONAS: Like everything else, the NIH has its mafia and its politics.

RICH: Oh-ho! We are on a *rampage*!

JONAS: We are *not* on a rampage!

RICH: We are a buffalo herd, I swear! What the hell is . . . ?!

JONAS: We are on a rampage because *The New England Journal of Medicine*, in two separate articles in the last six months, presents irrefutable evidence—Fitzer and the goddamn NIH to the contrary—that . . . !

RICH: Jonas, you are—excuse me—on a fucking *tear*. Really! I mean, excuse me again, but you cannot be a Golden Boy, you know, *forever*. *(A beat or two—Jonas moving)* . . . Am I wrong?

JONAS: *(More subdued, more internal)* Of course you're wrong. You're always wrong. You did your residency in Palo Alto.

RICH: Good. *Now* it comes out!

JONAS: You bet your ass.

RICH: The hideous, *slithering* truth from beneath the rocks!

JONAS: Absolutely. Damn right.

(Polly moves into the room just at the entrance)

POLLY: *(Overlapping Jonas)* Jonas, the Kabuki prints are amazing. Meg showed me. Rich, go see them. Meg has them out —hurry.

RICH: Yes, Ma'am.

POLLY: Don't be fresh.

RICH: Yes, Ma'am.

POLLY: *(To Rich)* Jonas flies to medical meetings—he brings home Kabuki prints. You fly, and you bring back herpes.

RICH: Well—no insinuations, of course. But that's not *my* herpes, Sweetheart.

POLLY: Be kind.

RICH: . . . All I know how to be. What else? Kabuki prints —amazing gifts from the Orient—then we're off.

(He exits. Polly studies Jonas)

POLLY: Don't take any of that literally.

JONAS: Well . . . I am only what I am . . . which is, of course, extraordinarily literal and extraordinarily real.

POLLY: Jonas, please.

JONAS: "Jonas, please," what?

POLLY: You know what I'm saying. Don't not be my friend. *(Jonas doesn't respond. He pours more bourbon into his glass)* Jonas, I couldn't bear it to have the knowledge that you and Meg weren't ideal. I don't want to believe *ever*, let alone know, let alone know in my *body*, not just my mind—that you . . . had ever acted unfaithfully . . . Especially if I had to live with the fact that the person that you had acted unfaithfully with was . . . Do you understand what I'm saying?

JONAS: But it was sure great fun bringing me to the *edge* of all that, *wasn't* it?

POLLY: Jonas, play fair.

JONAS: "Play fair"! You know, there's a *word* for *[that describes]* you.

POLLY: Jonas. Please. Don't . . .

JONAS: There's a *word* for you!! And it is not particularly polite.

POLLY: You've had a lot to drink.

(Jonas looks at his glass, at the bottles and ice bucket set out on the dry-sink bar)

JONAS: . . . Is that information you didn't think I had?

POLLY: I suppose I'm implying that . . .

JONAS: Don't lord any presumptions over me. Understand?!

(Silence)

POLLY: I don't think it's a good thing that you didn't go to Carter's game today. *(Jonas eyes her hard but doesn't respond)* . . . Meg talked to me. She's worried about it. She's hurt. She's angry. She's very afraid. *(Again, no response from Jonas)* Your son broke four passing records that you set when you went to his school. And you didn't go. You didn't choose to be there. To watch. To see him do it.

JONAS: Well, he's only a junior. I'm going to have any number of other opportunities.

POLLY: He's very bright, too.

JONAS: You've noticed that.

POLLY: I have.

JONAS: Well, his body and his mind have been living in reasonable proximity for a while at least. Gifts, so to speak, get picked up.

POLLY: I just think it's a cruel choice for a father to . . .

JONAS: I don't want any pathology-of-cruel-choices shit from you, lady! All right?!

POLLY: . . . You sometimes have a very vulgar mouth.

JONAS: Which specific acts are we . . . ? Actually, I *frequently* . . . *(A gratuitous smile)* Just so's we understand our relative positions.

POLLY: You know, If you're not careful—you could become a very sad and a very pathetic man.

JONAS: You like that adjective, "very," don't you. Excuse me — was that a prediction? Was it a promise?

POLLY: What it *was*, was . . . ! I mean, my God, Jonas, what kind of man goes around to all his childhood *haunts* and buys their jukeboxes?!

JONAS: . . . Well, we save what we can. *(Pause)* . . . I mean, you're still trying to save what lift you've got left—aren't you? I mean, it seems to me—given the things you wear— that . . .
(Polly tosses whatever's left in her cordial glass in Jonas's face. Meg comes to the door of the room)
MEG: Rich has your coat. I think he was disappointed that the prints weren't more erotic . . . ! *(She takes in Jonas with the Drambuie on him)*
JONAS: My left eyebrow had suddenly broken into flame. It happens sometimes when the optic nerve synapses *arc.* Polly rushed into the breach, so to speak. I'm very grateful. "Very."
MEG: *(Trying to recover and be light)* . . . I know . . . She does that. The "breach," I mean. Rushes. She's very good at . . .
(They all laugh uneasily. Jonas plays with it slightly, perhaps pushing the laughter to the point where they both understand his is mocking) [NOTE: In this section of the play, one, then another of the jukebox songs will run out without Jonas continuing them]
JONAS: Yeah, Polly's a peach. Or an artichoke, or an avocado, or something like that. Aren't you, Polly?
POLLY: Jonas is drunk.
JONAS: You don't think it's possible to be unattractive . . . without being drunk?
(Rich arrives at the door, carrying Polly's coat)
RICH: Are we starting over again?
JONAS: *Can* we?
POLLY: *(To Rich)* Let's go.
MEG: *(Her hand out to Jonas)* Let's say good bye.
POLLY: That's fine.
MEG: Jonas . . . ?
POLLY: Jonas obviously has other agenda.
RICH: *(Wishing it would be funny)* Agendae.
POLLY: *(To Rich)* Please.
MEG: Jonas. For heaven's sakes!
JONAS: *(Smile, wave)* Bye, guys.
RICH: Bye, Doctor.
POLLY: *(Leaning forward, kissing him on the cheek)* Night, Jonas. We love you.
JONAS: Thanks for putting my fire out.
(Polly looks at Jonas)
MEG: *(To Jonas)* You're really not coming to the door?
JONAS: Not tonight.
(Polly leaves first)

RICH: See you in that service meeting, Monday.

JONAS: Absolutely.

(Rich leaves. Meg follows—But not without some kind of hands signal intended to read, "We need to talk."

Jonas sits alone. He touches the spot on his face where the Drambuie was thrown. Tastes his fingers from the touch.

He gets up, gathers some change, studies a section of his wall, some pictures there, touches the glass of an award or two. He starts up only one of the jukeboxes, pours himself another drink, moves to and studies another section of the wall.

Meg comes to the door, studies him)

MEG: Why are you acting this way? *(He doesn't turn)* Why are you being so irritating and mean?

JONAS: *(He turns in to her)* Excellent questions.

MEG: I'm very serious.

JONAS: I know . . . I know.

MEG: Are you going to tell me? *(Jonas moves inside himself)* . . . Would you ever have an affair with Polly? Do you find her attractive?

JONAS: *(Brought out)* Where does that question come from?

MEG: From my watching the way she tries to play with you. She teases you. She gets very coy.

JONAS: There is a *word* for her.

MEG: Which is?

JONAS: *(Near overlap)* Not one which you would like hearing, I think.

MEG: Why are you acting the way you are?

JONAS: *(Smile)* I'm just an irrepressible guy.

(Meg moves to make herself a light drink)

I'm *not* an irrepressible guy. I was *once* an irrepressible guy. Somewhere in the weave of all that . . . is a probable truth—I'm not a genius any more. I'm not a hero. Neither god nor king! So we have the initial stages of adjustment to . . . It will be a brief but mean-spirited transition period in my life. I will try to keep it mildly tolerable, but, given the dimensions of my particular history, it may get out of bounds.

MEG: . . . That was a devastating thing you did to Carter.

JONAS: Which?

MEG: Today.

JONAS: Specifically.

MEG: Not going.

JONAS: How do you know?

MEG: It would be a devastating thing for any young man ... to have a moment of triumph and have his father choose not to be present!

JONAS: ... And you've talked with him?

MEG: No. Well, actually ... No, he ...

JONAS: He what?

MEG: He called. There were a series of parties. Victory parties. Celebrations. He said he didn't know, really, when he'd ...

JONAS: And he said, "Why didn't Dad come? I'm devastated."?

MEG: Oh, for God's ... !

JONAS: Well, did he *say* he was crushed?

MEG: Stop being such a bloody scientist!

JONAS: "I yam ... who I yam!"

(Pause)

MEG: *Are* you having an affair with Polly?

JONAS: I love it! ... No.

MEG: *Have* you had one?

JONAS: No.

MEG: Would you *like* to have one?

JONAS: No.

MEG: Would you like to have one with *anybody*?

JONAS: I choose ... Ann Margaret or Marie Curie! *(A beat)* or Loretta Lynn. *(A beat)* Or ... if I can't have Loretta Lynn, I choose Sissy Spacek ... Or ...

MEG: Let's go to bed. We can pick up in the morning.

JONAS: Go ahead.

MEG: Jonas, please ... !

JONAS: No.

MEG: Are you waiting for Car? *(No response)* Are you? Are you going to apologize to him?

JONAS: Go to bed. You can pick up in the morning.

MEG: I hate you when you're like this.

JONAS: Thank God, it's so seldom.

MEG: I'm not sure.

JONAS: Take my word for it.

(Meg glares at him)

(Direct) Take my word for it.

MEG: People used to say you were charming. *(Jonas nods)* You don't have any response to that?

JONAS: Which people were they? And how long ago did they stop saying that?

MEG: ... I'm going.

JONAS: To?

MEG: Bed.

JONAS: Good.
(A beat. She leaves) (After her) Meg?
MEG: *(Appearing, leaning back in the door)* Yes?
JONAS: Why can't you just *love* me through this? Not make a multiple-choice test out of it. Just . . . ride quietly with me through?
MEG: You're being "quiet?"
JONAS: No. But why can't you?
MEG: Because I think it's a cliché. "Middle-age Crisis." Because everybody's read all about it in Sheila whats-her-name's book.
JONAS: *Passages.*
MEG: Yes. And because you're very bright . . .
JONAS: Thank you.
MEG: . . . And you should just see it for what it is, the cliché that it is, and be above it.
JONAS: Meg?
MEG: Jonas?
JONAS: Why can't you just *love* me through this cliché? Take the ride quietly?
MEG: *(Leaving)* Good night!
JONAS: . . . Good night.
(Jonas sits in the chair a moment. He gestures with his hands—as though he's having a discussion, a very REASONABLE discussion, with himself . . . or Meg . . . or someone.
He gets up, meanders, starts up one or two of the jukes, freshens his drink, turns the lights off so that the only lights in the room are the jukes)
(Still standing) You don't radiate! Why would you radiate?! How long do you think a person can radiate?! You radiate and that's the *end* of you; it's all you can *do*: radiate, radiate, radiate. So, you go *in*. You take the sword in your bloody, fucking hand, and you go . . . !
MEG: *(From a distant room)* Jonas . . . ?! *(Jonas stops)* . . . Jonas . . . ?!
JONAS: Yes?!
MEG: Is Car home?!
JONAS: No!
MEG: . . . Are you talking to yourself?!
JONAS: Yes!
(Silence)
(To himself) You go in. "Mistah Kurtz—he daid." In and *in*! You use a . . . And you use a . . . You watch the flotsam. You

watch the foreign bodies floating on any of the visible channels. Fitzer has *fish* in his brain!

(Sound of a car outside, pulling up the driveway and into the garage. Jonas turns the lights back on. He takes a book from the shelf)

(Self conversation) "To whom should one attribute the theory of *innate heat*?" "Galen!" "Wrong. Aristotle!" "Wrong. Hippocrates!" "Who's right here?!" "What *is* the theory of *innate heat*?" "Pneuma!" "'Pneuma'! A *word* can't be a theory!" Then: "That's what distinguishes the living from the dead in any organism . . .": *Innate heat.* "Good! Good, Doctor! Yours is not the ordinary mind!" "Well, all my life, I have striven to be . . ." "Excellent! Strive!" "Thank you."

(Sound of a garage or back door closing. Jonas moves to his chair, sits in it, flips open his book: he pages through it. Several beats pass. From the kitchen, sounds of Carter rumaging the fridge.

Carter appears in the doorway to the den. He holds a half-filled half-gallon of milk. He wears Levis and a cutoff sweatshirt. He watches his father for a few beats)

CARTER: . . . Hi.

JONAS: Hello.

CARTER: You still up?

JONAS: If this is still me—then I guess I'm still up. Yes.

(Carter nods. He wanders into the room, takes another chair, drinks from his milk)

CARTER: . . . Have a busy day?

JONAS: Nothing extraordinary, I don't think. *(Carter nods)* . . . Where were *you*?

CARTER: Me?

JONAS: Yeah.

CARTER: When?

JONAS: Now.

CARTER: Out.

JONAS: Where?

CARTER: Around. *(Jonas nods)* . . . Some people had some parties.

JONAS: I see. *(Carter nods)* Which people were those?

CARTER: Just people. *(Jonas nods)* People I know.

JONAS: It's reasonably late.

CARTER: *You're* up.

JONAS: We've established that.

(Carter rises and starts to leave the room)

Where're you going?

(Carter stops, he pauses. He turns back to his father)

CARTER: Are you confused . . . about what the room is
. . . that's next to this room? I'm going into the dining room first
. . . which is next to this room. And then I'm going through the
door . . . between the dining room and the kitchen. And then I'm
going *into* the kitchen . . . Can I get something for you?

(A beat)

JONAS: There's some Brie cheese . . . in the cheese drawer in
the fridge. I'd appreciate a piece of Brie cheese, please—if you
would.

*(Carter nods and leaves. A moment of silence. Jonas gets up
from his chair, starts up a jukebox or two, moves around.
Carter comes back with a wedge of cheese between his fingers,
extends it for his father)*

No crackers?

CARTER: You asked for crackers?

JONAS: . . . I didn't. No.

CARTER: *(Pushing it further toward him)* Well, I just carry out
my assignments.

JONAS: *(Taking it)* Who had the parties?

CARTER: You and Mom for one—right?

JONAS: We had the Amblers over.

(Carter nods)

CARTER: Which is no party.

(He goes and looks into one of the jukeboxes)

JONAS: Who had *your* parties?

CARTER: Would you mind if I changed the songs in these jukeboxes? Put new sides in?

JONAS: Yes.

CARTER: They're out of date.

JONAS: Time is a mystery—and a continuum.

CARTER: . . . Right.

JONAS: Who had *your* parties?

CARTER: Don't screw around with me tonight—okay?!

(Silence)

JONAS: . . . Maybe you want to go to bed. *(Carter nods)*
. . . Do you think that maybe . . .

CARTER: That's one of the options—yes! One of the others is
—that I *don't* want to go to bed. One of the others is—that I have
no opinion or attitude one way or the other about bed. I think there
are still *other* possibilities . . . but it bores me to go through them.
(Jonas nods) . . . Maybe I'll just come in here some afternoon
and *change* all these records anyway.

JONAS: You can't "change" the Everly Brothers.

CARTER: Well, they said a lot of things couldn't be done.

JONAS: Or Hank Williams.

CARTER: . . . But people do them.

JONAS: So you had a good afternoon on the "gridiron"—my sources say.

CARTER: Yes, I did.

JONAS: Broke a few of the existing school records.

CARTER: True.

JONAS: Well, could they have been much . . . if just some *junior* in high school managed . . . ?

CARTER: They've been around!

(Jonas moves and studies a grouping of pictures on his wall. Carter studies him)

. . . They've been around almost twenty years.

JONAS: Twenty-*three* years.

CARTER: Twenty-*three* years—good for you.

JONAS: Do you feel competitive with me? *(Carter hoots)* Did I miss something?

CARTER: Unlikely.

JONAS: Did *you* miss something?

CARTER: Very little.

JONAS: You've no interest . . . in heading off to bed?

CARTER: Why do I get the sense . . . that this conversation is cyclical?

JONAS: "Cyclical"—that's a very good word.

CARTER: Well, I'm bright . . . *And* athletic. Apparently there's a gene pool. *(Jonas smiles, nods)* Why didn't you come? *(No immediate response)* You weren't called in. You weren't operating. You'd gotten home. I've checked that out already. Why weren't you there?

JONAS: How'd you check that out?

CARTER: You've got your sources; I've got mine.

JONAS: We going to have an argument?

CARTER: This *is* an argument. So I'd suggest you . . .

JONAS: How about a fight?

CARTER: Physical fight?

JONAS: Or an argument pushed to the *point* of a good physical fight?

CARTER: How about just a physical fight? . . . I mean, after all, I broke all your records of heroic achievement on the playing field this afternoon. And I'm just seventeen. I could probably whip your ass.

(Meg appears unexpectedly at the door in a dressing gown)

MEG: Excuse me, but what exactly is this exchange *about*?

JONAS: Just basic "ass-whipping" talk, darling. Don't pay no mind.

CARTER: (*Chagrined, to his mother*) . . . Hi, Mom I'm sorry.

MEG: Are you coming to bed?

JONAS: (*Aside to Carter*) I think what we have here is a less-than-instant replay of a conversation which . . .

MEG: I meant *both* of you—now that you're *both* home.

JONAS: Well, we have been *wrestling* with that issue. And it seems that neither of us are prepared to see it quite to closure.

MEG: (*To Carter*) How *are* you.

CARTER: Good.

MEG: Congratulations.

CARTER: Thank you.

MEG: (*Of Jonas*) He's being a shit.

CARTER: He's been a shit before. It's all right.

MEG: Get in a lick for me, while you're at it.

CARTER: I will.

MEG: Fading stars, you'll find, begrudge the losing of their light.

CARTER: Well . . .

JONAS: (*To Meg*) You may have made your point.

MEG: But my analyist friends tell me . . .

JONAS: Right: "Understanding is the first step only." Very good. Point/match. Sweet dreams.

MEG: . . . (*To Carter*) Whip his ass.

(*Meg exits. Several beats pass. Perhaps some independent movement. Readjustment*)

JONAS: . . . You don't date much—*do* you. (*A Beat. Carter looks at him*) . . . No. Scratch that. Unfair. Garbage shot . . . Garbage shot; garbage shot . . . How did it feel? . . . This afternoon.

CARTER: (*Cautious*) . . . It was fine.

JONAS: Triumphant?

CARTER: I think I said "fine."

JONAS: So you did.

CARTER: . . . It was no big deal.

JONAS: All in an afternoon's . . .

CARTER: I'm just saying I knew I'd do it. I wasn't that far. It was pretty much given . . . at that point. I wasn't worried that it might not happen. And if it hadn't happened today—it would have happened first game next year. So . . .

(*Jonas nods*)

JONAS: . . . Uncomplicated.

CARTER: I didn't say that ... I mean, I would have preferred ... that someone other than my father ... you know, won the statistics that I was after.

JONAS: I don't think so.

CARTER: Well, I do.

JONAS: No.

CARTER: Hey, excuse me, but I think I said ...

JONAS: *You attack what you are, my man! You attack your life. Don't pretend otherwise!*

CARTER: ... I see.

JONAS: ... I'm glad.

CARTER: ... And you're sure.

JONAS: I'm pretty damn sure. Yes. Yeah. And I think that if you *aren't* anything ... or are confused about what your life *is* ... then you make something up. And attack that!

CARTER: ... Sounds pretty sour grapes to me.

JONAS: Well, you take your wine any way you can get it, I think.

CARTER: ... And ... so ... is that the voice of experience?

JONAS: Well, there *is* a certain empiricism in it—experience—yes.

CARTER: Well, then, so ... what are *you*?

JONAS: The question?

CARTER: Say what?

JONAS: You're asking?

CARTER: I'm asking: What's *your* life? What are *you* ... that *you* attack ... all the time the way you do?

JONAS: ... I am ...

CARTER: Yes?

JONAS: ... A man trying to fill a hole.

CARTER: I see.

JONAS: I'm glad.

CARTER: And what's that mean?

JONAS: "Man"? "filling"? "hole" ...? Which word ...?

CARTER: What hole? "Hole" where? What hole?

JONAS: The hole that's not there! ... which is why it's a hole. Right? That's logical ... Look—forget it. I'm outwitting myself. I'm losing what I thought would be my focus—I did *have* a focus ... I'm mixing metaphors as well ... or in danger of it. I didn't come today ... because I didn't want you to have to have your father in the stands. I wanted you to attack *cleanly* ... and without confusion. You shouldn't have to *attack* something that's cheering for you. I thought it needed to be *your* day. Not some am-

biguous father and son picnic. Those were the *good* reasons. There
were ugly and small reasons as well. But you would do best to imagine those . . . because they'll take on more size and importance if
you do. And that can hone your attack. And you see—even my
good reasons *weren't* good reasons, because, by and large, all I did
was succeed in creating a *hole*, absence, vacuum for you . . .
which is what *I* have spent an up-until-this-moment lifetime trying to
fill. And it's quite clear where it's gotten me. I am a man past forty
with old songs in his . . . den . . . old "mementos," old
records. I am a ranging, off-center, energized, eclectic even what
they sometimes call "creative" mind in my profession—which was
fresh and attractive through my mid-thirties . . . but which has
come to be . . . arrogant and edgy, irritating, at my present station. I keep trying to fill a hole . . . which is no longer a hole
. . . if it ever was. And so here I am . . . I wanted you to have
a clean shot. *(A beat or two, then a smile)* Of course—with me—
there is always the chance that that's all just elaborate bullshit. Isn't
there? Another one of my verbal arias . . . that those around me
. . . have grown so accustomed to. Who can say . . . Anyway
—you now own several records! . . . and the attack is on! Right?
(Jonas smiles. Carter studies him) That a fair statement? . . . of
our two positions? *(Carter shrugs)* Don't shrug!
    CARTER: Is that one of the rules? . . . of experience? . . .
"Don't shrug"? *(Jonas doesn't respond. He refills his drink)*
. . . What happens when you shrug? What are the dangers of
shrugging . . . in the contemporary world? . . . Don't drink!
Don't drink so fucking much! I think that's a better rule than "Don't
shrug."
    JONAS: Of course. You're in training.
    CARTER: And you're *past* training.
    JONAS: Yeah. That's right. "Past-training," "post-training"
. . .
    CARTER: And what *for?*
    JONAS: For "The Event." Always for "The Event." You give
up *everything* . . . so that you can eventually be in The
Event . . . and let everything go.
    CARTER: I see.
    JONAS: No, you don't. But you will. Or you may. Or, then
again, one of the other possibilities is . . . *(Jonas puts his hand to
his head, hard massages his eyes)* . . . I drink too much. That's
true . . . But I'll drink too much and then I'll stop . . . practically
altogether, probably. That's my way . . . to excess . . . and
then very little at all . . . To excess . . . then finally in
moderation. *(Jonas looks at Carter)* Are you like that?

CARTER: *(Honest)* . . . I don't know . . . I don't think I've been around long enough to find out.

JONAS: True. You have to . . . *test* for patterns . . . To know that something isn't just a *phenomenon* . . . and not a pattern. I'm my own "control group" . . . Congratulations. On this after-noon.

CARTER: You already said that.

JONAS: No, I didn't.

CARTER: Yes, you did.

JONAS: I'm sorry—but that was your mother.

CARTER: *(Remembering)* That's right . . . I forgot.

JONAS: *(Small smile)* Good.

CARTER: Are . . . you and Mom having problems?

JONAS: . . . Such as?

CARTER: Uh . . . Do you think you might stop this *precision* shit . . . for just a minute . . . and answer my question?

JONAS: . . . Probably not . . . Probably not . . . Did you hear that?

CARTER: What?

JONAS: An echo. Or maybe I was answering both your last questions: "Are you and Mom having problems?" "Probably not." "Do you think you could stop this precision shit?" "Probably not." Maybe if I don't shrug and if I *drink* enough, I might possibly . . . Good! There! I did it! I didn't finish a sentence! You see— raggedness and imprecision are coming upon me! When I least expect! I think that's splendid!

CARTER: I think you do a lot of entertaining of yourself.

JONAS: That's true.

CARTER: I'm going to bed. *(He starts out)*

JONAS: *(After him)* Do you think I love you?

(Carter stops. He doesn't answer the question)

Do you think I *don't* love you?

CARTER: *(Simple, honest)* . . . I can't talk to you.

JONAS: That's not the question.

CARTER: Well, it may not be *your* question—but it's *my* question. *(Carter exits)*

JONAS: *(After him)* But it's not even a question! . . . You made a statement! . . . A statement's not a question! . . . Although it may have an implicit question in it!

(Jonas will set all his jukeboxes "in motion" during this final speech)

Carter, I try to instruct the world—and myself, through the reminders of that instruction—in the elegance of what any of us might reach for! What's attainable! . . . My communication tends to ... I use a baroque language, because I feel that a baroque language, possibly, is best-suited for ... ! Be sure that milk's put away! I'll take responsibility for the cheese. When you wake up in the morning, in the dawn of a new day, I guarantee that the Brie will be in its proper place! ... Don't shrug! Don't slouch! Don't break training! And if you try to change any of the records in *this* room—I'll be waiting for you! So plan your attack! ... Or attack your plan! And remember—that any of us are our own plans! So execute well! Because I am not alone! And Hank Williams is *armed*. And Don and Phil Everly are *contenders* again.

(Jonas is picking up items in the den, attending to the music, stopping occasionally to see something on his wall. Carter, passing to go upstairs, stops and watches his father, who doesn't know that Carter's there. Then to himself)

"I coulda been a contender." *(Out)* Who *said* that?! ... Wrong! It was *not* Rocky Balboa ... Well, I *do* love you! If I'm forced to answer my own question—which has generally been the story of my life. I also do not *not* love you! So there! There! All my questions are answered! All my holes are filled! *Some* of my holes are filled! *(To himself)* And some of my holes *better not* be filled ... or I'm in trouble. Because I tend to do things "in excess" when the first blush is on ... and then, ultimately, in moderation. But I love my son—and that will have to do for this evening, thank you. "Thank you." "Thank You." "You're welcome, I'm sure. Goodnight."

(Jonas looks up and sees his son)

CARTER: Good night.

JONAS: ... Well, yes ... Good night.

(Carter nods)

CARTER: ... Operate well tomorrow ... if I don't see you in the morning.

(Jonas nods)

JONAS: Yes. You too ... "Operate well." I like that.

(Carter nods. Jonas nods)

... Operate well.

(Carter moves away. Jonas stands alone in the room. He nods. He nods again. He nods more and more ... as the lights dim)

The End

Katharine Long

ARIEL BRIGHT

Katharine Long

Ariel Bright, a charming period fantasy about an aspiring actress and her psychic mortician mentor, premiered at the Depot Theatre in Westport, New York in August of 1983. It was subsequently produced in New York City in May, 1984 as part of the Marathon '84 Festival of One-Act Plays, presented by the Ensemble Studio Theatre (E.S.T.). The E.S.T. production directed by John Schwab with the author's husband, Bill Cwikowski, as Hiley Bedsal and Melodie Somers as Ariel Bright, was revived a couple of months later for The Best of Marathon '84 for the Pepsico Summerfare Center for the Arts at the State University of New York at Purchase. In reviewing the E.S.T. Marathon production for *Stages*, Debbi Wasserman writes, "Heading the list is the extraordinarily moving *Ariel Bright* by Katharine Long which fantasy whisks us back to 1912 and a world in which dreams come true ... In their brief encounter, we are treated to a dialogue that reveals two lonely, yearning souls. Long possesses a skillful writing technique that uses language sparingly-but-effectively to evoke character, mood, and story."

The background for *Ariel Bright* like Ms. Long's earlier plays (also produced by E.S.T.), *Unseen Friends* and *Two-Part Harmony,* is the American Midwest, where the author was born (in Champaign, Illinois in 1954) and where her parents had been raised. The playwright reports that the small town atmosphere of these works reflects the influence of her parents "nostalgic reveries of their home state, Missouri."

Ms. Long's first play, written at age twelve, was a grisly one about a strict teacher who hung her students. Her early fascination for the macabre is a pulsating tone in the work published here.

Associated with the E.S.T. since shortly after her graduation from Kenyon College in 1977, Ms. Long began as Office Manager in the playwriting department, reading and evaluating scripts, and within a year was serving as Script Development Director for the organization. Ms. Long considers this experience with a group dedicated to new plays as a valuable experience in her own development as a playwright.

Through one of those legendary quirks of last-minute casting changes in an E.S.T. workshop production, Ms. Long found herself acting in a play opposite her actor husband, and has even played the role of Ariel Bright with him. More recently she has acted in a new play, *Becoming Memories* by Arthur Giron, presented by the Pittsburg Public Theatre in 1985.

Also teaming up with her husband, Ms. Long teaches a writing course at E.S.T.'s Institute that focuses on the development of character through writing and acting techniques. Additionally, Ms. Long teaches writing under the auspices of The Dramatists Guild's Young Playwrights' Festival, an annual showcase of new plays by writers under the age of nineteen.

Another play by Ms. Long, *The Attic*, was a finalist in the 1977 Great American Play Contest, sponsored by the Actors Theatre of Louisville. Ms. Long has also written for daytime television series, *As the World Turns* and *Search for Tomorrow*.

Ms. Long dedicates *Ariel Bright* to her mother, Ruthanna Long.

Characters:

HILEY BEDSAL, *Mid- to late-thirties; medium height, slight build; moves quickly—always busy—adds personal touches to everything he does; rarely spends time among the living*
ARIEL BRIGHT, *thirty-five; six-foot-one, slender, graceful, ethereal; dressed in white; heads turn when she walks down the street; a gifted actress, ahead of her time*

Time:

5:00 a.m. on August 6, 1912.

Locale:

Grayson, Missouri, a small town located in the western part of the state.

Place:

The back room of Hiley Bedsal's funeral parlor. The back room is where bodies are prepared for their final departure. A drawn curtain, hanging upstage left, leads to the funeral parlor. Caskets can be purchased there when a funeral is not in progress.
As the lights go down, the first few bars of "What a Friend We Have In Jesus" softly plays to a ragtime beat. As the lights come up, Hiley Bedsal is standing before the "work coffin," holding a playing card up to the corpse. Most morticians prepare their clients on a table, but Hiley feels that a work coffin helps acclimate the body to his or her new permanent home. This work coffin can be anything from a pine box to a portable tin bath, but whatever the style, it must conceal the body within. Mrs. Moxem is within and her white hair is visible.
Hiley has designed the back room to meet his specific needs. To the left stands a tall shelf containing cosmetics and other items. On the desk, upper right, is a typewriter, a filing box, and a few additional objects that denote "organization." A tombstone is on display—so is a clothes dummy, wearing a festive

red gown. The gown is something a madam in a cat house might wear, and that is where Hiley got it.

HILEY: (*Holding a card before Mrs. Moxem*) Choosing a card is one thing. Finding it (*Returning the card to the deck*) after hiding it (*Dispersing the deck into the base of the coffin*) . . . now that's something else. The trick is concentration . . . (*Reaching into the coffin, he pulls up not only the card, but the entire deck which falls into the shape of a "card castle"*) . . . which isn't a trick at all. (*He removes a loose card from the top of the castle and shows it to her*) Your card, dear lady. Thank you. (*The cards slip back into the base of the coffin. Hiley gathers the deck together*) Last one. Lights out. Oh, you may not be tired now, but you will be—and tomorrow's a big day.

(*A long arm appears from behind the curtain. Hiley stares in astonishment as the curtain parts. The arm belongs to a woman who is alive and well and lying in one of Hiley's display caskets*)

HILEY: Miss Sneed!

ARIEL: Good evening.

HILEY: Good morning.

ARIEL: Is it morning already? How long did I sleep?

HILEY: How long have you been there?

ARIEL: You weren't here when I arrived. What time is it now?

HILEY: Four minutes past five.

ARIEL: Oh, thank goodness. I thought it was after six.

HILEY: How did you get in?

ARIEL: The parlor door was open.

HILEY: I beg to differ. It was locked.

ARIEL: The parlor door was easy to open. (*She starts to get up; Hiley helps her out*) I hope you don't mind that I let myself in.

HILEY: As a matter of fact, I do.

(*Ariel notices the corpse*)

ARIEL: Did someone die while I was napping? I crossed my fingers that no one would. Dead people give me the willies.

HILEY: Just what are you doing here?

ARIEL: I'm waiting for the train.

HILEY: This is not the depot.

ARIEL: I tried waiting at the depot, but I arrived too early—hours ahead of time. So, I decided to take a walk—stretch my legs. By the time I reached your display window, I just felt compelled to lie down . . . That is one comfortable coffin. Cushions must be made of silk.

HILEY: They are.

ARIEL: From the street it looked like silk, but I couldn't be sure until I climbed inside.

HILEY: As a rule, I don't permit that. If I let everyone test out the caskets, why the cushions would tear and the wood would get scratched. (*He takes a cloth and begins wiping the wood of the casket she'd been in*)

ARIEL: I understand the dilemma and I won't do it again. I promise.

HILEY: (*Handing her his business card*) Good. Then you're always welcome in the parlor, when it's open, during shop hours. Of course, I don't open until 9:00 a.m.

ARIEL: (*Politely returning the card*) During the day I'd be wasting your time. I'm not shopping to buy. I don't really need one . . . How much are you asking for this particular model?

HILEY: Three hundred dollars.

ARIEL: Good heavens! Sarah Bernhardt has one just like it. I wonder if she paid that much. Of course she bought hers in France. Things might be less expensive there.

HILEY: I wouldn't know.

ARIEL: Neither would I. But I would assume Miss Bernhardt could afford almost anything. I read in a recent article that she runs an extravagant household. Wild animals, including a leopard, occupy her salon. Salon is the Parisian word for parlor.

HILEY: Where does she keep this coffin?

ARIEL: In her bedroom.

HILEY: What's it doing there?

ARIEL: That's where she sleeps.

HILEY: In a coffin?

ARIEL: A bed for Miss Bernhardt would be mundane.

HILEY: Why?

ARIEL: She's the greatest actress of our time.

HILEY: What does a coffin have to do with it?

ARIEL: I'm not sure . . . perhaps it relaxes her. In preparing for a demanding role, an actress must find solace somewhere. What could be more peaceful than the bed of eternal rest? (*Ariel smiles; Hiley doesn't*) The article didn't say exactly why she slept in one, but she does what she pleases and I admire everything she does. (*Hiley is not convinced*) I'm sorry I jimmied the lock. I'll never do it again. (*She shakes his hand*) Good-bye, Mr. Bedsal. (*She starts to leave*)

HILEY: Hold on there!

(*Ariel stops dead in her tracks*)

Call me Hiley.

ARIEL: Good-bye, Hiley. Good-bye ... (*Tentatively approaching the work coffin and peering in*) ... Mrs. Moxem? Is that Mrs. Moxem?

HILEY: Who did you think it was?

ARIEL: I just assumed it was ... I don't know, some old tart.

HILEY: Why?

ARIEL: (*Referring to the clothes dummy*) The dress. Is that her burial gown?

HILEY: (*Smiling proudly*) Don't you like it?

ARIEL: (*Politely*) It's nice—it's festive. But what would Mrs. Moxem think?

HILEY: I picked it out with her in mind.

ARIEL: But is it appropriate?

HILEY: For what?

ARIEL: For death.

HILEY: Almost anything will do.

ARIEL: But for a funeral. Her friends will be shocked.

HILEY: Her friends won't be there. She outlived everyone she liked. Everyone's gone, except me. And I wanted to go home earlier than I did, but she kept offering these cheddar cheese things and the card game lasted until 2:00 a.m. ...

ARIEL: You were at her house this evening?

HILEY: Of course.

ARIEL: Who else was there?

HILEY: Just me.

ARIEL: How did she die?

HILEY: Laughing—at something I said. I don't remember being funny, but I guess she thought I was.

ARIEL: Is that why you ...

HILEY: What?

(*Ariel peeks at the body*)

Checking for marks?

ARIEL: Why would I do that?

HILEY: You think I killed her.

ARIEL: What a thought. It never occurred to me until you said it just now.

HILEY: I said, I just happened to be with her when she died.

ARIEL: Have you notified the authorities?

HILEY: I know how to do my job. I do it very well as a matter of fact. Do you think I really like cheddar cheese puff balls? I just ate them to be polite. And she cheats at cards. I knew that before we started playing—but I let her win. Everyone deserves a final pleasure. (*He begins brushing Mrs. Moxem's hair*) And if I hadn't been with her, she would have died alone.

ARIEL: This evening?

HILEY: Oh, yes.

ARIEL: How did you know?

HILEY: That she'd die tonight? It's hard to say.

ARIEL: It does seem strange that you just happened to be in the vicinity. And this isn't the first time I've noticed the coincidence. I'm referring to the untimely demise of Mr. Hopper.

HILEY: Of course I was around when he keeled over. Everyone in town was. It's not hard to be nearby in Grayson.

ARIEL: But you never paid him a speck of attention until the week before he died—and all that week you were pruning his bushes and mowing his lawn . . .

HILEY: It needed doing and he wasn't going to get it done.

ARIEL: And what about Miss Twitchell?

HILEY: What about Miss Twitchell?

ARIEL: I was sure you were courting her, and then two weeks into the courtship . . . need I say more?

HILEY: I wasn't courting Miss Twitchell.

ARIEL: You took her to the horse show and you bought her that beautiful hat.

HILEY: I wanted to give her a final pleasure.

ARIEL: How did you know she needed one!

HILEY: I am not the kiss of death.

ARIEL: Then who are you! . . . Please don't take offense, but in my opinion there is something unusual about you. (*Hiley seems confused*) Surely I am not the first to notice your distinction. (*Hiley nods*) Haven't you ever been told, by a close personal acquaintance perhaps that . . .

HILEY: I don't have a close personal acquaintance.

ARIEL: Oh.

HILEY: Most of my friendships are made in passing.

ARIEL: I see. Then let me be the first to say that you are remarkably different from anyone I've ever met.

HILEY: Thank you. You are too. Delightfully so.

ARIEL: Sometimes different is not delightful. Sometimes it's just plain odd.

HILEY: Please don't think that I would ever use that word to describe you.

ARIEL: Hiley, I'm using that word to describe you.

HILEY: How strange that you would come to that conclusion, considering we've never been formally introduced.

ARIEL: We didn't have to be. I've been watching you for quite some time.

HILEY: (*Pleased*) You have? Why?

ARIEL: You know things.

HILEY: Pardon?

ARIEL: You know more than a person should. Actually, you're more than odd. You're . . .

HILEY: Odd is breaking into a funeral showroom and mussing up the caskets!

ARIEL: I only slept in one.

HILEY: Just the idea of doing what you did—laying in a coffin before your time. That is more than odd. That is grotesque.

ARIEL: Sarah Bernhardt does it!

HILEY: In Paris, France. You are from Paris, Kentucky.

ARIEL: How did you know that?

HILEY: I have a card on you in my file.

(*Hiley motions to the desk. Ariel picks up the file box. Hiley nods and she opens it. She skims through the cards*)

ARIEL: Why, you have a card on everyone in town.

HILEY: Filed alphabetically.

ARIEL: Why?

HILEY: I like organization.

ARIEL: But cards . . .

HILEY: Listing birthdates and other pertinent facts. Can't order a tombstone unless I know when a person was born.

ARIEL: For the inscription?

HILEY: Believe me, it comes in handy. Everyone deserves a marker, but not everyone remembers to order one.

ARIEL: (*Regarding the tombstone on display*) Did you make this yourself?

HILEY: No . . . I order my tombstones from a company in Kansas City.

ARIEL: (*Reading the inscription*) "Mary Louise Moxem. Born August 6th 1813. Died August 6th . . ."

HILEY: 1912. Ninety-nine years old today. I brought a cake to her party. Made that myself. But we had those cheese puff things instead.

ARIEL: The tombstone arrived with the inscription?

HILEY: Oh, yes.

ARIEL: When?

HILEY: Last week.

ARIEL: Now see what I mean. That is down right uncanny!

HILEY: I don't think so. Mailed the requisition form in last March.

(*Ariel returns to the desk and frantically begins looking through the file*)

Can I be of assistance?

ARIEL: I'm not in here. I don't exist.

HILEY: Of course you do.

ARIEL: Then where am I? Seevers, Sinclair, Sleeper, no Sneed . . .

HILEY: Try looking under Bright. Ariel Bright. You do prefer that don't you to Enid Sneed?

ARIEL: (*Taken aback*) Ariel Bright is not my Christian name.

HILEY: It's your stage name.

ARIEL: That's a secret.

(*He finds the card and sets it on the lid of the box*)

HILEY: Ariel Bright.

ARIEL: It lists my birthdate and where I was born but it doesn't say anything about . . .

(*Hiley crosses to the shelf and picks up several cosmetic tins*)

HILEY: When you're going to die? No, I don't list everything.

ARIEL: But you know.

(*Hiley smiles and returns to the work coffin*)

If you know, tell me. It's soon isn't it? I knew it all along. I haven't been feeling or looking my best. My hands are always cold —even in August and occasionally I feel this twinge . . .

HILEY: Slow down. No need to rush things. You're not going to die young.

ARIEL: It's too late to die young. I'm thirty-five.

HILEY: You'll live to be twice that and more.

ARIEL: (*Takes a deep breath*) How much more?

HILEY: A lot more.

ARIEL: How do you know?

HILEY: I just do.

ARIEL: I have time?

HILEY: Yes.

ARIEL: To do what I want to do? (*Her hand caresses the curtain. She runs her fingers along the wood of the casket she'd been in*)

HILEY: If you set your mind to it. Quit fussing with that. Ariel, come away from there.

ARIEL: (*Returning from behind the curtain*)
"Grave sir, hail! I come
To answer thy best pleasure; be't to fly, to swim, to dive
into the fire:
To ride on the curl'd clouds; to thy strong bidding task . . .
(*She curtsies*) Ariel and all her quality."

HILEY: (*Applauding*) That was very good.

ARIEL: Do you really think so?

HILEY: Oh, yes.

ARIEL: I've never been on stage, but I've memorized every line from every play Shakespeare's ever written.

HILEY: And you say those lines with distinction.

ARIEL: Have you seen many plays?

HILEY: No. But I admire the theatre profession.

ARIEL: So do I. More than I admire any other. Not to cast aspersions on what you do—but acting—if I had my way, I would see a play every night.

HILEY: Or be in one.

ARIEL: That goes without saying.

HILEY: What time is your audition tomorrow?

ARIEL: (*He's beginning to know too much*) . . . 3:00 p.m.

HILEY: Then you'll be catching the 6:00 a.m. train. You are going to Kansas City aren't you—to audition?

ARIEL: I don't remember discussing this with you.

HILEY: You didn't.

ARIEL: You just knew? (*Hiley nods*) It's bad luck to even talk about it. (*She knocks on the wood of the work coffin*) It's foolish to call it an audition. I don't consider myself a professional actress. Audition is a professional term.

HILEY: I've never seen you as anything but an actress. You have a wonderful carriage. You're a pleasure to watch.

ARIEL: (*Surprised*) Thank you.

HILEY: (*Smiling*) You're welcome.

ARIEL: First time I've heard that. I've been auditioning for a while now—fifteen years. And in all that time no one has said, *"Thank you, Miss Bright. You're a pleasure to watch."*

HILEY: Not even a thank you. (*Ariel shakes her head*) That's rude.

ARIEL: Not rude. Rude means uncouth, uncultivated, unpolished. The Royal Kansas City Shakespeare Touring Company is anything but that. Are you familiar with their work?

HILEY: No, but I'll be sure to acquaint myself when you join their company. (*Afraid he has said too much, he begins to scout about the room for something*) There's a wonderful bottle of nail paste hiding somewhere.

(*Ariel spots the jar on the desk and picks it up*)

ARIEL: Looking for this?

HILEY: Yes.

ARIEL: (*Hands it to him*) I thought it was a bottle of blood.

HILEY: Blood isn't really this color.

ARIEL: Nail paste matches the dress.

HILEY: That's why I bought it.

ARIEL: Sure you want to color her nails?

(Hiley is coloring Mrs. Moxem's nails)
HILEY: Yes.
ARIEL: I don't believe Mrs. Moxem wore nail paste.
HILEY: She didn't. But that doesn't mean she didn't want to.
ARIEL: *(Cautiously)* If someone asks where I am tomorrow—not that they will—but you will keep it a secret.
HILEY: If you like.
ARIEL: Good. Those kids I teach have teased me before. And their parents don't care for me either. One child reported that her mother said, "Enid Sneed gives herself airs." When she said that I felt like hiding.
(Hiley is standing on his toes, trying to reach something on the top shelf)
What do you need?
HILEY: Emery board. I don't know why I put it up so high.
ARIEL: I don't know how you got it up there. *(She hands it to him)*
HILEY: You are tall.
ARIEL: Grotesquely tall?
HILEY: No.
ARIEL: Without shoes I'm six-foot-one.
HILEY: *(Impressed)* That's tall.
ARIEL: *(Not pleased at all)* For a Thespian it's unheard of. Actors are the tiniest human beings I've ever seen. And they don't grow. Actor-managers are even shorter and they're the ones who do the hiring. Mr. Madox, he's the manager I hate the most and last summer I was so tired of being turned down I said to him, "I could pick you up and drop you and from the height you'd be falling from, it would hurt!" He's dead now.
ARIEL *and* HILEY: *(Simultaneously)* Trolley car.
ARIEL: A great actor—but a rotten pedestrian.
HILEY: Maybe someone taller took his place.
ARIEL: I doubt it.
HILEY: Seems to me . . . yes, I remember reading about his replacement. Frank Ramsay. Isn't he the new actor-manager for the Royal Kansas City Shakespeare Touring Company?
ARIEL: Yes.
HILEY: Said in the article he was real tall.
ARIEL: It did not.
HILEY: Did too. Didn't you read that article?
ARIEL: No, and you didn't either.
HILEY: Guess you don't subscribe to the *Mortician Observer*.

ARIEL: There's no such paper. And you didn't read any article about Frank Ramsay being tall. Besides, even if he is tall, that doesn't mean he's going to hire tall people.

HILEY: But if he's six-foot-three, his leading lady could be six-foot-one or six-foot-two if she wore shoes.

ARIEL: That is, if he's six-foot-three.

HILEY: He is.

ARIEL: Don't say things like that to me, Hiley. I don't want to know.

HILEY: Of course you don't. Mind handing me the cold cream. (*Ariel brings it to him*)

ARIEL: Getting ready to do the face?

HILEY: It won't be easy. She wants to look a certain way.

(*Hiley has laid the cosmetics out on the table. Ariel begins to peruse through them and there are quite a lot to peruse*)

ARIEL: I see you have the complete Lady Beechum collection. Heavens, look at all this. If I used cosmetics, which I don't, I would purchase Lady Beechum. What a delightful lip rouge. Lovely shade. Did you buy this at Norwood's?

HILEY: Yes.

ARIEL: Well, I must pay the drugstore a visit. Not to buy, just to try it on.

HILEY: You could try it on here.

ARIEL: It looks like you've used it before.

HILEY: I haven't worn it.

ARIEL: No, but you've applied it to the lips of others.

HILEY: Yes.

(*Not wishing to put it on, she still finds it difficult to put down*)

ARIEL: May I put it on Mrs. Moxem?

HILEY: You'll have to touch her.

ARIEL: I know.

HILEY: Dead people give you the willies.

ARIEL: But cosmetics don't. I'll use this. And this. And . . . oh, violet eye powder. May I use this too? No, no, it wouldn't be right for Mrs. Moxem.

HILEY: Sure it would. That's why I have it out.

ARIEL: I can't use everything.

HILEY: I would.

ARIEL: If I do, she might look a bit brash.

HILEY: That's fine.

ARIEL: This is a woman who taught Bible classes.

HILEY: I know. (*To Mrs. Moxem*) I attended them. (*To Ariel*) Be generous.

ARIEL: Well, all right.

(She begins to prepare the collection in the order it will be used, occasionally glancing at Mrs. Moxem to see if her choice is appropriate)
"Her vestal livery is but sick and green
And none but fools do wear it, cast it off.
It is my lady, O it is my love.
O that she knew she were.
She speaks, yet she says nothing: what of that?
Her eye discourses. I will answer it. *(Tries to dab powder on Mrs. Moxem's eyelid)*
I am too bold." *(Pulls back)*
I don't think I can touch her. *(Dying to put the makeup on, she overcomes her fear)* I did.

(Hiley is busy arranging flowers. He takes the vase and heads for the parlor)
Hiley, don't go away . . .

HILEY: I'm just going to bring these flowers out front. I'll be back. Mrs. Moxem, you behave yourself. *(To Ariel)* She has a tendency to squirm around. *(He disappears behind the curtain)*

ARIEL: Hiley! *(Touching the body with caution)* I'm going to apply just a touch more of this. *(With more confidence now)* A bit more of that. *(Truly enjoying herself)* And as much eye powder as your lids can hold. Before I'm through, you are going to look better than Julia Marlowe. Everyone says she's so striking—so professional . . . *(Sing-song voice)* But she talks like this . . . And she sweeps at the air with her arms . . . *(Ariel's arms sweep at the air)* . . . I saw her do *Much Ado About Nothing* and that's exactly what it was.

(Hiley returns with a small satchel in his hand)
HILEY: Don't get carried away. Remember, you have a train to catch.

ARIEL: The 6:15.

HILEY: The 6:00 a.m.

ARIEL: That's right.

HILEY: How long are you planning to stay in Kansas City?

ARIEL: Well, if I'm hired, I'll tour the country. We'll head west first and then we'll move south and from there we'll travel to New York City. By the time we return to Missouri—that could be a year from now. And I might not even come back to Missouri. I might go on to Europe instead.

HILEY: You certainly travel light for a person doing so much traveling. Is this your suitcase?

(Ariel nods and crosses to him, taking the bag and placing it on the desk)

ARIEL: Thank you. I didn't want to leave it behind.

HILEY: Do you have things packed at home that you can send for if you get the job?

ARIEL: I suppose. I used to pack a suitcase, but I don't do that anymore.

HILEY: If you're hired, just send me a telegram and I'll rush over to that boarding house and pack up everything you have.

ARIEL: You are the sweetest man, Hiley, truly you are.

HILEY: Thank you.

ARIEL: But don't waste your day waiting for that telegram.

HILEY: Oh, I'll be here anyway.

ARIEL: But I can't say for sure that I'll attend the audition.

HILEY: Pardon?

ARIEL: I'm not saying I won't. I just can't envision being turned away again.

HILEY: This year you may not be.

ARIEL: I won't permit myself that thought—and for two weeks I haven't slept just for thinking about it. I don't know why I put myself through it anymore. It's not a pleasant experience. Last year they wouldn't even see me. I waited all day—waited all year for the opportunity to reacquaint them with my talent. I told a fib when I said I told Mr. Madox off.

HILEY: I know.

ARIEL: I would have picked him up and dropped him, but that man was so minuscule, I didn't even see him leave.

HILEY: Trolley car didn't see him either.

ARIEL: In fifteen summers I only met him once. He employed a lot of people who kept telling me I was wasting his time.

HILEY: Who says those people are working for Frank Ramsay?

ARIEL: Who says they aren't? People don't change.

HILEY: No one's forcing you to go to Kansas City.

ARIEL: I bought a train ticket, but it can be refunded.

HILEY: Possibly.

ARIEL: What! Won't J.C. Ewalt give me my money back? (*Hiley shrugs*) Oh, he's like everyone else in Grayson. I wouldn't be a bit surprised if he did deny me my refund. Never has a town been populated by a greater collection of unkind, inconsiderate, small-minded . . .

HILEY: Not everyone fits that description.

(*A beat. Ariel smiles*)

ARIEL: No, not everyone.

(*Ariel catches his glance. Hiley breaks the mood*)

HILEY: As I said, just let me know what you want packed.

ARIEL: Yes, Hiley.

HILEY: Do you have anything you'd like sent that isn't in your room? A pair of your shoes are at the repair shop, I believe.

ARIEL: I'll buy new shoes if I become a famous actress.

HILEY: Yes, you will.

ARIEL: Buy new shoes, or become a famous actress?

HILEY: Pardon?

ARIEL: You aren't suggesting, are you that . . .

HILEY: I didn't say anything. Now when you send that telegram, address it to Hileah Bedsal, not Hiley—That's just a nickname.

ARIEL: You act like I'm going to get the part. (*Hiley smiles*) What's so funny? . . . I am going to get the part?

HILEY: I didn't say that.

ARIEL: Then what are you saying?

HILEY: I mustn't say.

ARIEL: Hiley!

HILEY: It's not as if you're going to die. If you were, I'd tell you whatever you wanted to know—just to give you a final pleasure. But . . .

ARIEL: (*Cornering him*) It's not fair to hint at something and then not say it.

HILEY: You're right. It's wrong to hint and I have a tendency towards it, so I don't socialize much. But when I like someone the way I like you . . . there's such a temptation. For instance . . . (*Breaking away*)

ARIEL: Hiley!

HILEY: I met Claude Polmeir going into the post office and I could have saved him the trip by telling him, "You don't have any mail." But I didn't. I let him go right on in and find out for himself.

ARIEL: I'm not going to get the part.

HILEY: No, no . . . that's not what I said.

ARIEL: Then say what you are trying to say.

HILEY: I can't tell you what it is.

ARIEL: You mean, you refuse.

HILEY: I refuse.

ARIEL: If you don't tell me . . . (*She spots a bottle on the shelf and grabs it*) If you don't tell me, I'm going to drink this bottle of embalming fluid.

HILEY: Ariel, don't.

ARIEL: "Eyes look your last!
Arms, take your last embrace! And, lips, O you
The doors of breath, seal with a righteous kiss
A dateless bargain to engrossing death!"

(*She throws her head back—ready to drink*)
HILEY: You'll get the part!
ARIEL: What?
HILEY: Frank Ramsay will hire you.
ARIEL: Oh, my. Oh, my . . . Hiley!
(*She rushes to embrace him. He wraps his arms around her. She lets go*)
ARIEL: Did I hurt you?
HILEY: No.
ARIEL: This is the most wonderful thing that's ever happened to me.
HILEY: That will happen to you.
ARIEL: And it will happen?
HILEY: Yes.
ARIEL: I'll be part of the company? Playing all sorts of roles?
HILEY: Oh, yes.
ARIEL: All the time?
HILEY: Shakespeare—every night of the week except Sunday.
ARIEL: Shakespeare?
HILEY: That's right.
(*Ariel collapses on the stool*)
What's wrong?
ARIEL: I've forgotten all my Shakespeare. Every last verse. I must have swallowed some of that embalming fluid. Not enough to kill me, just enough to totally destroy my mind.
HILEY: (*Checking the bottle*) You couldn't have. The cap was on.
ARIEL: (*Backing away*) Vapors . . . vapors escape.
HILEY: (*Approaching her*) You better sit down.
ARIEL: Don't touch me! You've touched a dead person with those hands.
HILEY: So have you.
ARIEL: (*Furiously wiping her hands together*) What part will he give me tomorrow?
HILEY: Lady Macbeth.
ARIEL: They're doing the Scottish play? Bad luck from day one. Lord help me.
HILEY: I don't know why you're getting so upset.
ARIEL: You don't know? You mean there's finally something you don't know?
HILEY: I wish I'd kept my mouth shut. (*Returns to Mrs. Moxem*)
ARIEL: So do I.
HILEY: I just wanted to brighten your spirits.

ARIEL: It didn't work.

HILEY: I'm usually so good at it. Made Mrs. Moxem laugh tonight.

ARIEL: She was about to die. I have a long road of misery ahead, and I truly regret knowing about it.

HILEY: But you'll be acting.

ARIEL: With those tiny little people. Scurrying about the stage. Getting in my way.

HILEY: Frank Ramsay's six-foot-three.

ARIEL: And the biggest idiot I'll ever meet. Choosing an amateur to play Lady Macbeth. Only an amateur would do such a thing. My high regard for the Royal Kansas City Shakespeare Touring Company has been put to rest—completely.

HILEY: I'm sorry to hear that.

ARIEL: So am I.

HILEY: You planning on missing that train?

ARIEL: What time is it?

HILEY: 5:29.

ARIEL: No time to pack.

HILEY: Sure there is.

ARIEL: They'll expect me to come with costumes. And I haven't any to speak of. I made a few over the years but they're starting to look peculiar.

HILEY: If you're low on clothes, I could lend you some. Really, I've got three dresses in this chest just gathering dust.

ARIEL: Doubt they'll fit.

HILEY: You could let out the hem.

ARIEL: Those dresses belong to dead people.

HILEY: Eventually, but not yet. I'm a whole year ahead in funeral plans.

ARIEL: That's sweet, Hiley—but I'll bring what I have. If I decide to go.

HILEY: Not much time to decide.

ARIEL: I'm aware of that. I have a great deal to think about. My teaching career, for one. I do get the summers off. That's not something you just throw away.

HILEY: And you'll work all the time as an actress.

ARIEL: (*Nonchalantly*) Oh?

HILEY: Yes . . . all over the world. And when you're not working, you'll be with friends. You'll have one of those saloons like Sarah Bernhardt has.

ARIEL: A salon?

HILEY: Just jammed with interesting people. Painters, sculptors, dancers, writers—lounging on your furniture, eating your food

—talking to you night and day. My, what a whirlwind you'll be part of.

ARIEL: They'll all be famous?

HILEY: So will you.

ARIEL: Heavens.

(*Hiley rushes to her*)

HILEY: What?

ARIEL: I think I'm going to be sick.

(*He walks her to a chair and kneels next to her*)

HILEY: Hold my hand now. Yes, just relax. You've had a terrible shock. It's not every day a person learns they don't have to be unhappy.

ARIEL: You do have a soothing touch. I bet you're a marvelous mortician.

HILEY: (*Gently*) I'm the best.

(*Ariel stares at him for a moment too long*)

Ariel, you all right?

ARIEL: (*She's not*) Yes, I'm fine.

HILEY: Sure?

ARIEL: I just had a flash of something.

HILEY: (*Concerned*) Pain?

ARIEL: No. It's not that. Never mind. I'll be fine.

HILEY: Feel well enough to travel?

ARIEL: I guess.

HILEY: Well, time's awaiting, lady fair.

ARIEL: I know. I just had a flash that if I stayed . . .

HILEY: (*Abruptly*) Yes, well, can't think about that.

ARIEL: But I am. I know what would happen.

HILEY: So do I.

ARIEL: And you still want me to leave?

HILEY: (*No*) Yes.

ARIEL: Would I make you that miserable?

HILEY: I'm not the one who'd be miserable.

ARIEL: Oh.

HILEY: It's really for the best.

ARIEL: I suppose . . . It is a shame.

HILEY: I know. I've thought about it often.

ARIEL: You have?

HILEY: Yes.

ARIEL: I don't have to leave.

HILEY: No, you don't.

ARIEL: Tell me what to do.

HILEY: You decide.

(*A beat. They kiss*)

You are indeed a pleasure, Miss Ariel Bright.
(*Ariel turns to him and smiles. She starts to get up. Hiley extends his hand to help her*)
ARIEL: Thank you. (*Gently, she lets go of his hand and crosses to the desk*) What time is it getting to be? . . . It will take me five minutes to get to the boarding house. Fifteen to throw something in the suitcase. Should I take time out to wash my face? Does it look like I've been emotional?
HILEY: No . . .
ARIEL: How much time does that leave me to get to the train?
HILEY: I'll drive you in the hearse. There's room to lie down in the back if you start feeling sick again.
ARIEL: What about Mrs. Moxem? Is it all right to leave her here?
HILEY: Do you want to bring her along?
ARIEL: Do we have to?
HILEY: No, I'll pack her in ice.
(*Hiley exits through the curtain. Ariel calls after him*)
ARIEL: How long will that take?
HILEY: (*Calling back*) No time at all.
(*Hiley returns with a pair of earmuffs, a scarf, and a bucket of ice. Ariel watches as he begins assembling Mrs. Moxem in a winter wardrobe*)
ARIEL: Do you want me to go on ahead?
HILEY: No. I'll drive you over as soon as I'm done.
ARIEL: Would you like me to crank up the hearse?
HILEY: No, I'm the only one who can get her to start. She was working earlier today. That's a good sign.
ARIEL: Maybe you shouldn't drive me then.
(*Now that Mrs. Moxem is warmly dressed, Hiley gently pours ice about her*)
HILEY: I'll get you there. (*A beat*) Train's running a little late. Ran into a snag up in Rushville. (*A beat*) Six-minute delay. (*He turns to Ariel who smiles. He begins to search his pockets*) Pocket money. Pocket money. You're going to forget your purse.
ARIEL: (*Holding her satchel*) No I won't. Now that I've been reminded.
(*Unable to find any pocket money of his own, Hiley grabs a wad of bills from the bust of the dress dummy*)
HILEY: Just in case.
(*Hiley stuffs the money in his pants pocket and then crosses to the hat rack to get his morning coat. Ariel puts her satchel down, in order to help him on with his coat, and in doing so*)

forgets to pick it up again. She heads for the curtain. He follows. She stops)

ARIEL: Wonderful dress.

HILEY: *(Admiring it as well)* So you do like it.

ARIEL: Never said I didn't.

HILEY: You think it will make her look like a tart?

ARIEL: Absolutely.

HILEY: Good. *(He smiles at Mrs. Moxem)* That's what she wanted to be.

(Hiley puts on his mortician's hat, with the long black ribbons that trail past his shoulders. The first few bars of "What A Friend We Have In Jesus" softly plays to a ragtime beat. He quickly surveys the room with his eyes, turns and then follows Ariel through the curtain. The lights fade)

The End

Gina Barnett

BLOOD BOND

Gina Barnett

With the publication of *Blood Bond*, Gina Barnett makes her debut in *Best Short Plays*, and the play appears in print here for the first time. One of the hits of Marathon '84, produced by The Ensemble Studio Theatre (E.S.T.) in Manhattan, *Blood Bond* is described by *Stages'* reviewer Debbi Wasserman as a play that "... sparkles with insight. This tender story about the love between a lonely adolescent girl and the equally lonely family maid, captures the confusions of childhood with razor sharp precision."

Gina Barnett's first play, *Hiding Places*, was performed in E.S.T.'s 1982 OCTOBERFEST. Other plays of hers include: *Alone At Last*, produced by the Manhattan Punchline Theatre and the Actors Theatre of Manhattan; and *Thank You M'am*, an adaptation of the Langston Hughes' short story, commissioned by the Triplex Theatre, produced in the spring of 1986. She was also a contributing author and research assistant for the book *Space for Dance*, published by the Cultural Resources Center.

Most of Miss Barnett's work in theatre has been as an actress or acting teacher. She is a long time member of E.S.T., and in the E.S.T. Institute for Professional Training she teaches acting technique, auditions techniques, character work, and improvisation. She has also taught acting in the theatre department at Sarah Lawrence College and conducted private classes in acting, script analysis, and scene study. Her additional professional affiliations are with the Dramatists Guild and Actors Equity Association.

Characters:

FLORENCE JONES
KAREN GERARDO

Scene:

Lights come up on Florence Jones, a middle-aged black woman. She is in her bedroom in a large suburban home where she works as a housekeeper. She is watching a soap opera on TV and ironing. The TV announcer's voice is heard on the set.

ANNOUNCER: *Eternal Love,* brought to you by UNIQUE! "You'll know her by UNIQUE! the perfume that sets her apart." UNIQUE! Perfume, toilet water and soap, for you! UNIQUE! . . . And by NO-SCRUB, the cleanser that does all the work for you. NO-SCRUB lets mother be in the know! NO-SCRUB!
(After a few moments Karen Gerardo enters. She is white and twelve years old. She is wearing a long flannel nightgown)

FLO: What are you doin' outta bed?

KAREN: I couldn't sleep.

FLO: Baby, you're sick. Sleepin's got nothin' to do with it. You're supposed to stay under the covers.

KAREN: Can I stay with you for a little while?

FLO: No slippers on, you're gonna get a chill.

KAREN: I just can't stay there any more.

FLO: Where's your mamma, why don't you go st—. . .

KAREN: I don't know. She slammed the back door, drove off real loud.

FLO: All right. Hop in. (*She peels back the covers on her bed and tucks Karen in*) Oh, now wait a second, Karen!

BRENDA: (*On soap opera*) Nathan, hello . . . Come in.

NATHAN: (*On soap opera*) You look tired. Do you feel all right?

BRENDA: I'm fine. (*A beat*) Would you like a drink?

NATHAN: Please.

BRENDA: Scotch?

NATHAN: Yes. So, did you get the results?

BRENDA: Relax, Nathan, all right?

NATHAN: Well, what did the doctor say?

BRENDA: Please, Nathan, don't push me. This isn't easy for any of us.

NATHAN: You don't have to tell me.

BRENDA: Well, then, please . . .

KAREN: What?

FLO: Shh. I gotta see this part so I can report it on to Valerie. *(They watch the TV as Brenda in the soap opera reveals the baby's father. Flo interjects)* Come on . . . come on!

BRENDA: *(Continuing, as Flo turns up the volume)* Please try to understand, Nathan. It's FRANK'S baby.

NATHAN: WHAT!

BRENDA: Yes, Frank's. And I'm going to have this baby. WE are going to have this baby. FRANK and I.

(Soap opera music up)

NATHAN: Brenda, you can't be serious.

BRENDA: I've never been more serious in my life.

(Soap opera music ends)

ANNOUNCER: We will return to our story after these messages. *Eternal Love* has been brought to you by UNIQUE! "You'll know her by UNIQUE! the perfume that sets her apart," and by NO-SCRUB, lets mother be in the know.

FLO: *(Switching off the TV)* Ummmmm, ummmmm, ummmmm. Tsk, tsk. Lord!

KAREN: Mom says these shows are dumb. "Trash made to rot the brain."

FLO: *(With an edge)* Your mamma's a smart woman.

KAREN: So why do you watch them?

FLO: One man's poison is another man's meat.

KAREN: Huh?

FLO: Eternal Love, baby. That's my program. You got to get with the program! *(To herself)* So it was Frank's baby. Ummmm, ummmm, Valerie's gonna have herself a conniption.

KAREN: How come?

FLO: Well, she was sure Brenda was lying about being pregnant. That it was just some jive she was using to get away from Nathan. Ha, ha! Course, it still could be . . .

KAREN: What's jive again?

FLO: It's made up stuff, just a lot of hooey.

KAREN: Oh . . . like Daddy's trip to Chicago?

FLO: What?

KAREN: Mommy said that Daddy just SAID he had to go to Chicago for his business, but that really wasn't true. It was jive. REALLY FLO. She told me.

FLO: Your mamma told you that? When?

KAREN: Well . . . it wasn't to me exactly. She was on the phone . . . (*Flo gives Karen a look*) I was in the tub in her bathroom and she was on the phone and I just heard it.

FLO: Ummmm hmmmm. (*A beat*) Here, help me button. (*She hands Karen some shirts and starts to exit*)

KAREN: You won't tell her that I overheard, will you?

FLO: No, baby. Come on, cover up. (*She tucks Karen in*)

KAREN: I love your bed, Flo.

FLO: I'll be right back.

(*Flo exits to bathroom. Karen picks up a bottle of nail polish on Flo's night table and starts playing with it*)

KAREN: (*Calling to Flo*) When's Daddy coming back, Flo?

FLO: (*Offstage*) Don't know, darling, soon's he's done with his business, I suppose. (*She enters with water*) Now where's the nail polish I bought you? (*Karen puts the polish down abruptly*) You want some?

KAREN: No, thanks.

FLO: You want some apple juice?

KAREN: I hope he never comes back.

FLO: How 'bout some lunch? You got to eat, darlin', get your strength up.

KAREN: I hope he dies there in Chicago, or wherever he is.

FLO: Hey, now don't say tha—

KAREN: WELL, I DO!!!

FLO: You want the Boss to hear you talk like that? She don't mean it, Lord. She's got a cold in her head.

KAREN: I don't care what God thinks. I don't believe in him anyway. I'm an atheist!

FLO: Well, bully for you!

KAREN: And I do hope Daddy dies.

FLO: Well, death comes to everybody, hopin' or not.

KAREN: Good!

FLO: Everything's gotta end sometime, ready or not.

KAREN: I know!

FLO: Everything happens according to His will. Amen.

KAREN: Well, I can still wish for stuff.

FLO: Well, wishin' for your Daddy to be called is the wrong kind of wishin'.

KAREN: Why? Mommy does. IT'S TRUE. I heard her. She said, "I hope the bastard rots in hell."

FLO: Nooooooo!

KAREN: Yeah! (*A beat*) This shirt is missing a button.

FLO: It is?

KAREN: See? Here.

FLO: Now how'd I miss that?

KAREN: Musta been when Brenda was giving Nathan the big send-off.

FLO: I'm telling you that Brenda just be struttin' her stuff front of anybody be fool enough to look . . .

KAREN: "Just be struttin' her stuff."

FLO: You makin' fun of me, girl?

KAREN: NO! No, not at all. I love the way you talk.

FLO: You do, huh.

KAREN: You never say stuff like "struttin' her stuff" in front of my parents.

FLO: It ain't like I don't with them. I just do with you, right? (*She winks*)

KAREN: Yeah . . . When are you leaving for Christmas?

FLO: Next week.

KAREN: That's soon!

FLO: Ummmm, hmmmm.

KAREN: How long you gonna be gone?

FLO: Ten days. Ten glorious days!

KAREN: What're you gonna do down there?

FLO: I'm gonna raise hell and put a chunk under it.

KAREN: You gonna miss me?

FLO: Maybe.

KAREN: You gonna miss me so much you'll wish I was there?

FLO: Maybe.

KAREN: So . . . can I go with you?

FLO: Say what?

KAREN: Can I go with you to Charlotte for Christmas?

FLO: Now where'd that idea come from?

KAREN: Can I?

FLO: Well, I don't know, honey. What would your mamma say?

KAREN: I think she'd like it.

FLO: You do, huh. You think your mamma'd approve of you bein' on the loose with a bunch of colored folk for ten days? (*Laughs*) I don't know.

KAREN: Yup.

FLO: Besides if you WAS to come down South all you'd do is grumble because you'd have to go to church.

KAREN: I wouldn't grumble . . . maybe I'd find the Lord.

FLO: That'll be the day.

KAREN: Maybe I'd testify in front of the whole congregation. I FEEEEEEL YOU LORD. PRAISE JESUS. PRAISE ME! PRAISE EVERYBOD—

FLO: YOU CUT THAT OUT BEFORE I GIVE YOU A WHIPPIN' YOU AIN'T LIKELY NEVER TO FORGET!! (*Karen freezes*) You think you can make fun of my people? Hmmm? Answer me when I asks you a question, child.

KAREN: No.

FLO: Then you quit this here foolishness right now, you hear me?

KAREN: Yes.

FLO: Now I said get under, and settle down.

KAREN: I didn't mean anything by it, I was just . . .

FLO: It don't matter what you mean. It's how you act. If you was to pull that in front of my mamma she'd . . .

KAREN: I wouldn't. NEVER. I swear . . .

FLO: I mean we may be poor, and we may not have all this here "higher education," but we was raised right and we stick together. That's right. The Hendersons is one tight clan through thick and thin. Which is more than I can say 'bout some people round here.

(*Pause*)

KAREN: Well, what about Raymond? If all you Hendersons stick together so much . . .

FLO: Raymond ain't no Henderson. He's a Jones. Remember my married name is Jones?

KAREN: Oh, that's right. But if you marry somebody . . .

FLO: I'm not talkin' 'bout marriage. I'm talking family: mother, father, sister, brothers.

KAREN: Yeah, but if you marry somebody, he becomes family, too.

FLO: It ain't the same thing. Marriage ain't binding in the same way. You know what I'm saying? It ain't blood.

KAREN: But it is the same thing. Families have to start somewhere. You get married, that makes a family just as much as if you're born into one.

FLO: Not if it's barren.

KAREN: Huh?

FLO: If it's barren. If there's no children. Children's what makes the blood bond. The glue. No children, no blood bond.

(*Silence. Something heavy falls between them*)

KAREN: Well, how come you and Raymond didn't have any kids . . . huh?

FLO: You know you look a little flushed to me. (*She feels Karen's forehead*)

KAREN: I'm okay.

FLO: No, you feel a little warm darlin'.

KAREN: I'm okay. Come on, why?

FLO: Why, what?

KAREN: Why didn't you and Raymond have any . . .

FLO: Because for reasons that are not for young girls' ears, that's why.

KAREN: I am not "young." I'm gonna be in high school soon, and they "do it," in high school, you know.

FLO: Girl, you start "doin it," before you're ready, and I'll . . .

KAREN: Come on, Flo, I'm old enough to know these things.

FLO: That so? (*Holding thermometer*) Come on, open up.

KAREN: Not till you tell me.

FLO: Yeah? (*Karen nods with glee*) Well, I ain't gonna tell you till you open up. (*Karen opens her mouth, Flo sticks in the thermometer*) Under your tongue, darlin'. Okay. Keep it shut. (*Flow goes back to her ironing and starts to hum*)

KAREN: Flo . . . Flo . . . Come on . . . THAT'S NOT FAIR! THAT'S NOT FAIR, FLO!! YOU SAID YOU'D TELL ME IF I . . .

FLO: ALL RIGHT! Settle down. Settle down. Girl, you wear me to a thread sometimes. We couldn't have no children 'cause I got trouble with my female parts.

KAREN: Oh . . . Well, what kind of trouble?

FLO: Well, what kinda trouble . . .

KAREN: Come on, Flo . . .

FLO: What you want some kinda blow by blow? (*Karen nods vigorously*) Well, there ain't none. (*Flo starts to hum*)

KAREN: So that's it? The end?

FLO: You know you got to learn to appreciate signals better.

KAREN: Huh?

FLO: Now I already told you, people don't like it when you get nosey. When somebody gives you a signal, it's your job to just shut your mouth and look like you're already busy thinking on something else. (*Flo hums again*)

KAREN: Oh. So that was it for you and babies, huh?

FLO: Lord, this child. Yes. That was it for me and babies, huh. The end.

KAREN: You could've adopted . . .

FLO: Gimme that thing since you're spending more time blowing on it than . . . (*Karen hands her the thermometer*)

KAREN: Lisa Sablow at school's adopted. That's the first thing she always says when she meets someone. "Hi, my name is Lisa Sablow. I'm adopted." Very creepy.

FLO: Ummmm hmmmm. Not too bad, 100 degrees. Come on, stay covered-up.

KAREN: So did you ever think of that? Adopting?

FLO: Not really . . .

KAREN: Oh.

FLO: See . . . Raymond got another woman pregnant, and decided that's where God meant him to be.

KAREN: So he left you? (*Flo nods. A beat*) So you moved in here.

FLO: Well, yeah. But not right away.

KAREN: But when I was just a baby?

FLO: Ten months!

KAREN: So you adopted me.

FLO: In a way. Yeah, I guess I did. Lord, you were the cutest little thing I ever did see. You had little bitty hands, they was no bigger than, than . . .

KAREN: Look now. (*Karen holds up her hand*) Gimme yours. (*Flo puts her hand up to Karen's*) Almost as big as yours!

FLO: Well, not quite.

KAREN: Soon though.

FLO: Oh. Let's see now, any new developments. (*She looks at Karen's palm*) Ummmm hmmmm, ummmmm, hmmmmm, ummmmm . . .

KAREN: Tell!

FLO: Ooooooh, looks like romance on the horizon!

KAREN: Yuk! No way!

FLO: Well, I see it, right . . .*there!* (*Slowly tickling her way up Karen's arm*) And . . . I see maybe a looooong trip to someplace special . . . (*Karen starts to giggle. Flo starts to lightly tickle and pinch Karen, an old game between them*) Where there's itsey bitsey bugs and itsey bitsey bites, and . . . (*Karen breaks into peals of laughter as Flo tickles and hugs her*) . . . itsey bitsey gobbledygooks that go . . .

KAREN: Stop! Stop!

(*Laughing they both settle into each other's arms. After a moment Karen stiffens and begins to move away*)

FLO: What?

KAREN: Nothing . . .

FLO: Karen? . . . Honey? . . . I swear, you acting just like a weather vane in a hurricane.

KAREN: Daddy says we're too close.

FLO: Who, you and me? (*Karen nods*) He tell you this?

KAREN: No, I heard him tell Mom. Remember the night they were yelling so loud I asked if I could come eat with you?

FLO: Yeah, I remember.

KAREN: Well, later I heard him say that I spend too much time with you and that it's "unnatural."

FLO: Unnatural. What'd your mamma say?

KAREN: She didn't agree. She said something like "You're not stuck in the house all day like I am. I need relief and Flo's a good woman." God . . . it made me feel awful to hear them talk about us that way. But I don't know. Maybe he's right. Maybe if I spent more time with them . . . Oh, God, I don't know.

FLO: Baby, listen, the fact is he's got to be here for you to spend time with him. Right? I mean, he's just not around very much now, is he?

KAREN: I was scared if I told you what he said you'd go down to Charlotte and never come back.

FLO: You know I'd never do that to you, don't you? Hmmmmm?

KAREN: No.

FLO: Well, I wouldn't. So what should we do?

KAREN: What do you mean?

FLO: You wanna start meeting in secret?

KAREN: Huh?

FLO: You know, see you in the basement 'round midnight, up in the attic to dawn.

KAREN: Yeah!

FLO: Maybe we'll just pack up our act and hit the road!

KAREN: That'd be cool!

FLO: Well, then, come on. And a one, and a two . . . (*She starts singing "Darktown Strutter's Ball."*) Come on . . . Come on. Let's see if you remember it like I taught you. (*Flo starts to sing again, and Karen joins in. They sing together for a few moments and then Flo drops out and watches as Karen continues on alone. Karen begins to dance around as well*) SMOKIN'!!! Girl, you been working on it, you're getting it down now!

KAREN: I've been practicing in the shower so nobody'll hear me.

FLO: That's my girl. You gonna be a star some day, I tell you.

KAREN: This is my favorite part. (*Karen sings the last verse of the song and continues dancing, this time wrapping a blanket around her like a boa. When she finishes the lyrics to the song, she does a rousing bit of scat singing*)

FLO: (*While Karen performs*) Sing it out now . . . (*Applauding when Karen's finished*) Yeah, girl! Yeah! You are too much. Ummmm. Ummmm. Ummm.

KAREN: Aren't I? They're gonna love me down South, I just know it!

FLO: You do, huh.

KAREN: Yup. Especially your mamma.

FLO: My mamma?

KAREN: She'll be real proud of our song, won't she, Flo!?

FLO: Hard to tell . . .

KAREN: Well, there's just one way to find out, isn't there? Take me with you to Charlotte, Flo.

FLO: Now wait just a durn minute.

KAREN: Pleeeeeease. Please. Pretty please. I won't be any trouble.

FLO: Stop your whining.

KAREN: Floooooo.

FLO: Karrrr-eeeeennnnn . . .

KAREN: But, I know already.

FLO: You know what?

KAREN: I know Mom's offered you three hundred dollars to get rid of me over Christmas.

FLO: WHAT? Where did you come up with this? Lord, this child . . .

KAREN: Don't pretend. Come on, I know. She told me.

FLO: All right! Now you listen to me, and you listen to me good. Your mamma asked me to take you home with me over Christmas, and she offered to pay me a babysitting fee and some money for your food.

KAREN: Okay, so money for . . .

FLO: And I told her that IF I decided to take you with me, which I still have not done . . .

KAREN: (*Interrupting*) But what about the money. Don't you need the money?

FLO: The money ain't got nothing to do with it. If it makes your mamma more comfortable to think I'd do it as a job, then fine. It is not my job to change your mamma's ways. But I don't do nothing I don't want to on accounta' no money.

KAREN: Three hundred dollars just wasn't enough, was it?

FLO: I think it's time you got back into your own bed now, Karen.

KAREN: No.

FLO: Yes, darlin', come on.

KAREN: Why? Why all of a sudden?

FLO: Because I said so, you're getting overheated.

KAREN: I'm too old for "I said so." Something's going on around here, and you know what it is and you won't tell me. Nobody will tell me. Nobody's TALKING to me. Mommy spends more time on the phone and rearranging the furniture than she does with me. And where's Daddy? He called me this morning, and he sounded like he was on the moon or something. He kept saying "goody-bye angel, I love you, pussy cat," like I was dying or something. Am I dying, Flo? Is there something wrong with me? Did I do something?

FLO: You didn't do nothing, honey. It's not you at all. It's something between them.

KAREN: Well, what is it? I know you know.

FLO: It's your mamma's place to tell you. I can't be tellin . . .

KAREN: NO! *YOU* TELL ME! YOU! GOD!

FLO: Where you going Karen?

KAREN: I don't want to talk to you anymore!

FLO: No. Stay, tell me what's on your . . .

KAREN: DADDY'S RIGHT. DADDY'S RIGHT!!

FLO: What?

KAREN: I SHOULDN'T SPEND SO MUCH TIME WITH YOU.

FLO: Karen!

KAREN: I shouldn't spend *any* time with you at all anymore!

FLO: What are you saying?

KAREN: IT'S ALL *YOUR* FAULT . . .

FLO: WHAT'S MY FAULT!!

KAREN: YOU TOOK ME AWAY FROM THEM.

FLO: WHAT?

KAREN: YOU TOOK AWAY THE BLOOD BOND. I WAS THEIR GLUE, AND YOU TOOK ME AWAY FROM THEM.

FLO: I DIDN'T TAKE YOU FROM NOBODY.

KAREN: YOU SAID IT YOURSELF, YOU ADOPTED ME. YOU CAME HERE RIGHT AFTER RAYMOND LEFT YOU WHEN I WAS JUST A BABY, AND YOU ADOPTED ME. MOMMY JUST NEEDED HELP WITH THE CLEANING, SHE DIDN'T NEED YOU FOR ME. I COULD'VE HELD THEM TOGETHER.

FLO: NOW YOU STOP AND YOU LISTEN TO ME. Nobody was paying you no mind. If I hadn't looked after you as much as I did . . . Lord! Do you understand what I'm saying? You couldn't a done diddley-squat cause *they wasn't around.*

KAREN: Maybe they'd been around more if you hadn't come and . . .

FLO: WELL, HOW WE GONNA FIND THAT OUT? HMMMMMM? YOU TELL ME NOW, how are we going to find that out? . . . We ain't. We are where we are and I did what I did.

KAREN: Yeah, and fuck everybody else.

FLO: DON'T YOU *DARE* TALK TO *ME* WITH *THAT* MOUTH! (*Pause*) I love you, and I don't care what you say, there ain't no sin in that. My loving you didn't stop nobody else from loving you or each other. Now if you think I'm to blame because your parents can't live together no more, you'd better open up them big eyes of yours and look around. 'Cause there's lots of white folks splitting up who ain't got no colored ladies living with them to clean up their shit, pardon my language. And I'm telling you now, you are in for some hard times ahead. That's right. So I'd think twice about making me the bad guy. You hear me? You hear me when I'm talking to you, girl?

KAREN: YES! I HEAR YOU! I ALWAYS HEAR YOU!

FLO: Well, then don't turn on me. We're all we've got here. You understand? Do you?

(*Karen keeps silent, refusing to look at Flo*)

KAREN: Yessum.

FLO: Don't you "yessum" me unless'n you mean it.

KAREN: Yes, Ma'am.

FLO: You know, you think you're the only one around here who don't get her way. Well, I got some news for you. Nobody does. Right now your mamma ain't getting her way, and your poppa ain't getting his. And I sure as hell don't get mine none too often neither.

KAREN: Yes, you do. You get to go home. You get to go to Charlotte.

FLO: Yeah, well, if I'd had my way, I never woulda' left in the first place. But that's just the way it is. The Lord's got his plan for everybody, and he brought me to you . . . And I thank him for it every day. (*Pause*) Now I made my choice. And I stand by my choice. You think on that. And you go ahead on and make yours. But may the good Lord have mercy on your soul if you come up with the wrong one.

(*Pause*)

KAREN: Is Daddy really gone?

FLO: Seems like.

KAREN: Why didn't they tell me?

FLO: Scared, I guess.

KAREN: Scared of what?

FLO: I don't know, baby, I told your mamma I thought she should tell you something, but she wanted to wait until everything was final.

KAREN: You mean he might come back?

FLO: I don't know. You never know with those two. But . . . I don't think so, honey. (*Karen remains silent*) You hungry yet? You all right?

KAREN: Yeah . . . it's better just to know.

FLO: I hear you, darlin'. Come on, cuddle up.

(*Karen gets back into Flo's bed*)

KAREN: Flo?

FLO: Hmmmm?

KAREN: What about Charlotte? (*Flo can't respond*) You're scared to tell me no, aren't you? (*Pause*) You wouldn't have anything to be ashamed of. I'd do you real proud.

FLO: I know you would, darlin'. You do already.

KAREN: Then why can't I go with you? I could see that orchard and the old school . . .

FLO: Sssh, sssh, baby, listen now. It ain't you I'm concerned with, hear? It's them. They don't know you like I do. And they's my family . . . you understand?

KAREN: Yeah. I guess.

FLO: Come on, don't worry yourself about this now. Try to sleep a bit.

KAREN: What's gonna happen to Mom?

FLO: What do you mean?

KAREN: For Christmas.

FLO: Tell you the truth, I think she's plannin' on takin' herself a little vacation.

KAREN: Where to?

FLO: Don't know. Someplace warm.

KAREN: She can play tennis.

FLO: Ummmm hmmmmm.

KAREN: So if I don't go to Charlotte with you, do I have to go with her?

FLO: Probably. (*Karen buries herself under the sheets and moans*) Come on now, baby, nobody's gonna leave you stranded. Maybe I'll just stay up here, and you and I can do something real special. Go to the city or something like that. Wouldn't that be fun?

KAREN: You mean it, Flo?

FLO: We'll see.

KAREN: But what about your family?

FLO: Well, they'll all be around for a while.

KAREN: So, it's just you and me, isn't it?

FLO: For now, baby. For now.

(*The lights fade to black*)

The End

Janet Neipris

THE AGREEMENT

Janet Neipris

Janet Neipris (Wille) makes her debut in *Best Short Plays* with *The Agreement*, a witty and poignant play, which provides a timely comment on contemporary divorce arrangements. The play, originally commissioned by the Public Broadcasting Service (PBS) as a radio drama, was broadcast in both the United States and Australia. The stage adaptation premiered in the Philadelphia Festival for New Plays at the Annenberg Center in the spring of 1985. Additional presentations have been made by the Westport (Connecticut) Arts Council and the Women's Project of the American Place Theatre. *The Agreement* appears in print for the first time in this anthology.

A writer of considerable accomplishment, Ms. Neipris is an Associate Professor at New York University's Tisch School of the Arts, where she chairs the Dramatic Writing Program. Her other plays include a series of one acts, *Statues, Exhibition*, and *The Bridge at Belharbour;* and four full-length plays, *Separations, The Desert, Out of Order,* and *Almost in Vegas,* the latter work presented to glowing reviews in New York in 1985 by Off-Broadway's Manhattan Punch Line. Her plays have had over fifty productions with professional stagings at many regional theatres including the Arena Stage Theatre in Washington, D.C., the Goodman Theatre in Chicago, Center Stage in Baltimore, the Milwaukee Repertory Theatre, and the Pittsburg Public Theatre. In New York City her work has been produced at the Harold Clurman Theatre, the Cubiculo, the Thirteenth Street Theatre, the Manhattan Theatre Club, and the Women's Project of the American Place Theatre.

For the PBS radio drama series EARPLAY, she has written a number of scripts including *The Desert, The Piano,* and the radio adaptation of *The Agreement.* Ms. Neipris has also written scripts for television, including a pilot series developed for ABC, worked for three years as a major writer for the public service series, *The Baxters,* and has numerous documentary credits.

A composer as well as a playwright, Ms. Neipris co-authored and wrote the score for a full-length musical, *Jeremy and the Thinking Machine.* She has also composed music for Kevin O'Morrison's play *Requiem,* incidental music for a recent production of Arthur Miller's *Death of a Salesman*, and the score for Circle Repertory Theatre's First Playwrights' Benefit.

The training for her work began at Tufts University where she received a B.A. in English. She then received an M.A. in English from Simmons College, and later a Masters in Fine Arts in Playwriting from Brandeis University, where she received a Sam Shubert Playwriting Fellowship. She continued her writing assisted by a Fellowship in Playwriting from the National Endowment of the Arts, awarded to her in 1979-1980, and she is currently working on a new musical.

Characters:

SYBIL MATCHETT
SIGMOND MATCHETT
ALICE BAILEY, *her lawyer*
LESTER OSTERMEYER, *his lawyer*
BORIS, *Sybil's date*
ALICIA, *Sigmund's date*
JUDGE ALBERT BELLOWS

[CASTING NOTE: The same actor may play both Boris and Judge Bellows.]

Scene One:

Time: Early evening.

Place: California. Sybil Matchett's apartment. Sybil is with her date, Boris. Her children are in an adjoining room.

SYBIL: (*Holding up a glass*) To rainy nights in California.

BORIS: (*Holding up his glass*) To rainy nights (*pause*) *and love* in California. So, do you find it exciting writing for the movies?

SYBIL: Love it, and I've certainly never met a live stunt man before. What's the hardest stunt you ever did?

BORIS: (*As in "Ooh, this is hard"*) The hardest stunt?

SYBIL: The hardest stunt . . .

BORIS: Well, I did this horror film and there's this forest fire . . .

SYBIL: (*Cutting him off and turning to the direction of the children*) Stop it! Stop it! Just eat your sushi! (*Back to Boris, shrugging*) Kids. They like to shred it to aggravate me. Excuse me.

BORIS: No big deal. (*Continuing*) *So,* the entire world is enveloped by this forest fire . . . (*Imitating the fire starting in spots over the world, jumping around*) Woo . . Woo . . . Woo! Everything's burning! Poof! (*Pause*) Actually, just the parts that have forests.

SYBIL: Naturally.

BORIS: See, it starts out as this *love* story. What I'm talking about is . . . let me show you . . . (*Getting ready to jump*) This is *perfectly* safe. Don't worry.

SYBIL: No. I'm *perfectly* calm. (*To the children*) I hear you in there! If you're not going to eat it, stop throwing it! (*Back to*

Boris) This is really hard. *They're* jumping around, and *you* are
. . .

BORIS: *SO*, it's this *love* story, and his girlfriend is down there in this forest burning, and he has to put her out . . . so he parachutes . . . like this (*Parachuting, landing on the couch beside her, listing towards her*) Terrible film . . . But what do you think of my landing?

SYBIL: I'm impressed. (*To the children, without getting up*) Just go watch Big Bird! *(Back to Boris)* In the winter, Sigmund— that's my ex—takes them to Florida to his mother's mobile home where they play Bingo all week at her Activity Center. This year he brought his girl friend, Auntie Bambi. The children said she combed her hair a lot. She also got bored with playing Bingo, so they went to Disney World where Sigmund and she wore matching Mickey Mouse shirts. (*To the children*) You are nearing the end of my rope!

BORIS: Here, let me help you. (*Getting up, yelling at the children*) Hey kids! Listen to your mother! HEY! HEY! (*Back to Sybil)* So when do they go to sleep?

SYBIL: When they get tired.

BORIS: When is that usually?

SYBIL: It varies.

BORIS: I think it would be good if we could relax.

SYBIL: I am certainly trying.

BORIS: (*Breathing in on the "Re" and out on "lax"*) Re-lax. Re-lax. (*Sybil follows him, and they do the relaxation exercise in unison*) Re-lax. Re-lax. Now when's your trial?

SYBIL: It's a pre-trial. Next week in New York. Thank you for asking.

BORIS: And how long have you been separated?

SYBIL: One year, eight months.

BORIS: Been dating?

SYBIL: I haven't slept with anybody yet if that's what you mean.

BORIS: How come?

SYBIL: Nobody's asked me.

BORIS: I'm asking you.

SYBIL: Boris, do you think I'll get the Russian samovar his Aunt Millie gave us, because it was *his* aunt, but she gave it to me, but I think I'm going to give him the pictures of the kids, seeing I have the real thing.

BORIS: (*Exasperatedly*) RE-LAX. RE-LAX, LAX, LAX.

End of Scene

(Lights fade down slowly on the above scene then up on the next scene)

Scene Two:

Time: Early evening.
Place: Sigmund Matchett's Manhattan apartment.

Sigmund and his date, Alicia, are eating, almost finished with dinner.

ALICIA: Marvelous spaghetti avec pesto sauce, Sigmund.

SIGMUND: Thank you. It's my specialty. Don't bother twirling it around the fork. Just let it hang. So I have this house on the island which costs me a thousand dollars a month upkeep and it rains every damn weekend this summer.

ALICIA: What a shame. Pauvre (*Pronouncing the "e" as in "eggs"*) Sigmund.

SIGMUND: A thousand dollars a month shame.

ALICIA: I thought psychiatrists were rich, the urban population à la Woody Allen being trés neurotic.

SIGMUND: Not ones paying for the past *and* the present.

ALICIA: That sounds very psychological.

SIGMUND: It isn't. More scotch?

ALICIA: Merci, but no.

SIGMUND: An after dinner drink? Crème de cacao, crème de menthe, Manischewitz?

ALICIA: One scotch was fine. Beautiful view you have of Central Park.

SIGMUND: Thank you ... It's curious, Alice ...

ALICIA: (*Interrupting*) Alicia.

SIGMUND: Forgive me.

ALICIA: My name's Alicia.

SIGMUND: Alicia.

ALICIA: Thank you.

SIGMUND: You know, it's curious, Alicia ... I forgot what I was going to say, I got so concerned with the name. Oh yes, I was going to ask you if you were free next weekend.

ALICIA: I don't care for the Hamptons, thank you. They don't touch me.

SIGMUND: I see. They don't touch you.

ALICIA: And I think touching's important. How long were you married, Sigmund?

SIGMUND: Ten years. Well, perhaps we can make other arrangements.

ALICIA: I've never been to the Virgin Islands.

SIGMUND: Neither have I. The Virgin Islands touch you?

ALICIA: Vastly.

SIGMUND: Vastly . . . Could you watch your ashes, Alicia. That's French country fabric on the sofa, $18.99 a yard.

ALICIA: Have you ever been to Europe?

SIGMUND: When I was in the Army.

ALICIA: My former husband was in Korea.

SIGMUND: Good for him.

ALICIA: His name was Stanley, as in Marlon Brando in *Streetcar Named Desire.*

SIGMUND: Good for Stanley.

ALICIA: He had a dark fear of intimacy, unlike Brando. So what do you think about the Virgin Islands?

SIGMUND: I can't. I have a pre-trial coming up.

ALICIA: Oh. I thought you were already divorced.

SIGMUND: Well, for all purposes, I am.

ALICIA: Well for my purposes I wish you'd told me, because I only date *completely* free men, though I have to tell you, you make a terrific pesto sauce. (*Starting to leave*)

SIGMUND: I grate the cheese myself. Asiago. That's my secret. Not Parmesan. Asiago—A-S-I-A-G-O.

ALICIA: Well, I certainly admire that.

SIGMUND: But make sure it's fresh. Sometimes they say it's fresh when it's not fresh at all. Deceit is a dreadful thing in our society, you know.

ALICIA: And when you're free absolutely, sans doubt, I'd consider a return. I'll just catch a cab. Goodnight, Sigmund.

(*She exits as Sigmund muses, unaware, in a way, that she's gone, more preoccupied*)

SIGMUND: Unfortunately, *she* took the Cuisinart, because that's the way to *really* pulverize cheese, but I'm demanding it back because I know she never uses it because she never figured out which parts go where on anything. Sybil's very unmechanical. I also want the little Mexican god we bought in Guadalajara because she insisted it looked like me. It's actually a rendering of the god, Quetzalcoatal. She called him "Quetzal." It rhymes with "pretzel." Do you know she was late for our wedding ceremony? We had to pay overtime for the hall.

End of Scene

(Lights fade down, fade up on Manhattan courtroom interior)

VOICE: *(Over loud speaker system)* Court of the Southern District of New York, Probate Division, Judge Albert Bellows presiding. First Case, Farrow versus Farrow.

Scene Three:

Time: Morning, one week later.
Place: Manhattan Courthouse Corridor. We see Alice Bailey.
Sybil enters, breathless, somewhat disheveled.

SYBIL: Am I late? The plane was late. There were seagulls on the runway.

ALICE: Relax. We're fifth in line. We'll just go over some things here in the corridor.

SYBIL: I'm sorry, Mrs. Bailey. I'm always late. I was late for my own wedding.

ALICE: Beautiful day for a divorce, Mrs. Matchett. We'll probably be here all day. They're booked solid.

SYBIL: It drove Sigmund crazy, my being late, because he's so compulsive. He said it was part of my complicated neurosis.

ALICE: Just take a seat on the bench until we're called. And Judge Bellows may not call you and Dr. Matchett in on a pre-trial. He dislikes being involved with the inevitable emotions of the adversaries.

SYBIL: What does that mean?

ALICE: The judge gets the information from the lawyers, and then we lawyers translate the information to you, and you say yes or no. *(Pause)* It eliminates the middle man.

SYBIL: Us.

ALICE: Precisely. You wait outside while the lawyers talk to the judge. Now what were the taxes on your house in California last year?

SYBIL: Well, I should think it would help the judge if he could see the real people.

ALICE: The taxes . . .

SYBIL: They're somewhere here . . . *(Dumping out the contents of her bag)* The children gave me this candy bar *(Pulling out a melted candy bar and credit cards)* as a goodbye present at the airport, which was cute, but it's melting all over my credit cards.

ALICE: This is no joking matter, Mrs. Matchett. I need the tax figures.

SYBIL: I think I'm not hearing you on purpose because I'm scared.

ALICE: *(Sharply)* Well, no one would know it. You look awfully gorgeous.

SYBIL: Thank you. It's an Oscar de la Renta. He does this dot thing.

ALICE: You might have done better to dress down.

SYBIL: You mean to dress a little poor.

ALICE: Precisely. It would be in better taste.

SYBIL: What a dilemma, because I wanted to feel good too. *(Still searching)* Here it is ... *(Taking out the paper)* Two sixty-four Mullholland Drive, four thousand, six hundred dollars.

ALICE: Good.

SYBIL: Why is it good?

ALICE: It's high. Your expenses are high. That's good. We'll have a better case against the enemy.

SYBIL: The enemy ...

ALICE: Regarding medical and dental, are your children currently undergoing orthodonture or do you plan orthodonture?

SYBIL: Are you kidding? Have you looked in their father's mouth?

ALICE: Truthfully, I'm thorough, but no.

SYBIL: Awful. The children have dreadful malocclusions, and Sigmund comes from a long line of malocclusers, so it's his side that they get the bad bite from, so I feel he ought to be responsible.

ALICE: We're not talking about right or wrong here, Mrs. Matchett.

SYBIL: *(Breaking in)* But their bite ...

ALICE: I can only promise a good fight, not justice.

SYBIL: God!

ALICE: There's no agreement made in heaven. A good agreement is only what's good for both parties.

SYBIL: That's very philosophical, Mrs. Bailey.

ALICE: Thank you. And your husband and Mr. Ostermeyer, his counsel, are late.

SYBIL: And Sigmund has awful vision. I think we ought to put something in the agreement about future opthomological care. When you think about the things that *could* happen in the future because *he* was their father.

ALICE: Just wait until you meet your husband's counselor, Lester Ostermeyer, if you think you've got trouble now. And I thought your husband was always on time.

SYBIL: He might have a queasy stomach. Sigmund's stomach turns over when he's nervous. I used to make him hot water and lemon juice.

ALICE: Dr. Matchett is also asking for his exercycle, Mrs. Matchett.

SYBIL: That's ridiculous. He hasn't used it in ten years. He hasn't used a lot of things in ten years.

ALICE: Divorce has wrought many changes.

SYBIL: Someone said he gained twenty pounds after I left.

ALICE: He looked quite trim when he came to my office.

SYBIL: Was he wearing a vest? I bet he was wearing a vest.

ALICE: He could have been. Yes.

SYBIL: Well, watch out. He hides everything under vests. Do you think he's attractive?

ALICE: Are you kidding? Those blue eyes? That head of hair?

SYBIL: Head of hair? He must have had a transplant. Was he wearing glasses?

ALICE: Not that I recall. What were the utilities last year, Mrs. Matchett?

SYBIL: I knew it. Contact lenses. He probably had plastic surgery too. I may not even recognize him. He's a very vain person, Mrs. Bailey. I think the judge ought to know this. I had to fight him for the mirror every morning. Did you notice his nervous tick?

ALICE: Quite frankly, I found his eyes distracting, so I tried not to look into them.

SYBIL: No. It's in his left knee. It goes off at three minute intervals. It developed shortly after we married. All of a sudden the knee just pops out like a cockoo clock.

ALICE: I wouldn't mention that.

SYBIL: Mention what?

ALICE: That it happened *after* you were married. Discretion is the name of the game here.

SYBIL: Well I'm certainly not responsible, Mrs. Bailey, for everything that happened *after* we were married.

ALICE: Potentially.

SYBIL: God!

ALICE: Dr. Matchett also mentions a sheep dog.

SYBIL: Snowflake.

ALICE: He just stated *The* Sheep Dog.

SYBIL: He slept with it.

ALICE: Every night?

SYBIL: Uh huh.

ALICE: Let me get this down. *(Writing)* Slept with sheep dog
. . . Were you in the same bed with Dr. Matchett and his sheep
dog?

SYBIL: *(Adamant)* Our sex life was very *(Hesitating)* hot. I
tested out of the range listed in *Cosmopolitan's* quiz.

ALICE: I'm trying to make a case for you here, Mrs. Matchett.
That is the name of the game. Now you understand this could quali-
fy as sexual deprival and/or depravity. What exactly did Dr.
Matchett do with this dog, Mrs. Matchett?

SYBIL: I bought Snowflake in the stuffed animal department of
F.A.O. Schwartz. Sigmund kept it on top of the bed as you would
a toss pillow.

ALICE: That *is* a bummer.

VOICE: *(Offstage)* Next case . . . Connely versus Connely.

ALICE: *(Reading from her list)* The Sam Francis painting of
Point Bobo at Sunset.

SYBIL: Point *Lobo*, Mrs. Bailey, *Lo-Bo*.

ALICE: *(Reading)* Also asking for the Cuisinart, the sailboat
. . .

SYBIL: *(Surprised)* What?

ALICE: Well, he can *ask* for anything he wants.

SYBIL: Whose side are you on, Mrs. Bailey?

ALICE: It doesn't mean he's going to get it.

*(Lester Ostermeyer and Sigmund Matchett enter, deeply
involved in discussion, looking at papers)*

ALICE: There he is! That's Mr. Ostermeyer, his counselor, the
man with him. Don't worry, Mrs. Matchett. You know what they
say about me. That my knife goes in so quietly you never see the
blood.

SYBIL: Sigmund looks terrible. I hate the hair.

ALICE: Just be charming to him. A little honey never hurts.

SYBIL: His back is bothering him. I can tell by the way he's
walking crooked. Oh, God!

ALICE: Just be calm and don't give them any information. And
be advised that your husband's counselor, Lester Ostermeyer, is
going through a divorce himself.

SYBIL: *(Whispering as the men come nearer)* Is that good?

ALICE: Oh, no. That's bad. Very bad.

SYBIL: *(Repeating)* Very bad.

ALICE: He hates all women now. His wife ran away with her
secretary.

*(Lights fade out then up on corridor outside courtroom. It is
fifteen minutes later)*

ALICE: My client, Sybil Matchett, is requesting ownership of the sailboat, *The Sybil.*

SIGMUND: Sybil can't even sail.

ALICE: She could learn to sail, Dr. Matchett.

SYBIL: I could learn to sail.

LESTER: That boat gives *my* client inordinate seasonal pleasure.

ALICE: I'm sure. I understand he does a lot of "springy" entertaining on board.

LESTER: He's too busy working so he can make his payments to Mrs. Matchett.

ALICE: Not too busy working to take a vacation in Florida last year.

LESTER: To visit his aged mother.

SIGMUND: My aged mother.

SYBIL: My foot, Sigmund.

ALICE: And snuck a trip in to Disney World, four days at the folksy Dutch Inn, one hundred and forty dollars a night.

SIGMUND: I object! That was for two rooms and I had the children.

SYBIL: Auntie Bambi slept in *his* room I'll bet.

LESTER: My client has every right to participate in social contact with the opposite sex.

ALICE: Your client took some bunny on a trip.

LESTER: Bambi LeClair is a social worker.

ALICE: Oh I'll bet she is with a name like that. *(Turning back to the case)* My client, as noted in document one hundred and fifty-nine *(Reading)* is asking for the following: the property on West 83rd Street in Manhattan and the furnishings thereof, the summer property on Long Island and the furnishings *thereof,* the piece of land purchased jointly, and let me add hastily, in Spanish Lakes, located in the deserted desert of Arizona.

SIGMUND: Oh, boy, another tall tale.

LESTER: May I understand, Mrs. Bailey, the only thing *not* under contest is the children, custody awarded to *your* client.

SYBIL: *(To Alice)* Is that a win or lose?

ALICE: Please refrain from any comments, Mrs. Matchett.

LESTER: That's right, Mrs. Matchett, a little restraint here and on your MasterCharge.

SIGMUND: I'll drink to that.

ALICE: You're out of order, Mr. Ostermeyer, and your client.

LESTER: You're never going to get what you're asking for, Mrs. Bailey. You must think I'm representing Rockefeller here.

ALICE: You're going to be weeping in your scotch, Lester Ostermeyer. I'm warning you.

LESTER: Blow it out your bloomers, Alice. Where are we on the list?

ALICE: Two more cases before us, and I doubt we'll come to any agreeable agreement here today since your client is making outrageous demands.

LESTER: Just wait until we get into her artsy-crafty life in sunny California.

ALICE: Who *is* Bambi LeClair?

LESTER: We understand Sybil Matchett associates with women —*a lot!*

ALICE: Sybil Matchett is a model mother.

LESTER: But can she bake an apple pie?

SYBIL: Yes, I can.

SIGMUND: Yes, she can! She certainly can. I was married to her, so I know.

SYBIL: I wish this was over, Sigmund.

SIGMUND: It takes a lot of digging to bury the past, Sybil.

VOICE: *(Offstage)* Next case, Wolf versus Wolf.

(Lights fade, spot on Sigmund downstage)

SIGMUND: The day I asked her to marry me, in Truro, Massachusetts, which means "truth" and is on Cape Cod, was sunny. We were invited guests for that weekend. It was August, 1969, and the nights were already beginning to get cold. Sharon Tate and her friends had just been murdered, John Kennedy had been dead for six years and Robert Kennedy for one. That weekend in Truro, we rowed across the lake in a brown wooden boat to a beach where the sign said "Private, No Trespassing." It was hazy and the fog was beginning to roll in. I thought then that I wanted to be with you forever. "I'll love you forever," I said. The name of the boat was "Someday."

(Lights down on Sigmund and up on Sybil downstage)

SYBIL: If you want to know why I married him, the beginning of everything, I would have to tell you pea soup. He was a senior at Amherst and had an apartment over Russo's Liquors. He invited me for the weekend. I was a junior at Wellesley and it cost eleven dollars round trip on the Peter Pan Bus Lines. I arrived in a well-underway snowstorm and we made soup together, he peeling the carrots, me adding the peas. We ate it, sitting at a four-legged maple table by the window, with French bread, which we dipped. Outside the snow was falling on the spruce trees in the public park. It was green and white outside and in. Afterwards we made love, of course.

(Lights fade, then up again on courtroom corridor)

SYBIL: It was a B minus over C plus marriage which was hard to leave.

SIGMUND: We had our differences.

SYBIL: Which are nobody's business.

ALICE: The specifics would be helpful, Matchetts.

SIGMUND: No touching privates, please.

LESTER: I don't know how you expect us to fight this case without ammunition.

SIGMUND: God, all we want is an agreement.

ALICE: Cut the baloney, doctor. You preyed on this woman, demanding favors, refusing coffee of the instant type, laughing at her large buttocks.

SYBIL: Mrs. Bailey, please!

SIGMUND: Thank you.

SYBIL: No dirty linen.

SIGMUND: We'll wash our own.

SYBIL: And I don't have large buttocks.

SIGMUND: No, she doesn't.

SYBIL: Thanks, darling.

SIGMUND: The pleasure's mine.

LESTER: *(Officially)* The marriage has irretrievably broken down.

ALICE: *(Officially)* Non-aligned chemistry.

SIGMUND: We simply grew in different ways.

SYBIL: Like a cactus and a violet.

ALICE: My client is also demanding the bicycle built for two.

LESTER: My client is not shipping a tandem bike cross-country.

ALICE: Then *my* client will forget to send *your* client the slides. They'll slip her mind.

LESTER: Which you must admit is already pretty slippery. Things just fall in and out of it.

SYBIL: Wait a minute. You're talking about me. He's talking about me, Sigmund. He's insulting me.

SIGMUND: All's fair.

SYBIL: What's fair? How you came in the middle of the night and absconded with our entire set of classical records?

SIGMUND: It was three o'clock on a Sunday afternoon, I'd just flown in from New York, I was visiting my two children, and she said "Take anything, I don't care."

ALICE: *(To Sybil)* My God, is this true? You said, "Take anything"?

SYBIL: I didn't care at the moment.

ALICE: My client was crazed from temporal disappointment.

SIGMUND: Sybil was never crazed. She is a very rational woman.

SYBIL: Thank you, Sigmund.

SIGMUND: You're welcome, and she lives in California, so what would she want with classical records?

SYBIL: Right. We're too busy tossing about on the tennis courts.

LESTER: I suggest they split the collection—he'll take Bach through Liszt, and she'll get Mozart through Wagner.

ALICE: I object. Then my client loses Rachmaninoff and Tchaikovsky.

SYBIL: And I love the Russians.

SIGMUND: God, you can't have the world!

SYBIL: He has all our books, a green leather bound version of *The Rubaiyat of Omar Khayyám* which he inscribed "To my sweetheart, and the night shall be filled with music," boxed in his mother's basement.

SIGMUND: Safe in Mamaroneck.

SYBIL: Molding away. How is your mother?

SIGMUND: She had a heart attack and is in a recuperative home.

SYBIL: A home! My God! Couldn't your sister Helen take her in?

ALICE: Keep to the necessary confusions, please. We are about to be called. State your requests clearly.

LESTER: In tangible terms.

SYBIL: Twenty-five.

SIGMUND: Thousand?!

SYBIL: Until there's a change in my situation.

SIGMUND: Like what?

SYBIL: Success.

SIGMUND: I heartily wish it for you.

SYBIL: From the depths of your pocketbook, I'm sure.

ALICE: Let me remind you, visitation rights have to be settled.

SIGMUND: I want the children every summer.

SYBIL: Fine.

SIGMUND: For two weeks.

LESTER: In any state my client wishes.

ALICE: *(To Sybil)* You don't have to agree to any location lock-in.

SYBIL: Then I won't. I have no idea what state I'll be in.

ALICE: All my client wants is a sense of security. She wants Dr. Matchett to put his assets *not* in wine or women, but in his family. Trust funds.

SIGMUND: Security comes from within.

LESTER: A-men.

SYBIL: Sigmund always talks like a psychiatrist when it comes to money because he's cheap.

SIGMUND: If Sybil were to lay all the baubles I've given her in a straight line, they would stretch across the lobby of the Plaza Hotel where I took her on her honeymoon.

SYBIL: *Our* honeymoon, Sigmund, *OUR.*

(Lights fade out. Spot up on Sigmund downstage)

SIGMUND: I wanted everything to be perfect. I was very much in love with her. I ordered the bridal suite. There were mirrors on the ceiling.

(Lights down on Sigmund, up on Sybil downstage)

SYBIL: We brought our own candles. Hand dipped. I was nervous. The ceiling had mirrors. I couldn't look. I was very young and Sigmund was the world.

(Lights fade, then up on courtroom corridor)

SIGMUND: She kept telling me she felt sick, at fifty-five dollars a night in those days.

SYBIL: I kept telling him I felt nauseous.

SIGMUND: I told her I loved her.

SYBIL: I told him I thought I was going to throw up.

(Lights fade up on Sigmund)

SIGMUND: We had dreams, trips we wanted to make, children we wanted to have, how we were special . . . lucky.

(Lights fade, up on Sybil)

SYBIL: Sigmund was wise about things no one else was wise about, and he knew all the verses to "My Darling Clementine," which he sang to me lying in bed at the Plaza Hotel. He sang them off key, which was the only way he knew, lying there, the city sounds outside us . . . *(Singing a little off key)* "You are lost and gone forever, La dee da da, da da dee."

(Lights fade and up on Sigmund)

SIGMUND: We read *The Prophet* aloud to each other by candlelight in the beginning. Her hair was brown and silky, and we promised never to take anything for granted, like our luck. But it turned out that luck had nothing to do with anything.

(Lights fade back up on courtroom corridor)

SIGMUND: Mrs. Matchett threw up on our wedding night.

ALICE: I don't find that evidence of anything to my client's detriment.

SYBIL: Well, I was much better in the morning.

SIGMUND: The next morning I had breakfast sent up.

SYBIL: It came on a silver tray with a red rose.

SIGMUND: Which was wilting. I ordered fresh strawberries out of season. It was December.

SYBIL: It was snowing and carriages were lined up in the park.

SIGMUND: She said she wanted to go out for a ride in the snow, so we did.

SYBIL: Three times around the park. I said, "Let's ride until the sun comes out."

SIGMUND: Only it never did.

SYBIL: So we went back to the room.

SIGMUND: Back to bed.

SYBIL: They had white satin sheets.

SIGMUND: And she threw up again.

SYBIL: Well, it turned out I had the flu.

ALICE: My client requests full medical and dental.

SIGMUND: Only I refuse to pay for another gum job. She already had one gum job, and if she doesn't floss, it's not my fault.

SYBIL: I stimulate with toothpicks every night.

LESTER: My client does, however, deed to his soon-to-be former wife, their jointly owned cemetery plots.

ALICE: My client accepts.

SYBIL: I do not! They don't even have a view. He bought them in the most crowded part of the cemetery, way in the back, because it's cheaper.

SIGMUND: That's my Sybil! Always has to be a star!

SYBIL: I'm *not* your Sybil anymore, and I've decided to be cremated anyway. Everyone in California is cremated.

SIGMUND: That's the American way. Out of sight, out of mind.

LESTER: Let's just divide the plots evenly then.

SYBIL: I'm not being buried next to him.

ALICE: Then I'll take them. I have no need for front and center.

LESTER: Thank you, Mrs. Bailey.

ALICE: Let's get under way then.

LESTER: To proceed.

SIGMUND: I want the Cuisinart returned.

SYBIL: The Cuisinart's broken.

SIGMUND: *(To Sybil)* What did you do to it?

SYBIL: I don't think an avocado should harm a Cuisinart.

SIGMUND: No. Not unless you put it in with the pit. Where's the warranty?

SYBIL: I lost it.

SIGMUND: WHAT?

ALICE: My client says she has lost it.

SIGMUND: My lawyer can hear what your client, who is my wife, says. I'm telling you, Lester, she's highly irresponsible. I don't know, letting the children go off with her.

SYBIL: *(Sarcastically)* Then take them, please, Sigmund.

SIGMUND: *(To Sybil)* I wouldn't want to hog all the assets. On the other hand, candidly, Sybil is a highly eccentric and bizarre personality. And an oral compulsive. Twinkies by the ton, undercover.

SYBIL: He is a highly rigid and obsessive person, an anal compulsive.

ALICE: Sounds like the perfect match.

SYBIL: Mrs. Bailey, whose side are you on?

LESTER: How was your wife's eccentricity manifested, Dr. Matchett?

SIGMUND: When driving she would only make *left* turns, refused to make rights.

SYBIL: I'm afraid of rights. He knows that.

SIGMUND: We would just drive around and around and . . . it also severely limited our sexual activity.

ALICE: I should also mention, then, that Dr. Matchett, a highly revered psychiatrist, wears his bunny slippers to bed because he says they make him feel more secure. I mean he already has his stuffed sheep dog.

SIGMUND: I have poor circulation.

SYBIL: The bunny slippers have little blue furry ears and button eyes.

SIGMUND: Why don't I tell them how you slept with your mouth open.

SYBIL: I have a deviated septum.

SIGMUND: Which causes a loud locomotive-like sound.

LESTER: *(To Sybil)* In other words, Mrs. Matchett snores. And I also understand you have a hot tub in your backyard. Who's been in your tub lately, Mrs. Matchett? And how hot is it? Rub a dub dub, three men in a tub.

ALICE: I consider these innuendos highly unprofessional.

LESTER: Come on, Alice, you're defending a hot chick here. Admit it.

SYBIL: I am not a hot chick.

SIGMUND: My wife is definitely not a hot chick.

SYBIL: Thank you, Sigmund.

LESTER: *(To Sigmund)* I'm your lawyer and I'm simply trying to establish here that Mrs. Matchett is a rotten mother and that you owe her nothing.

SIGMUND: But that's not true. Sybil is a very dedicated mother
. . . scouts, cake sales, bedtime stories, the whole bit—four stars.

LESTER: Oh, terrific, Dr. Matchett, that's terrific! Keep it up!

ALICE: In my opinion, Mrs. Matchett is one of the most
beautiful women to ever come across my desk.

LESTER: *(To Alice)* Well, no one asked for your opinion.

ALICE: My colleague here seems to think my opinion is worth-
less.

LESTER: You women think you're the only ones in the world
who ever poached an egg, prepared a report, and looked gorgeous
—all on the same day.

ALICE: I think you should be disqualified for that sexist statement.

LESTER: I'm not quitting now, just when the juices are beginning to run.

SYBIL: Well, don't count on my juice, Ostermeyer.

SIGMUND: Mrs. Matchett and I came for an agreement, not a
carnage. I want this stopped, Lester.

LESTER: You want a case or not, Dr. Matchett?

SIGMUND: You're harassing my wife.

ALICE: You are, Lester. You are in contempt of the court and
my client.

LESTER: *(To Alice)* You haven't got a case and you know it.
Sybil Matchett's crazy, a highly eccentric personality, classified
according to the American Psychiatric Association under file #509,
"Bizarrity as a Classical Disorder."

ALICE: Come on, Lester, everyone knows all psychiatrists are
nuts, including your client.

LESTER: My client is paying me a hundred dollars an hour to
determine exactly who the crazy one is.

SIGMUND: Don't remind me.

SYBIL: *(To Sigmund)* You're shaking.

SIGMUND: It's my stomach.

SYBIL: No, I think it's your knee.

VOICE: *(Offstage, over loud speaker)* Next case . . . Matchett
versus Matchett.

SYBIL: That's us!

VOICE: *(Offstage)* Counselors only.

SIGMUND: What does that mean?

LESTER: The judge is going to try and mediate without you and
Mrs. Matchett there.

ALICE: Around the corner, there's a small cafe. You two go off
and have a drink.

LESTER: Have yourselves a Bloody Mary.

ALICE: We'll deal with the judge. We know what you're fighting for. And on the boat, *The Sybil*, Sybil, how much is it worth roughly?

SYBIL: Why don't you let Sigmund have it. To tell the truth, I don't know the bow *(Pronounced "ow")* from the rudder.

LESTER: Aha! She admits it!

ALICE: She admits nothing. Come on, Lester. The judge is waiting. *This* is war!

(Lights fade out)

End of Scene

Scene Four:

Time: One half hour later.
Place: "A Small Cafe."

Sybil and Sigmund are seated at a table. Jazz plays. They have a drink and a sandwich.

SIGMUND: I thought you don't drink.

SYBIL: I do now. I like your contacts.

SIGMUND: I got a transplant.

SYBIL: I'm working on a word processor.

SIGMUND: I've learned to cook on a wok.

SYBIL: I joined a spa.

SIGMUND: I'm taking a Great Books Course at Columbia. We read Plato last week.

SYBIL: I finally read *The Brothers Karamazov*.

SIGMUND: I miss the kids.

SYBIL: They miss you. Julie had the lead in the Thanksgiving Play. She was Pocahontas.

SIGMUND: I know. She wrote me.

SYBIL: I have the pictures. *(Taking them out)*

SIGMUND: *(Peeking a look)* She's pretty. She has your mouth. *(Then abruptly)* Beautiful day today. Warm. Sunny.

SYBIL: Feels like home, breathing in all those good Manhattan fumes. I miss New York.

SIGMUND: More happens on any given day *in a closet in New York* than in an entire city anyplace in America.

SYBIL: We don't have good jazz in L.A. Nobody's blue, I guess. *(Offering him a cigarette)* Cigarette?

SIGMUND: No, thanks. I gave up smoking too.
(Sybil lights up)
SYBIL: Too?
SIGMUND: Too. You didn't notice I wasn't smoking in the courthouse this morning?
SYBIL: I guess you weren't.
SIGMUND: No, I wasn't.
SYBIL: Well, I'm impressed.
SIGMUND: Well, you should be.
SYBIL: Please don't tell me what I should be.
SIGMUND: It was a long process. I was hypnotized five times. I'm in a trance right now. *(Pause)* I've decided not to ask for the other night table. I don't want to break up a matched pair.
SYBIL: Thank you.
SIGMUND: And I know you'll be sad to learn that my Uncle Al died last month. Zap. Just like that. I think he died of loneliness with Aunt Celia gone.
SYBIL: Gone?! Sigmund!
SIGMUND: I mean you go to the other side of the continent, you expect life to stop.
SYBIL: You could have called me.
SIGMUND: We *are* getting divorced.
SYBIL: Well, I still like your family. It was you I didn't like. *(Pause)* I don't know what to do with our wedding pictures.
SIGMUND: I don't know what to do with your father's pocket watch your mother gave me. Better head back for the courthouse. Maybe they've come to a decision. *(Calling)* Waitress!
SYBIL: *(Interior)* It was the thickest pea soup this side of Austria, and we ate it sitting at a four-legged maple table by the window.
SIGMUND: Before we go back, I have something to tell you. You were a winning wife. You're funny, you're warm, I love your face and your meatless moussaka and the shape of your mouth which is bowshaped which is what the kids are, and I don't know what happened. I just got crazy. I don't know what it is I wanted ... I still don't.
SYBIL: You wanted a divorce. You said you didn't love me anymore.
SIGMUND: I hate going to sleep by myself at night and waking up all alone on Sundays which are terrible. Where's the waitress? *(Calling)* Miss! *(Pause, then abruptly)* How's your social life?
SYBIL: Dating a lot. How's yours?
SIGMUND: Dating a lot. *(Pause)* It stinks. That's correct. I date a lot. I have dated twenty-two women in the past year, and I have noted a certain pattern; they jog, the drink white wine spritzers,

and make quiche on request. Oh, the quiches I've conquered, the millions of mushrooms and brocollae.

SYBIL: Well, no one can do eggs once over light the way you can.

SIGMUND: Last winter I went up to Bromley. I rode past our house. They let the maples get too high; they block the whole view of the mountains.

SYBIL: That was a good house.

SIGMUND: We made love that time in front of the fireplace after the kids went to sleep.

SYBIL: Stop. You're making me crazy. It's history.

SIGMUND: It's our history. *(Pause)* Why did you stop coming to bed when I went up to bed? Staying downstairs . . . ?

SYBIL: I was afraid you wouldn't ask me if I wanted to.

SIGMUND: But if you didn't come, how could I ask you?

(Lights fade)

End of Scene

Scene Five:

Time: Same time.
*Place: Lights fade up on judge's chambers. Judge Bellows,
Alice Bailey and Lester Ostermeyer.*

JUDGE: They all want it all, but you can't give them what there isn't nor can you divide what's indivisible.

ALICE: You can't fight over the contents of an empty pocketbook, your honor.

LESTER: And you can't argue over the water in an empty well, sir.

JUDGE: Precisely.

LESTER: What, then, is your proposal on the periodontal care, Judge Bellows?

JUDGE: Brush better. Brush three times a day. Your gums are your own responsibility.

ALICE: This agreement appears in order, judge. We'll present it to the Matchetts.

JUDGE: If they can't agree, tell them they'll have to come to court, but there's a four year back-up, by which time no one will remember *or* care anymore about who gets the pet cat.

ALICE: Dog.

JUDGE: See, I've already forgotten. And without passion there are no victories. Good afternoon, counselors. Pleasure to see the A Team together again, stopping at nothing. Oh, and Lester, how's yours going?

LESTER: Fine thank you, sir. Very civilized. Since we can't come to any decisions yet, my wife is occupying the bottom floor of our home, and I have the top. She's got the kitchen, so I'm simply taking all my meals out . . . but I got the bathroom, which seemed more essential.

JUDGE: I'd say so. Good luck with the Hatchetts. Tell them I said compromise is the cornerstone of conciliation.

ALICE: You bet, your honor.

JUDGE: And Alice, how's the big romance going? Any chance of wedding bells?

ALICE: Nothing ringing this year, your honor. Always hoping.

JUDGE: Just keep your sunny side up—NEXT!

(Lights fade out)

End of Scene

Scene Six:

Time: Immediately following.
Place: Courthouse corridor.

ALICE: There they are! *(Calling)* Dr. and Mrs. Matchett! Here we are! *(To Lester)* They're a handsome couple, don't you think? Wholesome.

LESTER: We're divorcing them, Alice.

SYBIL: What did Judge Bellows say?

LESTER: You'd better agree today. If you hesitate, you'll forget why you're getting a divorce in the first place.

ALICE: We may be coming very close to an agreement here.

[Note: Both lawyers write quickly on legal pads during next scene]

LESTER: *(Rapidly)* To him, all statuary.

ALICE: *(Rapidly)* To her, all paintings.

LESTER: To him, all loose lamps.

ALICE: To her, all fixed lighting.

LESTER: To each, all gifts from the other's family.

ALICE: As in *his* Aunt Millie's samovar to *her*.

LESTER: And *her* mother's silver service to *him* as *he* polished it.

ALICE: As the party of either side claims it was their charms which wooed the other's family, in contrast to their own.

LESTER: Wherein the adage familiarity breeds contempt.

SIGMUND: *(To Sybil)* I thought I might come out to California for Christmas.

SYBIL: Last Christmas Day the kids and I went to a movie with another divorced family. It was supposed to be a comedy, but it was very sad and we all cried.

LESTER: I think we're getting close on this agreement.

SIGMUND: I think you took my bathrobe when you left, Sybil.

ALICE: Before we tie things up here, Dr. and Mrs. Matchett, we'll have to renegotiate the life insurance.

SIGMUND: My green velour robe.

SYBIL: I wear it around.

SIGMUND: It's a *real* robe.

SYBIL: Yes, it is.

LESTER: *(To Sigmund)* If you let her keep the lithograph of Rodin's "The Screaming Woman" and the Cuisinart . . .

ALICE: *(Breaking in)* Which is broken. *(To Sybil who is staring into Sigmund's eyes)* Mrs. Matchett, pay attention here. Your whole future's at stake.

SYBIL: Hardly over a Cuisinart.

ALICE: We are working our way *up*, if you please. Now his lawyer's carved out a three year plan, at the end of which, he disclaims all responsibility.

SIGMUND: That's ridiculous. I don't disclaim responsibility in three years.

LESTER: Well, if you insist on continuous support, then Mrs. Matchett should give you some of the furniture as collateral. We are talking *the* major pieces.

ALICE: That's crazy.

SIGMUND: I agree. That's crazy, Lester. The kids and her have to live, sleep, work, eat, sit in a chair, do whatever it is people do every day to use up the time.

LESTER: *(To Sigmund)* This is a battle. We're fighting here to divide the spoils.

SIGMUND: We sound like vultures.

ALICE: No room for sentiment here. This is a courthouse. She gets to keep all the jewelry Dr. Matchett *gifted* her, without attachments.

LESTER: *(Writing it down)* No attachments.

ALICE: All liquid assets are divided equally since he is probably hiding what he *really* has in some bank in New Jersey.

LESTER: There is nothing in New Jersey.

SIGMUND: That's right.

LESTER: Try not to hold up progress, the two of you. We're committed to getting you a rock solid agreement. *(Quickly continuing)* He gets to keep the French Oriental.

SYBIL: Sigmund doesn't even *like* the French Oriental.

SIGMUND: I didn't even know we *had* a French Oriental.

SIGMUND: What about WAM? Do you still belong to WAM?

ALICE: All the real estate to her.

SIGMUND: Oh, nothing personal.

ALICE: Who wants an empty house?

SYBIL: Women Against Men? Yes, they have a West Coast Branch; but Sig, it's nothing personal.

LESTER: Then everything in the houses to him.

SYBIL: It's a political issue with me. And I joined because I was angry at you for making me punch a time clock.

LESTER: We are talking value here, not utility.

[Note: Above speeches should be timed to end at the same time. Though characters speak over each other, the lawyers don't miss a word.]

ALICE: He made you punch a time clock, Mrs. Matchett?

SIGMUND: I just wanted to equalize the load ... Why don't you ask her about the time she and her friends from WAM put a rabbit in the bed ... a live one, I might add.

SYBIL: Simply to remind you of *your* responsibility in the birth control process.

LESTER: She put a rabbit in your bed?

[Note: The next section occurs rapidly.]

ALICE: And on the insurance, he adds the dismemberment amendment, God forbid.

LESTER: God forbid.

SIGMUND: God forbid.

ALICE: *(Writing)* So on this twenty-fifth day of August, the party of the first part agrees with the party of the second part ...

LESTER: *(Breaking in)* You're really getting a fine agreement here, Dr. Matchett. Everything spelled out.

ALICE: So everyone goes away happy.

LESTER: Final check. *(Checking his list)* Routine clauses on cohabitation and other deviations from the norm will in effect negate this contract.

ALICE: Wipe it out.

LESTER: And we would simply start from scratch.

ALICE: *(Breaking right in)* Now if you'll both sign this paper, Mr. Ostermeyer and I will write it up and you could be divorced this afternoon. *(Pushing the paper at Sigmund)*

LESTER: In the next hour.

SIGMUND: As simple as that. *(He does not sign right away but ignores the paper)*

ALICE: This agreement will not be considered final, of course, for six months, so both of you would have to wait that period to remarry.

SYBIL: To remarry . . .

ALICE: Most difficult settlement since Ford versus Ford. I can't believe it's almost over. Just sign here, Mrs. Matchett . . . *(Holding out the paper to Sybil)* and you'll be divorced, out in the world with the rest of us, out in the marketplace. You'll receive a xeroxed copy.

(Sybil does not move to sign)

LESTER: *(To Sigmund)* Just sign your John Doe here and you're a free man.

SIGMUND: *(Interior)* The night she left I kept thinking, if I get up the next morning and start the day with orange juice, everything will be okay.

SYBIL: *(Interior)* I didn't stop crying until Indiana. And the moonlight does not shine along the Wabash. The kids were silent all the way across the country. Not one fight. Thank you, I thought, for something. By the time we got to the Black Hills, I couldn't remember why we had started out.

SIGMUND: Sybil, we're all alone in our lives and nobody knows. We could die of something and no one would know.

SYBIL: I know.

LESTER: People are waiting to lock up. *(Holding out the document to Sigmund)* X marks the spot. *(Handing him the pen. Pause. Sigmund signs)*

ALICE: Mrs. Matchett . . . *(Holding out the document and pen)* Your signature . . . *(Pause)* AND IT'S . . . *(Sybil signs)* OVER!

LESTER: It's over, Dr. Matchett! It's over!

SYBIL: *(Quietly)* It's over.

SIGMUND: All over.

SYBIL: Wait a minute! You forgot the children!

LESTER: The children.

ALICE: The children.

SIGMUND: How could you forget the children?

ALICE: Well, they're *your* children.

LESTER: You could have reminded us.

ALICE: *(Holding out her lists)* Look at all these items we're juggling. You need the memory of an elephant. *(Looking over the list)* She got the swings on the outdoor equipment clause.

LESTER: So he gets the children, no strings attached.

SYBIL: Wait a minute. I'm not giving up any children.

LESTER: We all have to make do with partial rewards.

SYBIL: Tell it to Santa Claus.

SIGMUND: The children are hers.

ALICE: I move we put the children on a rider.

LESTER: *(Writing) Ride* the children.

SIGMUND: I mean they're ours, but I can't make the home Sybil does. I think we'll arrange this between us. Don't you think, Sybil?

SYBIL: We prefer to arrange matters between us privately. *(Pause)* We'll separate and divide them ourselves.

LESTER: *(Packing up)* Everything then is in order and accord.

ALICE: *(Packing up)* Congratulations, Mr. Ostermeyer. *(Shaking his hand)*

LESTER: *(Saluting)* I salute you, Mrs. Bailey. A lovely agreement.

ALICE: Good afternoon, Dr. Matchett, Mrs. . . . *(Correcting herself)* Sybil Matchett. *(Looking out the window)* Blue skies, white clouds, birds singing . . . It's a beautiful day for a divorce.

LESTER: An exquisite day for a divorce.

(Lester and Alice exit. Pause)

SIGMUND: And it's over.

SYBIL: All over. *(Interior)* It was green and white outside and in. Afterwards we made love, of course.

SIGMUND: *(Interior)* I'll love you forever, I said. The name of the boat was *"SOMEDAY."*

SYBIL: Sometimes when I'm on a date, I call the man Sigmund by mistake. I forget. Maybe I'll always forget, or never forget . . . Oh, God, I'm embarrassed. Could you give me a lift to the airport?

SIGMUND: Maybe you never will. When I go to bed at night, I always make sure the pillows are together, even though no one's there. Come on, Sybil. *(Pause)* To the airport.

The End

RAMON DELGADO, EDITOR

This publication is the sixth edition of *The Best Short Plays* edited by Ramon Delgado, who continues the series made famous by the late Stanley Richards.

An experienced literary advisor, Dr. Delgado has served as chairman for new plays at the Dallas Theater Center, as a literary advisor to The Whole Theatre Company in Montclair, New Jersey, and as theatre consultant to Scholastic Magazine's *Literary Cavalcade*. Dr. Delgado has also been script judge for the Playwrights' Program of the American Theatre Association, the International Biennial Play Competition sponsored by Southern Illinois University at Carbondale, and is an adjudicator for the American College Theatre Festival.

Born in Tampa, Florida, and raised in nearby Winter Haven, Ramon Delgado started writing plays for marionette shows when he was eleven years old. By the time he had finished high school he had written two full-length plays and several one-act plays.

Recognition as a playwright has been received with honors in five regional and twelve national playwriting competitions, including those sponsored by Theta Alpha Phi, the University of Missouri, EARPLAY, and Samuel French. Three of his full-length plays— *Listen, My Children, A Little Holy Water,* and *The Fabulous Jeromes*—received honors in the David Library American Freedom division of the American College Theatre Festival. Seven of his short plays have been published, notably "Waiting for the Bus" in *Ten Great One Act Plays* and *Themes in the One Act Play,* and "Once Below A Lighthouse" in *The Best Short Plays 1972.*

In 1978 Dr. Delgado's one-act play "The Jerusalem Thorn" was chosen for the Dale Wasserman Midwest Professional Playwrights Workshop, and after expansion into a full-length script, the play was produced Off-Off Broadway by the Acting Wing, Inc., at the Shandol Theatre. Two of his short plays have had Equity showcase productions at the No Smoking Playhouse and at The Glines. The New York Hispanic theatre INTAR selected him as a Playwright-in-Residence in 1980. Three of his short television plays have been aired over PBS, Channel WSIU, Carbondale, Illinois.

Dr. Delgado began his education at Stetson University in Deland, Florida; then studied with Paul Baker and Eugene McKinney at the Dallas Theatre Center. He received an M.F.A. in 1967 from Yale School of Drama, studying playwriting there with the late John Gassner, and later with Christian H. Moe at Southern Illinois University at Carbondale, where he received his Ph.D. in 1976.

SEEDS OF MODERN DRAMA

Introduced and Edited by Norris Houghton

THERESE RAQUIN
ZOLA

AN ENEMY OF THE PEOPLE
IBSEN

MISS JULIE
STRINDBERG

THE WEAVERS
HAUPTMANN

THE SEA GULL
CHEKHOV

Five great forces · Chekhov, Hauptmann, Ibsen, Strindberg and Zola · dramatists whose work define, embrace and transcend the trends and genres of the modern stage, meet here in this extraordinary exhibition of their sustained and sustaining power in today's theatre.

The ideal text for any course venturing into modern drama, Norris Houghton's volume boasts five landmark plays in distinguished modern translations.

ISBN: 0-936839-15-5   PAPER: $9.95
448 pages, 5½ x 8¼

ORDER FOR FALL CLASSES TODAY!

CLASSIC DRAMA
From Applause

MARY STUART — FRIEDRICH SCHILLER

Like Mary Stuart herself and the legends which pursued her to her death, Schiller's drama continues to captivate the modern imagination nearly two centuries later. Eric Bentley's lean forceful rendering of the German masterpiece will command the attention of theatre audiences for many years to come.

96 PAGES, 5½ X 8¼
ISBN: 0-936839-00-7
(PAPER) $5.95

Adapted by Eric Bentley
Translated by Joseph Mellish

PHEDRA — JEAN RACINE

Racine's tragedy of a woman trapped in the web of a terrible diseased passion, unspeakable and irresistible, and the vehement contagion that spreads throughout her world.

Glenda Jackson currently stars in the highly acclaimed new stage version by Robert David MacDonald, slated for Broadway this Spring.

72 PAGES, 4½ X 7¼
ISBN: 0-87910-261-6
(PAPER) $6.95

translated by
Robert David MacDonald

CELESTINA — FERNANDO DE ROJAS

The central and pervasive situation is a simple one: a dirty old woman is helping a courtly young gentleman to seduce a girl. The wonder of the thing lies in the art with which Fernando de Rojas derives, from such commonplace materials, a towering tragedy—or rather tragi-comedy.

112 PAGES, 5½ X 8¼
ISBN: 0-936839-01-5
(PAPER) $5.95

Adapted by Eric Bentley
Translated by James Mabbe